IN SICKNESS AND IN WEALTH

IN SICKNESS AND IN WEALTH

Migration, Gendered Morality, and Central Java

Carol Chan

Indiana University Press

This book is a publication of

Indiana University Press
Office of Scholarly Publishing
Herman B Wells Library 350
1320 East 10th Street
Bloomington, Indiana 47405 USA

iupress.indiana.edu

The paper used in this publication meets the minimum requirements of
the American National Standard for Information Sciences—Permanence
of Paper for Printed Library Materials, ANSI Z39.48–1992.

Manufactured in the United States of America

Library of Congress Cataloging-in-Publication Data

Names: Chan, Carol, author.
Title: In sickness and in wealth : migration, gendered morality, and Central
    Java / Carol Chan.
Description: Bloomington, Indiana : Indiana University Press, 2018. | Series:
    Framing the global book series | Includes bibliographical references and
    index.
Identifiers: LCCN 2018019380 (print) | LCCN 2018021015 (ebook) | ISBN
    9780253037053 (e-book) | ISBN 9780253037022 (cl : alk. paper) | ISBN
    9780253037060 (pb : alk. paper)
Subjects: LCSH: Foreign workers, Indonesian. | Foreign workers'
    families—Indonesia—Jawa Tengah—Attitudes. |
    Indonesians—Employment—Foreign countries. | Women foreign
    workers—Indonesia.
Classification: LCC HD8708.5.A2 (ebook) | LCC HD8708.5.A2 C53 2018 (print) |
    DDC 331.5/440899922—dc23
LC record available at https://lccn.loc.gov/2018019380

1 2 3 4 5   23 22 21 20 19 18

Contents

Acknowledgments

This work would not have been possible without the patience and kindness of the residents of the three migrant-origin villages in Cilacap and Yogyakarta. I am deeply grateful for the opportunity to hear and witness the hopes, regrets, and sources of shame and faith that you have so generously shared with me, and hope that I have done your stories, lives, and struggles justice. Elsewhere in Java, I owe special gratitude to Ratih Pratiwi Anwar, who provided me with much intellectual, personal, and practical support from the very beginning of this project. I thank her for our engaging discussions on migration and development, for her countless invitations and introductions to migrant-related forums, activities, institutions, and contacts, and above all, for her deep friendship, care, and company. As a friend and occasional research assistant, Yuna (Pratina Ikhtiyarini) introduced me to several migrant labor activists and networks in Indonesia. Her companionship and insights during our field trips were invaluable.

The following organizations in Indonesia and Singapore have also been extremely helpful in the development of this work: Serikat Buruh Migran Indonesia (SBMI), Buruh Migran Yogyakarta (Infest), Wisma Bahasa (Yogyakarta), Koalisi Perempuan Cilacap, Yayasan Kembang, Solidaritas Perempuan, Daya Anisa, Nahdlatul Ulama, Indonesia Family Network (IFN), Asosiasi Tenaga Kerja Indonesia (ATKI), and Humanitarian Organization for Migration Economics (HOME). In particular, I would like to thank Jolovan Wham, Bu Erna Murniaty, Mas Hariyanto, Mba Maizidah Salas, Mas Aan, Mas Bobi Anwar Ma'Arif, Mas Fathulloh Muzamiel, Mba Fendy Sri Rahuyu, Pak Abdul Rahim Sitoris, Mba Erwiana Sulistyaningsih, and Nisrina Muthahari, for their time and patience, and for sharing their experiences as former migrants and/or persons who have worked for years with Indonesian migrant workers and relevant Indonesian state agencies. Institutional support during my extended fieldwork period in Indonesia was provided by the Center of Asian Pacific Studies (CAPS) at the University of Gadjah Mada Yogyakarta.

As an academic mentor and friend, Nicole Constable has continually inspired me to think, talk, and write about issues concerning gendered migration, precarious labor, and hope in critical and sensitive ways. Many aspects of this work grew out of and were shaped by her thoughtful and challenging questions, guidance, conversations, and editorial and writing advice over the years. This research also greatly benefited from the feedback and encouragement from other academic mentors, especially Joseph Alter, Andrew Weintraub,

Gabriella Lukacs, and Laura Brown. For motivating me to publish and refine aspects of this project, I extend much appreciation to Koichi Iwabuchi, Andy Chih-Ming Wang, Daniel Goh, Leslie Butt, Harriot Beazley, and anonymous peer reviewers of various journal articles and this book manuscript. Catherine Allerton's careful reading and pointers also contributed significantly in my revisions of this book for greater context and clarity. All remaining errors are my own.

Generous funding for my doctoral studies and fieldwork (on which this book was based) was provided over the years by the University of Pittsburgh's Chancellor's Research Fellowship in Chinese Studies, Social Science Doctoral Dissertation Fellowship, and the Institute of Money, Technology, and Financial Inclusion (IMTFI) research fellowship at the University of California, Irvine. Shorter field trips and conference travel were also possible thanks to the University of Pittsburgh's Anthropology Department, Gender, Sexuality and Women's Studies Program (GSWS), Asian Studies Center, and the Indo-Pacific Council, in addition to the Social Sciences and Humanities Research Council of Canada (Grant: "Southeast Asian Women, Family and Migration in the Global Era"), the Centre of Asia-Pacific Initiatives at the University of Victoria, Canada, and the Association for Asian Studies (AAS). Very special gratitude goes to Phyllis Deasy, Lynn Lantz, and Linda Howard at the Department of Anthropology at the University of Pittsburgh, for their knowledge, assistance, and patience in navigating university life and bureaucracy.

During the writing and revisions of this book, the following institutions in Chile generously supported me with space, time, and funds to complete the manuscript: the Programa Interdisciplinario de Estudios Migratorios (PRIEM) and the Department of Anthropology at Universidad Alberto Hurtado, and the Centro de Estudios Políticos, Culturales y Sociales de América Latina (EPOCAL) at Universidad Bernardo O'Higgins. I am blessed to have for company colleagues armed with intellectual rigor and humor. To Choon Yen Khoo and Kellynn Wee at the National University of Singapore, I am grateful for the time you have taken to engage with extracts from the manuscript; our e-mail conversations made writing from South America a little less isolating. A million thanks to Carl Pearson for the meticulous copy-editing, and the wonderful editors and assistants at Indiana University Press for making this book a reality, especially Jennika Baines and Stephanie Smith.

Very special thanks to Venera Khalikova, Xi Jie Ng, Arika Garg, Corrie Tan, Dolly Schwartz, Shauhrat Chopra, Wenqi Shi, Jody Handoko, Belinda Raintung, Larissa Ranft, Mindy Clarke, Jaimie Adelson, Kim de Wit, Suzanna Eddyono, Anis Nahrawie, Archana Garg, Rajan Garg, Wei Ling Neo, Jia Qi Tan, and

Carolina Ramírez. In so many different and profound ways, their support and humor have made this transnational six-year research and book project more enjoyable and possible. Finally, I am always indebted and thankful to Francisco Garrido, Yeow Khuen Chan, Phuan Seok Ee, Samuel and Colleen Chan, for their enduring love, support, and faith.

An earlier version of Chapter 2 appeared in *Sustainability* 6, no. 10 (2014), and some material in Chapter 3 was published as part of an article in *Global Networks* 14, no. 4 (2017). A shorter and different version of Chapter 6 was published as Chapter 8 in *Precarious Belongings: Affect and Nationalism in Asia* (2017), edited by Daniel Goh and Chih-ming Wang (London: Rowman & Littlefield International).

Note on Names and Indonesian Currency

Most personal names in this book are pseudonyms, except for officials quoted from news sources or official public speeches at events which I attended. This is in accordance with academic convention to safeguard the privacy and anonymity of those who spoke to me and participated in this research. For individuals facing particularly delicate social situations, I shared different aspects of their stories under two names, in order to deter possible identification. As per social convention in Java, where appropriate, I refer to persons with gendered honorifics of *Mba* (Miss or older sister), *Bu* (Mrs), *Mas* (brother), or *Pak* (Mr). For ease of reference and to ensure the anonymity of the sites and its residents, I refer to the main field sites in this book simply as either based in Cilacap or Yogyakarta, rather than assigning them specific names.

Regarding the Indonesian rupiah (IDR), I roughly convert the amounts based on the average and standard exchange rate of United States Dollar (USD) 1 to IDR 10,000.

Abbreviations and Terms

Abbreviations

BNP2TKI (*Badan Nasional Penempatan dan Perlindungan Tenaga Kerja Indonesia*) National Agency for the Placement and Protection of Indonesian Migrant Workers.

BP3TKI (*Balai Pelayanan Penempatan dan Perlindungan Tenaga Kerja Indonesia*) Office for the Service, Placement, and Protection of Indonesian Migrant Workers, a local branch of BNP2TKI.

MUI (*Majelis Ulama Indonesia*) National Council of Ulama Indonesia. The *ulama* is a body of scholars trained in Islamic law and science, usually perceived as the authority for interpreting Islamic doctrine and law. In Indonesia, this is usually represented by MUI, a body comprised of the majority of Indonesian Muslim groups with various approaches to Islam.

NGO non-governmental organization

SBMI (*Serikat Buruh Migran Indonesia*) National Migrant Labor Union of Indonesia

PPTKIS (*Perusahaan Penempatan Tenaga Kerja Indonesia Swasta*) Privatized/ Commercial Agency for the Placement of Indonesian Migrant Workers. Besides placing workers in jobs abroad, PPTKIS is also typically involved in recruiting and training migrants prior to their departure.

PRT (*Pekerja/Pembantu Rumah Tangga*) Domestic Worker/Helper

TKI (*Tenaga Kerja Indonesia*) Indonesian Migrant Worker

TKW (*Tenega Kerja Wanita*) Female Migrant Worker

Frequently referenced Bahasa Indonesian terms

Adat local customary law, which consists of both informal and semi-codified sets of moral regulations governing a community

Kejawen Javanese animistic practices and beliefs, sometimes also referred to as Javanese religion

Kodrat Islamic concept of nature and destiny. With regards to gender roles as natural and destined, *kodrat wanita* in Indonesia typically refers to a Muslim woman's natural duty to care for her children, husband, and domestic chores, while *kodrat pria* refers to the duty of a Muslim man to provide for his family.

Malu shame or embarrassment (for an in-depth discussion, see Chapter 4)

Nasib from the Arabic term "naseeb," meaning fate or one's share in life as given by God

Pahlawan devisa foreign exchange hero

Takdir from the Arabic word "taqdir," meaning destiny and predestination

IN SICKNESS AND IN WEALTH

Introduction: Faith in Migration

This book is about how and why residents of migrant-origin villages develop and sustain faith in transnational migration's uncertain promises, despite its many financial, physical, moral, and mortal risks. It begins with the day I took a four-hour bus journey from Yogyakarta city to Cilacap, an area in Central Java where many Indonesian transnational migrants are from. I was traveling with Sita, a self-defined labor activist in her early thirties who worked for various nongovernmental organizations on social justice issues, including women's health. Through mutual friends, we met in Yogyakarta, where, strikingly, as I told her of how I was raised by and among different migrant Filipina domestic workers in my home who were employed by my extended family in Singapore, Sita spoke of growing up in a rural village in Cilacap, where it was the norm for young women to migrate abroad for domestic work. Such work often encompasses cleaning, cooking, and taking care of the elderly and/or young children of an employer's household, where the worker is also expected to live with the family. Sita always knew that becoming a migrant domestic worker was an option for her, but none of her immediate kin had ever migrated at the time. She eventually became one of the village's few university graduates. We got off the bus in the middle of a small highway, where her brother and sister-in-law picked us up with their motorbikes. The road to their village and house was unpaved and rocky.

Here, almost everyone had one or more family members working overseas, who formerly worked overseas, and/or who were planning to work abroad, even for persons in typical "nonmigrant families" like Sita, whose younger brother (and later, his wife) had tried and failed to migrate several times. Her older brother married the daughter of a migrant woman who seldom returned to visit, but regularly sent them money. At the time of my fieldwork, this daughter (Sita's sister-in-law) was waiting for her mother's unlikely return, so that she, too, could work abroad. Women who migrated usually did factory or domestic work in Malaysia, Hong Kong, Taiwan, Singapore, or Saudi Arabia. Men labored on plantations in Malaysia, were private chauffeurs in Saudi Arabia, or worked in factories in Taiwan and Korea. Village neighbors heard about my arrival and soon came to Sita's house to chat or invite us to their homes. Some of them were Sita's extended kin: they included return migrants, migrant applicants (prospective migrants), migrants' close kin, and those who did not plan to migrate. Children and teenagers sometimes sat in on our conversations, occasionally participating. Everyone had an opinion or story about migration, especially regarding women's journeys.

On the one hand, most people, especially the middle-aged and the elderly, repeatedly said that migration was good. Many asked if I was actually a recruitment agent who could find them jobs. They said that the money was good and the work seemed easy. They talked about how local income-generating alternatives such as planting rice or running restaurants (*warungs*) yielded very little, hardly enough to cover necessary expenses. The more "successful" return migrants were present or nearby to validate these views: their remittances contributed to starting motorbike repair shops, building bigger houses, or buying land from neighbors. They also perpetuated images of "the good life" overseas. One woman who used to work in Singapore said to me almost apologetically, "Here are my children. Look at them, they're so dirty.... This is *kampung* [village] life. So dirty.... Not like modern Singapore, so clean."

On the other hand, when I asked about return migrants—those who had worked overseas and come back—the stories were more specific and grim. Characters from these stories were heard of, often in whispers, but seldom seen. Couples got divorced, mostly due to adultery by either the migrant woman or the left-behind husband. Single women came back pregnant with "mixed-race" children.[1] Many returned with mysterious physical or psychological illnesses, despite leaving in the pink of health. For example, some stayed in bed for months before passing away; others were depressed, stopped talking, or else went mad (*gila*) talking to themselves. A few died abroad, and little formal explanation was given to the families by recruitment agencies, foreign doctors, or Indonesian or foreign governmental representatives, beyond statements that "accidents" (*kecelakaan*) happen. Sometimes, the repatriation of these bodies took far too long. It was puzzling for me to hear these dark stories one moment, while the next, unhesitant affirmations that migration was largely a good and promising endeavour.

One evening, I took a walk to the nearby rice fields with Sita's young cousin. She was twelve, and very bright. She had been sitting in on many of our discussions on migration. I asked her what she wanted to do in the future, and she replied that she wanted to be a teacher. "Don't you want to migrate too?" I asked, "Everyone seems to think it is good, you heard." (In fact, her relatives had joked that it would be her turn someday soon.) She cried out immediately, "No, no, I don't want to." When I asked why, she said that it was obvious, and told me confidentially specific rumors of adultery, divorce, single parents, death, and sickness. She had highlighted the source of my confusion, so I asked, "Why is it that everyone knows these things yet still talks about how migration is good?" Without missing a beat, she replied, "Because when they talk about that, they're only talking about money."

Despite the widespread sensational news of migrant abuses, sicknesses, and deaths in destination countries of Southeast Asia and the Middle East, hundreds of thousands of Indonesians continue to migrate annually for work abroad.[2] Why do they continue to embark on expensive and uncertain journeys, to take on precarious jobs? What kinds of comparative risks or value are there in staying in the village or working in nearby cities? Although Sita's young cousin remarked that her fellow villagers are "only talking about money," I argue that money and migration are valued in moral terms, shaped by local discourses and attitudes towards gender and sexuality, local customary laws (*adat*), and Islam. Indeed, how money—specifically money earned by migrants abroad—is talked about illuminates essential moral dilemmas and landscapes that characterize the everyday lives and aspirations of many residents of migrant-origin villages, partly due to the tension for money to be both "an instrument of individual desire," and "an instrument of collective dependency" (Narotzky and Besnier 2014, 9; see also Zelizer 2000).

Residents, particularly women, are often caught between competing desires and embodied expectations that appear incommensurable, such as migrating to financially provide for children, parents, and spouses, or staying to physically take care of these same family members. This individual moral dilemma is complicated by the elusive nature of human intentions and desires, which provoke others' moral judgments or discussions about specific individuals' "true" selfish, altruistic, or socially acceptable motivations behind migrating or staying. Moral judgments and reputation matter to persons deciding whether to migrate, stay, or return, in a context of relatively profound social interdependence, in which the help, goodwill, and trust of neighbors and fellow villagers are central not only in times of need, but also integral to one's sense of social and self-worth.

While researchers and journalists have examined and described the experiences of migrants in countries where they work and live, less is known about how residents of migrant-origin locales perceive and experience migration. Migration is still largely understood in popular and scholarly discourses from the perspectives of those who move, or in broad structural terms such as poverty and unemployment. In contrast, this book traces the diverse and surprising ways that migrant-origin villagers evaluate migration, its associated promises, risks, and rewards, such as money and sicknesses or injuries.

Framing Transnational Indonesian Migration

An estimated six million documented and undocumented Indonesians currently work overseas, typically in the Asia Pacific region, and the Arab countries in the Persian Gulf.[3] These transnational labor migrants are powerful moral symbols in the national imaginary. They are simultaneously valorized and despised in national media: portrayed as "foreign exchange heroes," "oppressed" victims of poverty and abuse abroad, and selfish criminals. These migrants serve as moral symbols in the sense that they are publicly represented by state authorities and national media as embodying values or linked to practices that are perceived as socially desirable or undesirable, admirable or pitiful, right or wrong. In early 2015, for example, the Indonesian President Joko Widodo publicly expressed feeling "brokenhearted" and "ashamed" on behalf of the nation (*Warta Kota* 2015). Addressing reporters, politicians, and his countrymen, he announced plans to stop sending Indonesian migrant workers as domestic workers abroad. Alluding to widespread reports of the abuses against Indonesian migrant domestic workers, the President framed his decision in terms of protecting the nation's "pride and dignity."

Over the past two decades, the Indonesian state, commercial, and nongovernmental organizations (NGOs) have proposed and implemented various programs and policies targeted at Indonesians who are planning to work abroad, currently working abroad, or have returned from working abroad. These programs typically draw on or contest the often-assumed economic advantages of migration, justifying their financial, practical or discursive interventions by representing the organization or group's moral obligations to and the moral imperatives of migrants and their families—how they should respond to the phenomenon of migration. For example, state and NGO-initiated financial education programs or entrepreneurship training programs aim to fulfill the state's or NGO's duty to "empower" diligent or struggling migrants and their families. Media and public campaigns and reintegration programs act to "save" "victims of trafficking." Trafficking is often a highly moralized term indicating a punishable wrongdoer (the human trafficker or smuggling organization) and an innocent victim. It has been unevenly used to represent a variety of issues facing many Indonesian labor migrants, such as when recruitment agents or employers target them for financial fraud and abuses (Ford and Lyons 2012; Lindquist 2013a; 2013b; Palmer 2012). Additionally, negative sanctions by Islamic organizations and proposed plans by the state include calls to illegalize, "stop," or "ban" the migration and perceived exploitation of women as domestic workers.

Contextualized by these tendencies of institutions to moralize, categorize, and regulate gendered and precarious labor migration in Indonesia as well as globally, this book shows how migrants, their kin, and their neighbors actively engage with, reproduce, or complicate these broader discourses and interventions. First, I show that migration is a messy process that exceeds and complicates common categories of those who go and those who stay behind. Second, I show that attitudes toward migration—whether it is viewed as "good" or "bad," desired or undesired, a moral responsibility or a selfish risk—vary widely according to the positionality of villagers, NGOs, and state representatives. Third, by examining how migration and the multi-scalar discourses surrounding it are highly gendered, I demonstrate their significant impact on how migrant-origin villagers experience and perceive migration-related risks, success, and failure, in terms of gender and morality. I argue that these multi-scalar moral discourses and responses to transnational circulations of bodies, labor, and finance constitute *gendered moral economies of migration.*

Approaching migration in terms of gendered moral economies draws attention to how the transnational circulations of bodies, labor, and finance are not only strongly shaped by destination countries' migration policies and socio-economic inequalities (Kearney 1995; Massey et al. 2005; Schiller, Basch, and Blanc 2012). In addition, these circulations are also influenced by international political dynamics and powerful ideas about gender and morality, such as what kinds of migration or financial flows should be encouraged or stopped, regulated or criminalized (Ford and Lyons 2012; Heyman and Symons 2012; Killias 2010; Rudnyckyj 2004; Silvey 2004). Such broader discursive and structural processes mutually shape the everyday material and economic conditions of migrant-origin villages, as well as the embodied subjectivities of residents there. This book draws on participant observation and interviews conducted between 2012 and 2016 mainly in three migrant-origin villages in Central Java (particularly Cilacap and Yogyakarta), but also including various stakeholders in different parts of Java. I argue and show how precarious labor migration is practically and financially sustained, tolerated, or encouraged, to various degrees, in migrant-origin villages through gendered and moral discourses of shame and faith, despite the high risks and costs to villagers in terms of finance, health, and mortality.

Through ethnographic examples, I demonstrate how migrant-origin villagers develop and practice gendered shame and faith to negotiate the risks associated with migration, return, and staying behind. These villagers do so partially by circulating blame and shame to migrants, migrants' families, recruitment agents, or foreign employers and "cultures." Through narratives of fate and destiny, they also attribute agency to nonhuman and divine actors in determining migration outcomes. Many scholars, activists, journalists, and state officials see these narratives of shame, fate, and destiny in terms of ignorance. I argue instead that these narratives enable migrants and residents to negotiate arbitrary and risky migration processes by framing and explaining the past in order to act strategically on the present for better futures. Disputing common representations of migrant-origin villages as sites of ignorance and immobility, my objective is twofold. On the one hand, I argue that villagers mobilize and develop shame and faith to explain, justify, and critique migration's "collateral damage" to families and villages—unwanted side effects produced by migration or its pursuit, including familial separation, divorce, deep financial debt, and economic inequality. On the other hand, these narratives of shame, fate, and destiny also serve to sustain faith in migration's promises of redemption, development, and "better" lives. Discourses of shame and faith may sometimes take the form of ethical reasoning to justify staying or leaving as moral projects that will lead to worthwhile lives and livelihoods. Villagers' gendered practices of shame and faith thus critically shape the transnational flows of labor and money.

(Im)mobilities and Motilities

Many Cilacap and Yogyakarta villagers who never left the country identify and are identified by others as "former" or "ex" transnational migrants. Examining migration from the viewpoint of places where migrants come from reveals that common categories of "prospective," "current," "return" migrants, and "nonmigrants" are more complicated and messy. This book shows how these terms are used and linked to one another in a multitude of surprising ways, which reflect how Central Javanese villagers and return migrants perceive where migration starts and ends, or whether a migrant is successful or a failure. Migration studies have tended to look at the experiences of migrants in destination countries (Brennan 2014; Constable 2007; Hondagneu-Sotelo 1994; Manalasan 2003; Yeoh and Huang 2000), or to trace links between migrant destination and origin countries (Levitt 2001; Gamburd 2000; McKay 2012; Parreñas 2005; Pratt 2012; Silvey 2006). They also examine experiences of "return migrants" (Kloppenburg and Peters 2012; Long and Oxfeld 2000; Özden and Schiff 2007; Xiang et al. 2013) and "nonmigrants" or those "left behind" (Dreby 2009; Hannaford 2015; Hoang and Yeoh 2011; Toyota, Yeoh, and Nguyen 2007). In contrast, I examine how migrant-origin villagers relate to and use these categories in fluid and changing ways, linked to their own ambivalent desires to migrate or to stay.

Studies of migration have historically drawn from economic perspectives that emphasize "push" factors that motivate migrants to leave their countries (e.g., unemployment or political violence), in relation to "pull" factors that attract migrants to particular destination countries (e.g., labor shortages or the demand for cheaper migrant labor) (Massey et al. 2005). Current studies have largely shifted away from understanding migration in terms of what has been called a "sedentarist" view (Malkki 1992), according to which migrants "uproot themselves, leave behind home and country" to settle in destination countries (Schiller, Basch, and Blanc 1995, 48) and nonmigrants are left behind. Unlike these images or implications of stasis, stability, and settlement, migration has more recently been understood in terms of simultaneity (Levitt and Schiller 2004), relationality (Conradson and McKay 2007), or mobility (Hannam, Sheller, and Urry 2006). Scholars increasingly emphasize the fluidity of migrant categories and status: while current migrants may decide to return home to settle, return migrants may choose to migrate again, and nonmigrants are also potentially future migrants (Cohen and Sirekci 2011; Constable 1999; Ley and Kobayashi

2005; Toyota, Yeoh, and Nguyen 2007). Furthermore, migrants may go from being documented to undocumented, and vice versa over the course of days or a week, depending on their employment situations, or the contingent, unpredictable results of their appeals for residency, visa extensions, or renewals (Constable 2014; Paraskevopoulou 2011). Such variability and uncertainty resonate for many Indonesian migrants, many of whom work abroad only temporarily, on two- to three-year contracts, in destination countries where permanent residency or citizenship is largely out of reach.[4]

Despite these more complex understandings of migrants' agency, mobility, and fluid identities, the mobility and motility (potential for movement) of those considered "nonmigrants" have not been given the same attention. Migration research arguably still tends to privilege the agency and views of migrants over those who do not cross borders, as encapsulated by the commonly used term "left-behind" to refer to nonmigrants. The term "left-behind" suggests incorrectly that nonmigrants—including migrants' peers, kin and neighbors in places of origin—are necessarily abandoned or surpassed by migrants in geographical and socioeconomic terms. As Sara Ahmed puts it, "[The] idealisation of movement, or transformation of movement into a fetish, depends upon the exclusion of others who are already positioned as not free in the same way" (Ahmed 2012, 152). Clearly, nonmigrants are not merely "passive recipients of remittances, information, and care" (Reeves 2011, 557). This book contributes an ethnography-based understanding of the emotional and relational experiences of those typically considered "left-behind" in migrant-origin communities, persons who also interact with and shape the continuous cross-border flows of persons, money, and expectations linked to migration.

Migrant-origin villagers make or negotiate decisions to stay, although they might face overwhelming pressures to migrate, and have the opportunities and resources to do so (Bylander 2014). The term and framework of "motilities" is useful for understand this dynamic: it refers to individuals' *potential for transnational movements* (Kaufmann, Bergman, and Joye 2004).[5] The term emphasizes important aspects of transnational migration not fully captured by the dichotomy between "mobile" and "immobile" persons, or those who migrate and those left behind. As Mark Salter (2013) puts it, "any understanding of the contemporary circulation must account not only for the facilitation and incarceration of specific groups, but of all the non-cases of mobility, those who are stopped before they start" (Salter 2013, 10; Kellerman 2012). In the same vein, this book examines different kinds of "stops" and "starts," based on the views and experiences of migrant-origin villagers who decide to stay, those ambivalent about migration, and those who attempted but failed to migrate.

Acknowledging the fluidity of persons' mobility statuses, for ease of reference the following terms refer to their current statuses or statuses at the time of research. "Return migrants" or "former migrants" refer to those who have worked and lived in another country before returning to settle (either temporarily or permanently) in the country of origin; "migrants" refer to those currently working and living in another country; "nonmigrants" are those who have never left their country of origin with the intention to live or work abroad. Additionally, since this book focuses on transnational migrants, my use of the terms "migrant" and "migration" can be understood as transnational. When I refer to migration within Indonesia, I use the qualifiers, "domestic" or "internal." While being sensitive to the instability of the distinctions between "documented" and "undocumented" migrants, this book uses the terms to refer to those with or without the legal right to live and work in a destination country; and "semi-documented" for those who may have the right to live in a destination country but are working in violation of some or all conditions of their migrant status (Paraskevopoulou 2011, 118).

Morality, Ethics, and Development

What constitutes "good" or "bad" migration, "successful" or "failed" migrants, varies widely, especially among those working at state agencies, at NGOs, and residents of migrant-origin villagers. While state representatives tend to see migrant wealth and remittances as central measures of "successful" migration and "development," migrant-origin villagers see migrant money and debt in more complicated ways. Institutionalized and public discourses of Islamic and Javanese morality, religious piety, and fate inform and constitute many residents' views and practices of migration and its associated risks and rewards. These views feed into villagers' own desires, questions, and ambivalence about migrating or staying. As demonstrated in later chapters, formal and informal institutional attempts to wield power over the lives of individuals through gendered moral discourses about migration shape migrant-origin villagers' responses to migrant wealth and debt, health and injuries.

What constitutes morality, how it may be differentially applied to men and women, and the mutual effects and consequences of moral discourses and practices on migration processes and patterns are central concerns of this study. My focus on the diverse moral landscape of migration builds on but departs from current studies of morality and migration. These have typically focused on the moral obligations or pressures that motivate migrants (Constable 2014; Faier 2007; Fioratta 2015; Thai 2014), the moral surveillance of migrants and their remittance practices (Dreby 2009; Katigbak 2015; Velayutham and Wise 2005), or the moral surveillance of migrants' spouses or kin at home (Chu 2010; Gamburd 2000; Hannaford 2015). Instead, I examine how moralizing local and institutionalized narratives of migration have touched and shaped the lives, relationships, and subjectivities of migrant-origin villagers. Together, migrants and migrant-origin villagers engage with these broader discourses to produce and shape what I call gendered moral economies of migration.

The concept of moral economies is particularly useful to this study for its "capacity to highlight the ambiguous logics and values that guide and sustain livelihood practices" (Palomera and Vetta 2016, 415). The idea of a moral economy is most often attributed to historian Edward P. Thompson's (1971) influential studies of the widespread food riots by English peasants in the eighteenth century in response to unfair prices of a "free" market economy. Anthropologist James Scott later popularized this concept through examining the livelihoods of Southeast Asian rice farmers (Scott 1976). Both scholars sought to situate economic activities within the realm of politics, religion, and social relations, to understand how the collective actions of those then considered "premodern" or "precapitalist" were "grounded upon a consistent traditional view of social norms and obligations" (Thompson 1971, 76–79), and patterned "fears, habits, and values" (Scott 1976, 2–4). Current uses of the concept have moved away from these associations of moral economy with the "premodern."

Thompson and Scott's conceptions of the moral economy have been criticized as largely homogenous and presuming amoral or "less moral" capitalist economies. Current scholarship, in response, addresses the intersection of economic, social, and moral values under late capitalism, but yields little agreement on the boundaries of the moral and the economic (Simoni 2016). Nevertheless, my "economies" (plural) build on feminist substantivists who highlight the dynamic and contested nature of human relations and action and are reluctant to strictly define the "economic." This "feminist economic" approach critiques the assumption of rational and autonomous economic actors and behavior, pointing to the centrality of emotion and personal relations of interdependency as central to social reproduction.[6] Thus I understand the economic as always constituted by complex sociopolitical relations that are plural and heterogeneous across social settings. Attending to both the plurality of economies and moralities in Central Javanese migrant-origin villages, the term gendered moral economies captures two main points of this book.

First, highlighting the influence (and interplay) of sometimes conflicting moral discourses on human behavior articulates alternatives to rational choice theory. In this case, people migrate despite known risks, or stay at home despite pressures to migrate. Second, the framework of gendered moral economies makes explicit the diverse logics of obligation and responsibility by emphasizing the political economy of the expression, implementation, and utilization of moral discourses by Indonesian and international institutions to shape transnational flows of labor and capital. Attending to such logics illuminates how forms of exploitation can be rendered temporarily acceptable, and how forms of socioeconomic differentiation are sustained (Narotzky and Besnier 2014, 7), not only within Central Java or Indonesia, but on a regional and global scale.

A handful of scholars have explicitly looked at migration in terms of a moral economy, mostly in terms of moral imperatives for migrants to send money to their families (Katigbak 2015; Stevanovic 2012), sometimes alongside moral judgments against migrant mothers' separation from their children (Contreras and Griffith 2012). I take a broader approach, and emphasize the importance of gender in the ways migrants, their kin, and neighbors negotiate values and expectations associated with the circulations of money, labor, and bodies, including those who are injured or healthy. Differing from current research which focuses on the moral rationality of human behavior within migrants' transnational relations (except see Keough 2008), I take a multi-scalar approach to understanding how migration is mutually shaped by moral discourses surrounding it.

Rather than using the term "moral" in moral economy to refer to evidently positive characteristics such as altruistic, caring, and sharing behavior (Tufuor et al. 2015) or the development of trust and a positively normative social code (Wright 2016), I examine instead how people in particular contexts "conceive of, negotiate, and practice morality in their everyday lives" (Zigon 2008, 1). In Central Java and Indonesia, what counts as moral encompasses a broad spectrum of activities and behavior in everyday life, and is influenced by institutionalized discourses, public discourses, and embodied dispositions of individuals (Zigon 2010, 5–6).[7] Although this book focuses specifically on migration, migration is not the only realm of everyday life and politics in Indonesia that is moralized. However, at the time of my research, migration was an explicitly moralized phenomenon that concerned the everyday lives and hopes of many residents of migrant-origin villages. Migration, overseas remittances, and international abuses, were daily topics in regional and national newspapers.

Looking at how migration is valued—such as in terms of "success" and "failure"—from the perspective of migrant-origin villages, this book engages with ongoing discussions over the impact of migration on migrant-origin countries and communities. Such discussions are often concerned with whether migration leads to the social and economic development of migrant-origin countries and communities, or perpetuates under-development and exploitation of the often poorer migrant sending countries (Faist 2008). This debate—known as the "migration-development nexus"—is implicitly concerned with the moral consequences and impact of migration on origin countries and communities, by assuming that there is a universal shared common idea of the good life—referred to as "development." Generally, certain scholars and policymakers distinguish between "good" migration that should be encouraged nearly as a moral imperative for governments and migrants—that which leads to "development" or "better" lives for more people (Özden and Schiff 2007)—and "bad" migration that should be discouraged, reversed, or stopped—in recent years presented as "trafficking" or "modern day slavery" by some activists and journalists (see, for instance, End Slavery Now, the CNN Freedom Project, Slavery Footprint).[8] This book contributes to these timely debates and issues by examining instead how such gendered and moral representations of migration, and its potential rewards ("development"), or costs ("slavery"), are experienced, reproduced, complicated, or challenged by residents of migrant-origin locales.

While there have been debates over whether "the moral" constitutes a unique sphere separate from ordinary life or is intimately present and remade in everyday life, I agree with the latter view.[9] Moral discourse and action are context-dependent, and thus can at times be more explicitly verbalized and understood as a process of conscious reflection, and at other times, take the form of embodied, instinctive, and unreflective responses to the needs of intimate others around them. In the former scenario, interviewees and friends in Central Java sometimes perceived morality and justified particular decisions, actions, or consequences by appealing to what they considered an objective moral source, such as the Qur'an, government regulations, or local customary law (*adat*). Nevertheless, villagers' moral judgments of others are not always internally or collectively consistent, and people clearly do not merely follow or abide by fixed moral codes or rules, although there might be some agreement as to what the social norms are *generally*. The generality and broad nature of "objective" moral rules highlight that there are always ways for individuals to reconsider how applicable those rules are in specific and temporal circumstances confronting persons. These discussions, moral judgments, and pluralistic moral attitudes reveal the necessary remaking of explicit norms and implicit practices within everyday life and interactions (Brandom 2008, 20; Zigon 2014), partially through taking into account, assuming, and/or discussing the intentions of others (Duranti 2015; Keane 2007). I take seriously the observation that "freedom does not lie merely in the absence of rules" (Heywood 2015, 200), but that individuals continue to negotiate freedom and agency in relation to other people and to both formal and informal codes of conduct (Laidlaw 2002). In other words, a prerequisite of moral codes is their reliance on ethical reflexivity, where "the activities of gossip do not simply reproduce values but exert new pressures on them" (Keane 2014, 12, see chapter 6).

Moving beyond the current scholarly focus on what constitutes the production, rejection, or maintenance of particular moral attitudes, I pay attention to how such attitudes are mediated at various levels, such as when and to whom moral judgments are pronounced (Lambek 2010, 2; Das 2007). In Central Java, what counts as morality is highly gendered. Women and men are subject to different standards of appropriate and desirable behavior and actions, typically regarding work, sexuality, reproduction, and financial and care obligations to the family (see chapter 3). Also, people are "enmeshed in different relations that entail different demands and desires" everyday (Han 2012, 20). I encountered people who harshly pronounced moral judgments on fellow villagers as ungrateful or neglectful of family members, and yet provided or sought help and food from the same people. The "moral" in everyday life thus emerges from and is also woven into people's interactive responses to the lives and needs of others (Das 2015, 115; Han 2012). Such lives, needs, and moral responses are articulated within a broader global context of highly uneven capital accumulation and distribution (Palomera and Vetta 2016).

Migrant-origin villagers' moral discourses of migrants and migration, as illustrated in the chapters that follow, can also be read as their *ethical and practical responses* to the inherent risks and arbitrary nature of the migration process. On the one hand, explicit moral judgements (such as gossip and shaming) can serve as broad critiques or justifications of migration as an endeavour, and its socioeconomic impact on migrant-origin village residents. On the other hand, the ways in which people can simultaneously express or enact empathy and generosity to help others cope with migration-related shame or the threat of shame, reveal moral pluralism in everyday life, in villagers' understandings of the broader circumstances shaping individuals' migratory or staying "fates." Ideas about morality or appropriate ways to *present* oneself and *respond* to others are mediated and structured through situated forms of communication and material exchange. As the following chapters show, gendered moral economies of migration are constituted, remade, and sustained through seemingly mundane everyday village talk about and responses to migrant success and failure: their money, houses, debts, and sickness.

Gender and Migration

It is now a truism that migration processes and discourses about it are highly gendered, and shape the experiences and conditions of migrants' work and lives abroad. Globally, migrant women often do care work and service work, while migrant men typically perform physically dangerous or intensive work. Depending on how migrants are perceived in terms of race and ethnicity in destination countries, migrant women and men may have distinct experiences with regards to work and residency, discrimination and opportunities, harassment on the streets or at work, and romantic or marriage possibilities. But gender also clearly structures the experiences in migrant-origin locales, of those who do not migrate, those aspiring to migrate, those who fail to migrate, and migrants who return home. This book describes the subtle and multifaceted impact of transnational migration on everyday life, relationships, and subjectivities in these places, particularly with regards to the ways in which gender, ethnic identity, and religious faith structure their views and everyday interactions. Migrants who return from working in other Islamic and non-Islamic destination countries can present subtle yet significant challenges to local gendered expectations, moralities, and kinship. Everyday conversations about migration and discussions about foreign migrant-destination countries and cultures reveal how migration can create new differences and exacerbate existing ones. These differences include diverging moral behavior and views, religious views, and material wealth. Migration thus may present wider alternative venues and possibilities—liberating, dangerous, and ambivalent—to the ways in which villagers experience and understand village relations, the world, and their place in it.

Feminist scholars of gendered migration in the 1990s and 2000s were influential in prompting the examination of the social and emotional impact of migration on migrants, their kin, and their communities of origin (Donato et al. 2006; Mahler and Pessar 2006; Hondagneu-Sotelo 2000). By looking at how gender structures household dynamics (such as patriarchal relations) and macrostructural dynamics of labor industries, these scholars encouraged a shift away from particularistic (culturally essentialist), household, or economic analysis. Instead, they called for gendered analyses of the "politics and governance of migration," such as neoliberal or welfare state policies on migration and diasporas (Donato et al. 2006, 6). A key question these scholars have raised is whether transnational migration "create[s] even greater possibilities for the reinforcement of prevailing gender ideologies and norms, or, conversely, [if] transnational spaces provide openings for women and men, girls and boys, to entertain competing understandings of gendered lives" (ibid.; Piper and Roces 2003). To date, research has only yielded mixed, ambiguous conclusions, suggesting that transnationalism has uneven and contradictory gains for women and men.

Engaging with these ongoing discussions about gender, politics, and mobility in Indonesia and elsewhere, I examine how migrants' experiences abroad, as well as migrant-origin villagers' experiences with recruitment agents, NGOs, and predeparture migratory processes, present new ideological, practical, and physical opportunities and threats to relationships, identities, and lives. These opportunities and threats are often evaluated and experienced in gendered ways in Central Java, with reference to Islam, God, or "Javanese culture." Women's migrations in particular can threaten, revive, or reproduce Javanese ideals of masculinity and femininity, while the failures of migrant men to live up to these ideals tend largely to be publicly tolerated yet experienced profoundly by some men as an extreme source of humiliation (see chapter 4). Migration-related financial debt and earnings affect prospective and current migrant women and men differently in terms of access to credit and risks of financial fraud, wage nonpayment, and labor exploitation. Migration can thus provide opportunities for accumulating previously unimaginable amounts of wealth and property, or it can result in crippling debt. Migrant remittances may ensure nutrition and food for children, adults, and elderly, but also pose threats to the bodies of migrants and their kin, in terms of mental and physical illness, and in the worst cases, death.

Attention to the impact of migration on everyday life, aspirations, and gender relations in Central Java cautions against assumptions that labor migration necessarily enables the "emancipation" of Muslim women from "patriarchal" rural villages (Brettell and Simon 1986; Hondagneu-Sotelo 1994). This older view is increasingly untenable, especially as the past decade of transnational migration from Indonesia has also witnessed the increasing influence of Muslim religious discourse, organizations, and leaders in cultural production and consumption, education, and politics in Java (Fealy and White 2008; Hefner 2011; Salim 2015). In contrast to earlier studies of Southeast Asian women's migrations to participate in waged work in factories and cities in the 1980s and 1990s (Elmhirst 2002; Mills 1999; Silvey 2003a; Wolf 1988), the opportunities for or restrictions to women's transnational mobilities in the twenty-first century depend not only on the dynamics and relations between influential religious organizations in Indonesia and the state, but also on intergovernmental diplomatic relations and mutual obligations (see chapter 1).

Attending to the subtle dynamics of gender, labor, debt, and remittances in migrant-origin villages also challenges the common myth that labor migration in general will over time lead to economic prosperity or "better" lives for migrants and their kin. Instead, I show that migration confronts villagers with difficult questions about the risks of migration, and the "collateral damage" inflicted on migrants, kin, and friends as a result of the pursuit of wealth, knowledge, love, adventure, respect, and/or independence. Migration has introduced or exacerbated villagers' encounters with differences in terms of intersecting values framed in religious, moral, and gendered terms, even while these differences are negotiated, respected, or contained by some migrant-origin villagers.

Overview of the Chapters

The book's chapters are organized by the different ways in which Indonesian migration is valued and shaped by state and non-state institutions and representatives, migrants, and residents of migrant-origin villages. Chapter 1, The Politics of Morality and Identity in Central Java, first introduces the field sites in Cilacap and Yogyakarta, where the bulk of this research was conducted. The chapter also contextualizes the book's discussion of gender and religion in Central Java within a broader history and politics of morality and identity in Indonesia. Understanding the past and present dynamics of politics, religion, and morality in Indonesia illuminates how women's transnational labor migration constitutes changing and contested ideas about gendered and moral duties to the family and nation.

The subsequent chapters each deal mainly with ways of framing or locating responsibility or blame for migration's promises and ills, including the unequal distribution of wealth, debt, opportunity, and risk. Chapter 2, Mobilizing and Moralizing Indonesian Labor, asks why some cases of violence against migrants are highly visible in national and international media, and receive the attention of NGOs and states, while other forms of labor abuse and everyday suffering are rendered mundane, tolerable, and sometimes even necessary. Drawing from a range of sources including newspaper articles, speeches by and interviews with Indonesian state representatives and migrant activists, this chapter introduces the complex discursive and infrastructural landscape of transnational labor migration in Indonesia. I demonstrate how responsibility for migratory processes and injustices is often ascribed to many different actors and institutions. In the institutionalized dispersals of responsibility and blame among institutions and actors, I argue that women migrants tend to carry the burden of ensuring "successful" migration outcomes, and they endure the shame associated with failure.

Chapter 3, Evaluating Migrant Success and Failure, shifts the book's focus to migrant-origin villages of Cilacap and Yogyakarta. Providing an in-depth view of "success" and "failure" for migrants, former migrants, prospective migrants, and their peers and kin, this chapter shows how residents experience and perceive transnational migration in ways that are influenced by—and also constitute—public discourses. Migrant success appears both ubiquitous yet simultaneously elusive, as many villagers express a paradoxical ambiguity and certainty about migration's rewards. Looking critically at the dominant view that migrants move to make money, and that financial success is of primary importance to migrants' kin, I show how villagers make important distinctions between "self-evident" material markers of success (i.e., wealth, houses, and enterprises) and more elusive gendered moral requirements of success (i.e., fulfilling or performing gendered duties). I argue that villagers ultimately evaluate migrant success and failure based on moral judgments of migrants' character and actions, vis-à-vis their social relations and how migrants distribute their money and debt.

The second part of this chapter introduces and discusses individuals who occupy an ambivalent identity as "former" and "failed" migrants, despite never having left the country. Exploring how and why some villagers who tried and failed to migrate are perceived as "neither/nor" and "both/and" migrants and nonmigrants, I argue that their situations demonstrate the high expectations for all migrants to succeed once they decide to migrate. Villagers and former migrants locate ultimate blame for succeeding or failing in migrant individuals rather than point to the roles and/or complicity of recruitment agents and employers. Moral self-responsibility emerges as a fundamental and limiting theme in villagers' and former migrants' discourses on migrant success or failure.

Chapter 4, Shame, details the ways in which villagers variously identify shame (*malu*) or the threat of shame as a negative consequence of migration, failing to migrate, or staying. Discussing other existing analyses of malu in the Indonesian archipelago, this chapter shows how not only migrants but also migrants' families are blamed for migrants' failures constituting a "kinship of shame." The embodied experiences of shame, or the threat of shame, strongly shape people's decisions to stay, migrate, or return. Shifting from migrants' own moral subjectivities, I address how such moral evaluations of migrants also shape the desires, behavior, and shame of those who do not move (or have not yet moved). Work, money, and sexuality are tied to residents' sense of shame in terms of appropriate gendered moral behavior, relations, and identity. I move beyond the dominant scholarly and media focus on morality in relation to women's migrations, and ask how male migrants or female migrants' husbands experience and cope with their partner's migration, including experiences of humiliation and emasculation (see also Elmhirst 2007; Gamburd 2000; 2008). This chapter thus reveals what is morally at stake in gendered migratory and staying subjectivities, and why villagers express great ambivalence about whether or not to migrate.

Chapter 5, Faith, explores the central role that faith and fate play in villagers' responses to migration's promises and risks. Narratives about fate and destiny illustrate how and why migrants and their families can sometimes be absolved of blame and responsibility for "shameful" actions. Yet, when deployed at the level of institutions and their representatives, discourses of fate absolve the responsibility of states and institutions for the unbalanced level of uncertainty and risk that migrants bear in comparison to the level of control granted to recruiters, employers, and government officials (Prusinski 2016a). Focusing on faith and fate offers an alternative to the dominant focus in migration research on either human autonomy or on migration infrastructure. I argue that villagers' views of divine agency acknowledge the inherent risks, loose regulations, and arbitrary nature of the migration process. Their discussions and practices of faith cannot simply be viewed as fatalistic, as faith requires human effort. Narratives of fate and destiny mobilize individuals to practice self-discipline and piety or to perform solidarity through collective prayer and mutual care.

Chapter 6, Contesting the Terms of Belonging: Views Of/From Elsewhere, explores migrant-origin villagers' views of foreign places and the possibilities or threats they pose. Some villagers blame foreign employers and foreign states for things that go wrong for migrants abroad. Such discussions of "Indonesian" and "foreign" cultures can shift villagers' discussions of migration away from migrant self-responsibility or blame. I highlight the restlessness, ambivalence, or explicitly transgressive actions of prospective migrants and return migrants to suggest ways in which residents and migrants negotiate or contest local gendered and sexual moral expectations. As stories in this chapter reveal, alternative moralities and gendered subjectivities build on and grapple with notions of personhood and morality both here and elsewhere.

The concluding chapter, Gendered Moral Economies of Migration, returns to the book's key questions about the diffused responsibility and blame in relation to both the potential earnings and the potential injuries of Indonesia's six million migrants. Villagers rarely file official complaints against corrupt agents or protest or make formal demands for reform of failed policies. Yet, they are far from naïve or ignorant. This chapter links the ways villagers maintain faith in migration's promises to their cultivation of shame and discipline in response to the anticipated risks. Pointing to hopeful and current interventions by advocates for migrants' welfare, this chapter raises important questions about the wider relevance of gender, morality, and faith to migration studies.

Notes

1. This term is usually used to refer to children who appear visibly different from their mothers, often exhibiting features such as very dark or very light skin. However, in my experience, sometimes such so-called "mixed-race" children do not appear too physically different from other children. I suggest they might be referred to as "*campur*" partly due to gossip about how they were conceived.

2. In 2014, when this research was conducted, more than 400,000 Indonesians embarked on regular, documented migratory journeys. Statistics for 2015 and 2016 show a marked decrease in official rates of migration to between 275,000, and 200,000. However, it is difficult to tell if these reflect overall migratory trends or if migrants are instead turning to irregular and undocumented routes due to increasing restrictions and regulations. See chapter 4; BNP2TKI 2015, 2016, 2017.

3. Most data cited on the number of Indonesian migrants abroad are estimates due to the need to include irregular and undocumented migrants. The numbers tend to vary between 4.5 million to 6.5 million. Of this latter figure, Khoo et al. (2015) estimate that 5 million Indonesian migrants are domestic workers. The six million figure estimate is based on Anjalah 2015.

4. The pathway to citizenship or permanent residency in many of these destination countries, such as Singapore, Malaysia, Hong Kong, Taiwan, and UAE, is mainly through marriage to a citizen. Applications for permanent residency in these countries often depend on "points systems" which privilege higher income applicants with tertiary education backgrounds. Moreover, Singapore, for example, explicitly forbids migrant workers on specific work visas (e.g., domestic work visa) to marry Singaporean citizens, although anecdotally, some former migrant workers have been able to do so and thus embark on the path to citizenship, albeit through multiple appeals, international journeys, and complex bureaucracy based on nontransparent and discretionary measures. In Hong Kong, appeals by activists for migrant domestic workers to be eligible for permanent residency, like most other skilled foreign workers, have been rejected by the government. See Chen 2012.

5. The term "motility" is most commonly used in a physiological or biochemical sense, referring to a body or cell's embodied energy and ability for movement. It has been sparsely used in sociology by Zgymunt Bauman in *Liquid Modernity* (2000) to describe the ability to be mobile. The theorization of motility that I draw on is mainly that proposed by Vincent Kaufmann, Manfred Bergman and Dominique Joye (2004).

6. For a review, see Bear et al. 2015, and Narotzky and Besnier 2014; for other classic approaches to how capitalism and monetary economies are constituted in social and

gendered relations and inequality, see Daston 1995; Ong 2010; Rosaldo 1980; Strathern 1988; Weiner 1992; Wolf 1992, Zelizer 2000.

7. Institutions are formal and informal social organizations such as religious organizations; village, regional, and central governments; nongovernmental and international organizations. They wield varying degrees of power over the lives of individuals, but can never completely enforce their discourses about morality. Institutional moralities are plural, and can influence public discourse substantially, whether in encouraging the adoption of similar or counter-attitudes and practices. I use public discourse about morality loosely to refer to "public articulations of moral beliefs, conceptions, and hopes" by and through media such as television, print and online journalism, protest, the arts such as theatre or literature, intellectual debates, and everyday expressed opinions and that which is taken for granted as "common knowledge" (see Zigon 2010, 7). These may be but are not necessarily linked to institutional morality.

8. http://www.thecnnfreedomproject.blogs.cnn.com, http://endslaverynow.org, and http://slaveryfootprint.org.

9. See, for example, Das 2012 and Zigon 2008 for an overview of the debates.

1 The Politics of Morality and Identity in Central Java

COMING FROM SINGAPORE, I was keenly aware of the moralizing and sexualizing discourses in the media and everyday public discussions about Indonesian and Filipina migrant domestic workers. These notions of the migrant woman (and ethnic other) as a "seductress" to be wary of, "abused victim" to be rescued, or "sacrificial mother" supporting her own poor family and village are not unique to Singapore, but are also present in diverse cultural and geographical contexts of migrant destination countries. When I first arrived in Yogyakarta and Cilacap, I was thus naively surprised by how some of these stereotypes and tropes of Indonesian migrant women were also circulated and reproduced not only in Indonesian national media, but also among migrants' own kin and neighbors. Very quickly, my simplistic assumptions about grateful families as receivers of remittances were replaced by a necessity and desire to navigate the nuanced meanings, differences, and effects of such moralizing tropes about migrants in migrant-origin villages.

This chapter introduces the three main migrant-origin villages of Cilacap and Yogyakarta where the bulk of this research was conducted, in addition to other participants and places comprising this work. To contextualize the book's discussion of gender and faith in Central Java, this chapter also provides an overview of the history and politics of morality and identity in Indonesia. The centrality of morality in contemporary Indonesian politics, public discourse, and social life, is closely linked to struggles between groups and leaders over defining values and identities linked to Islam, gender, family, and the nation. The following sections address the history of migration in Indonesia, earlier ethnographies of Javanese gender and family paradigms, and the ways in which political and religious leaders and organizations in Indonesia have cooperated and clashed in determining and regulating moral discourse and behavior. Gender—which is closely tied to conceptions of the "family" and familial responsibilities—often takes center stage in mediating the relationship between "religion" and "the state." Alongside industrialization and the feminization of domestic and transnational migration, Indonesian women's activities and mobilities emerge as a key site and topic of enduring institutional and public contestations over morality, family roles, and ethnic, national, and religious identity.

Traveling Between Sites: Villages, Fairs,
Workshops, and NGO Offices

Most of the data for this research are based on participant observation and
130 semi-structured interviews conducted mainly in Java, Indonesia. A main
research period between September 2014 and August 2015 was supplemented
by shorter research trips in 2012, 2013, and 2016.[1] Most interviews and informal
conversations were conducted in Indonesian, with a minority in English (with
activists or former migrants who spoke English) and partial Javanese. The bulk
of ethnographic data for this book is based on fieldwork conducted in three main
migrant-origin villages, two located in Cilacap and one in Yogyakarta. All are
geographically based in Central Java.[2] In 2014, 21 percent of Indonesian documented migrant workers originated from the Province of Central Java, the second largest migrant-origin province nationwide (BNP2TKI 2015).

I was first introduced to Cilacap in 2012 when, while learning Bahasa
Indonesia in Yogyakarta, I met Sita, who was introduced at the beginning of this
book. Sita had lived in the city of Yogyakarta for about five years by the time we
met, and she shared my curiosity about why so many of her Cilacap neighbors
and fellow villagers migrated abroad, despite the many known risks. She invited
me to visit and stay with her family in Cilacap for a few days. With her help trans-
lating, due to my intermediate Indonesian and nonexistent understanding of the
Javanese language at the time, we conducted preliminary interviews with her kin,
neighbors, and two recruitment agents who also lived in the village. Each night
we discussed what we had observed, heard, and talked about. Like me, Sita was
struck by the pervasive and seemingly incompatible stories of violence against
migrants, and the general, almost self-evident, image of success associated with
migration. We noticed how frequently the idiom of *nasib* (fate) was invoked to
justify risky migration journeys, or migratory failures and sicknesses. It was Sita
who first associated the frequent use of nasib with her observations of increasing
Islamicization in her village and among the friends she had grown up with. She
associated the growing influence of Islam in social life with everyday references
to Islamic discourses or religious leaders' sermons, and the increased popularity
among Cilacap women to don the Muslim hijab as opposed to more loosely worn
Javanese *kerudung*. These initial observations and questions would come to be
central to my research. I have continued visiting Sita's village each year since,
staying for longer periods in 2014 and 2015.

My attachments to Sita's village in Cilacap, her family, and neighbors,
spanned a longer temporal period compared to the other two villages I lived
in. This allowed me to track the changing life circumstances and migrant statuses of its various residents. I arrived in the second Cilacap site in 2014 to visit
an acquaintance, Nurul. She had been a migrant domestic worker in Malaysia

and Singapore for over twenty years, and we met through Singapore- and Yogyakarta-based migrant-centered NGO networks.[3] Largely due to the circumstances of her return and her marital history, Nurul was subject to gossip and social marginalization in her community, and deeply sympathetic to others in her position. She was an engaging and opinionated storyteller, and expressed great interest and awareness of broader political and labor issues concerning migrants like herself. I met her small network of kin, acquaintances and neighbors, and a few close friends. Living with Nurul gave me a deeper insight into the daily experiences, interactions, and views of a return migrant, and how she and others like her negotiated gossip and harassment.

I was introduced to the third site, a migrant-origin village in rural Yogyakarta, in September 2014. BNP2TKI (National Agency for the Placement and Protection of Migrant Workers) had organized an event in the city of Yogyakarta to showcase successful Indonesian migrant-based associations and entrepreneurship. Selected return migrants and their fellow villagers from various parts of the archipelago were invited to attend. My interest in and engagement with the Yogyakarta site were sparked by a conversation with a resident and nonmigrant, Minah. When I told her about my research interests, she remarked, "Some migrants return with lots of money. Others become crazy. But many . . . are so arrogant, and they believe they are better than the rest of us. There is a problem of integration. Return migrants should undergo some kind of socialization program when they come back to their *kampong* (village)." Because Minah and I had a mutual friend, she invited me to visit her village. In contrast to the other two sites, Minah's village participated in various development and educational programs funded by the state and international development organizations, and facilitated by NGOs. Thus I was able to observe and participate in two such programs, and compare how such programs might impact participants and other villagers' attitudes to migration and migration-related institutions (e.g., BNP2TKI and relevant NGOs).[4]

The three sites share important similarities. I refer to them as "migrant-origin" villages, because statistically and anecdotally, transnational labor migration is prevalent. Nearly everyone has kin, neighbors, or friends who have migrated or tried to migrate, or who have themselves migrated. The three sites share geographic and infrastructural characteristics. All are near the South Java Sea, and depend on rice agriculture as well as fishing industries. Many residents also work in factories or construction projects in urban areas of Indonesia. The sites are all relatively rural; they are inaccessible directly by bus. This is significant when considering the amount of time and money required for residents to travel to the nearest BNP2TKI or BP3TKI office or district government office to obtain official information or advice about migration processes and regulations. Their relative inaccessibility also increases the residents' reliance (regarding migration-related procedures) on fellow villagers and available recruitment agents and agencies in their village or neighboring villages, as compared to urban dwellers who might be able to "shop around" for a trustworthy agent or a better agreement.

Fieldwork in these three villages included living with families of former migrants, current migrants, and prospective migrants, and participating in daily activities for women such as meal preparation and childcare; attending weekly Qur'an readings and prayer meetings (*pengajian*) and *arisan* (a local form of rotating credit and savings association); taking part in or attending weddings, births, funerals, and annual Javanese and Islamic festivities such as *Satu Suroh* (Javanese New Year), *Idul Adha* (Islamic Day of Sacrifice), and *Idul Fitri* (the day marking the end of the holy month of fasting). These daily and ritual activities facilitated the participation and observation of informal talk amongst women and men about personal and broader political concerns about their families and the village, as well as how ideas about gender and morality are closely tied to family dynamics, roles, and responsibilities. Fieldwork in the villages also allowed me to observe the organization of gender roles in households, and compare how migration was framed temporally and situationally in terms of gender, finances, and other material and moralizing terms. On-site fieldwork was also complemented by online communication with current migrants (mainly based in Singapore), Central Javanese residents, and migrant activists based in Indonesia and Singapore.

I also conducted interviews with representatives and staff of NGOs focused on migrant, labor, or women's issues. While it was difficult to contact and interview at length government representatives of BNP2TKI, I spoke to one who worked for a district branch (BP3TKI). I also closely followed, archived, and analyzed the multiple public speeches of and interviews with state representatives of BNP2TKI, the Ministry of Labor, and the Ministry of Foreign Affairs in the Indonesian press. These interviews and press archives helped me to understand the institutionalized approaches to and personal staff and representatives' experiences with migration-associated issues. Examining the multiple perspectives of institutions and their members illuminated diverse or common opinions about why migration was so popular, and to what extent individuals and groups condoned, vilified, or tolerated (aspects of) the practice. I also observed several programs, workshops, and conventions targeted at or concerning return migrants, prospective migrants, and their kin in multiple other migrant-origin villages in Wonosobo, Yogyakarta, and Cilacap.[5] These activities were variously organized and funded by the Indonesian state, foreign states, and/or development and aid institutions, and facilitated by NGOs, grassroots organizations, state agencies, and commercial companies.

Thanks to the generosity and patience of several former migrants and activists at SBMI (*Serikat Buruh Migran Indonesia*, or National Migrant Labor Union),

I stayed at their migrant shelter in Jakarta for a week in January 2015, after which I remained in touch with key members at other SBMI-organized events, and through email communication. SBMI is arguably the largest migrant welfare organization in the nation with dispersed subgroups across the archipelago, run by former migrants. On this trip I was accompanied by a friend and occasional research assistant, Yuna, whom I had met in Yogyakarta during interviews with herself and a colleague at a migrant-centered NGO where she worked. Yuna had also previously worked with SBMI, and introduced me to the organization and its executive committee and volunteers. Migrants who were deported or who failed to leave the country stayed temporarily at this shelter, while SBMI staff helped to mediate and resolve their problems with recruitment agencies or BNP2TKI. My experience here enabled me to meet some former migrants who had returned to Indonesia but who did not want to, or had not yet returned to their villages of origin. Conversations at SBMI helped to balance the views and experiences of return migrants at the shelter with the others "at home." In observing the interactions between SBMI staff (all former migrants themselves) and the more recently returned migrants, I was reminded that migrants often criticize and judge one another. Like residents in migrant-origin villages, they do not always share common experiences, interests, or views.

Yuna also accompanied me on two other trips: to a national SBMI conference in Wonosobo for three days, and once on a weeklong trip to Sita's village in Cilacap. Our conversations about migration from Indonesia, particularly NGO networks, enabled me to appreciate the various concerns, disagreements, and NGO- and state-proposed solutions to issues such as undocumented migration and inflated recruitment fees from Indonesia.

The "doing" of fieldwork for this research thus entailed frequent travel between migrant-origin villages, the national capital of Jakarta, and the city of Yogyakarta. I agree with the observation that "fieldwork itself is a work that selects and follows particular connections between people, places and other agents" (Hastrup 2012, 157). The various people, sites, and events constituting my fieldwork experience and data are connected by the ways in which they participate in and shape transnational migration processes from Indonesia, from migrants' predeparture to migrants' return, and possible remigrations. My mobility between sites was not uncommon for anyone I interacted with. Migrant-origin villages consist of many individuals who often come and go unpredictably. This includes those who cross national borders, those who move to nearby urban cities and return on weekends, or those who work on other Indonesian islands on project-based contracts and return annually or every two years. Workshops, conferences, and events organized by or for prospective and former migrants—such as "show-and-tell" entrepreneurship fairs for return migrants—were often fleeting and short-lived "sites." Due to the nature of their work in advocating for labor migrants' and women's welfare and the day-to-day facilitating of migrants' or women's immediate practical or legal problems, NGO staff and activists often had hectic schedules and multiple travel itineraries. Their weekly or monthly routes were often between various offices wherever they were based, or between Jakarta, migrant-origin villages, and even migrant destination countries. Thus, at any point in time, even when I was based in the villages, I communicated with friends, acquaintances, and colleagues in other sites and locales (see Hannerz 2003).

Doing fieldwork, particularly in the villages, required me to navigate various positions and misperceptions. As an ethnic Chinese-Singaporean who speaks fluent Indonesian, I was sometimes mistaken as a Chinese-Indonesian or a foreign recruitment agent looking for prospective migrants in the villages. At other times, I was taken as a foreign employer visiting a former migrant employee. On multiple occasions, men and women asked half-jokingly if I could sponsor their working visas in Singapore, or take them with me when I returned. Twice, I was approached to fund the businesses of return migrants. Most of the time, however, as an obvious "outsider," many residents approached me to share their experiences, stories, and views about migration. Some were eager to corroborate or explain rumors and gossip: "Is it true that a domestic worker can earn up to USD 6,000 a year?" "Why do Indonesian women become lesbians when they go overseas?" At times, people assumed I shared their assumptions and values about gender roles and morality as a fellow "Asian" and "non-Westerner." Other times, people were wary that, as a non-Muslim and foreigner, I might be "too open" in my views, that I might approve of homosexuality, premarital sex, divorce, or unmarried couples who cohabit. However, as a young and unmarried woman at the time, I mitigated potential views of my presence as threatening by always moving around the village accompanied by local female friends (and sometimes their children). Some residents sought information about migratory regulations and processes to Singapore and Korea in particular. Many others taught me a lot about migratory and labor regulations (or the lack of them) in Gulf Cooperation states, Taiwan, Hong Kong, Malaysia, and Indonesia. The stories, attitudes, and the questions, of everyone I met, shaped my understanding of the various perceptions and stereotypes of recruitment agents, employers, migrants, and their lives abroad.

My interest in issues of gender, morality, and labor migration was initially sparked by being raised by and among Filipina and Indonesian domestic workers in Singapore, where an estimated one in five households hire a domestic worker (Ministry of Manpower 2013, in Platt et al. 2013, 13). Between 2005 and 2007, I worked in cafes and restaurants in Singapore alongside migrant workers from China, Bangladesh, India, Nepal, and Pakistan, who were sometimes paid half my wages, with longer hours, and fewer rest days (if any). In 2011,

I briefly volunteered for and worked with the migrant labor NGO Humanitarian Organization for Migration Economics (HOME) and the Indonesian Family Network (IFN). During that time, I helped to facilitate and document cases of labor abuse, fraud, and forced repatriation that faced both male and female migrant workers in Singapore, particularly those who worked in the manufacturing, service, or construction sectors. These experiences in various positions and affiliations such as a dependent, employer, colleague, and NGO volunteer have given me a long-term view of the dynamics and issues concerning gender, labor, and migration, not only in Singapore, but also in Southeast Asia broadly.

Javanese and Indonesian Mobilities

Temporary migration within Indonesia has a long history. The internal and international migration of men in many parts of the Indonesian archipelago—often known as *merantau*—has since the early twentieth century been socially sanctioned as a rite of passage into adulthood for male youth, and linked to social expectations for men to financially contribute to the family as migratory "breadwinners" (Hugo 1982; Nas 2003). It was not uncommon for Javanese men to move temporarily to find work in neighboring areas, provinces, or islands within Indonesia, for periods as short as a few days to months to years (Hugo 1982). Women typically stayed behind to take care of agriculture and the children. Men's circular migrations to and from the household were seasonal, and their movements often occurred in between planting and harvesting seasons, when there was little work to be done (Hugo 1982).

The Suharto government's later institutionalization of transnational labor migration as a pathway to national economic development has a historical precedent in the state's *transmigrasi* (transmigration) program. As part of Suharto's broader project to engineer Indonesia's demographics in the pursuit of economic growth and national integration, from the 1970s to 1990s the Ministry of Transmigration was restructured to facilitate coerced mass-migration of Javanese peasants in populated areas to the outer islands, such as Irian Jaya (West Papua), Sumatra, and Borneo (Tirtosudarmo 2003). Informed by similar efforts in the nineteenth century of the Dutch before them, the Suharto government justified the program by pointing to overpopulation in Java as a main cause of Indonesia's economic stagnation and poverty (ibid.). Social science research on transmigrasi has focused on two key issues: indigenous rights and agrarian movements on the outer islands, and ethno-political conflict (Collins 2007; Li 2007; Potter 2009). Scholars criticized repressive state policies and the World Bank and other development agencies for funding the program, all of which were perceived as part of a broader mission to facilitate Indonesia's industrialization and incorporation into the global capitalist economy (Dove 1988).[6] The programs had an explicitly moral, heteronormative aspect: sponsored Javanese migrants "were required to be married, of good character ... and to have farming experience. Migrant families received a small house with one hectare of rain-fed cropland." (Frederick and Worden 1993, 172). Following the fall of Suharto's government in 1998, these programs virtually ceased.

Other forms of migration from and within Java were simultaneously starting to take place in the 1970s and 1980s. Industrialization in Indonesia during this time meant more job opportunities for rural and typically uneducated women. Despite initial general moral panic and parental disapproval, in the 1980s in Sumatra and Java, women from agriculture-based rural areas managed to migrate and live apart from their families to work in factories. In contrast to the migrations of men outside of the village, which were largely taken for granted, women's migrations created tensions among family members, and provoked moral judgments from some villagers. Resistance to women's migrations for work were framed in terms of their moral reputations as unmarried women being exposed to strange men in unfamiliar surroundings (Elmhirst 2002; 2007). For example, an ambivalent parent whose daughter worked in a factory considered that "a girl working in a factory isn't right", and is "dirty" (*kotor*) and "shames" the family (in Wolf 1988, 96). Nevertheless, many women managed to migrate by appealing to their parents' sense of duty to appear be "providing well for their daughters, to be 'modern'" (Elmhirst 2002, 155).

Parents generally did not expect financial support from "factory daughters," partly due to women's low wages, alongside gendered ideas that their income was only supplementary to men's contributions (Wolf 1988). Thus young women initially spent their earnings on 'modern' consumption goods, and remitted irregularly to families (Elmhirst 2002). However, with the normalization and institutionalization of such migration through villagers' social networks, families increasingly negotiated control over young women's earnings and activities (ibid.). While their new income enabled some Javanese migrant daughters to participate in household financial decision making, most of them still required permission from fathers or older brothers regarding wide-ranging aspects of their lives away from home, and relinquished bonuses or savings for their families' consumption upon demand (Wolf 1988, 100). In sum, women's internal labor migrations during the 1980s and 1990s created new relations of dependence and autonomy between parents and migrant daughters, which partially increased young unmarried women's bargaining power within households, but did not overtly challenge patriarchal family hierarchies. This was also generally true for women's migrations elsewhere (Mahler and Pessar 2006).

It was during this period of later industrialization—when rural women's migration for factory work was more accepted and common—that the Indonesian state began to promote transnational female labor migration, mainly targeted at rural, uneducated women. The shifting circumstances of and backlash against the state's promotion of women's migration (under various presidents) will be discussed below. Today, the majority of Indonesia's transnational migrant workers come from relatively rural backgrounds and have graduated from junior high or high school. Most participate in precarious work—work that is usually informal, flexible, characterized by low and uncertain wages, a lack of unionization or protective regulations, and job insecurity (Kalleberg 2013). Indonesian migration increased rapidly after 1998, during the time of the Asian Financial Crisis and the fall of Suharto's military-based, centralized government. By this time, agricultural work such as rice farming in Central Java was largely perceived as a less desirable and unviable livelihood among rural youth. The decline in manufacturing and industrial jobs in the turbulent social and political climate of the late 1990s, as well as comparatively higher wages abroad, contributed to the popularity of transnational migration.

The rise in demand specifically for Indonesian women's labor abroad from the late 1980s to the present day is linked to the entrance of professional women into the labor force of modernizing economies of destination countries such as Singapore, Hong Kong, and Malaysia (Constable 2007; Lan 2006). Recruitment agents from these countries partner with Indonesia-based agents who persuade women to work overseas—sometimes by paying them a small fee (Palmer 2010; Khoo et al. 2015)—and convince their families to permit them to go abroad (Rudnyckyj 2004). The perceived docility of migrant women compared to potentially disruptive men also influenced the migrant labor recruitment industry in Indonesia, with the perception that it is less risky to offer credit for women's journeys (where their work and mobility abroad were more likely to be controlled) as opposed to those of men (Khoo et al. 2015; Lindquist 2010).

As is the case in Cilacap and Yogyakarta, the majority of Indonesia's migrants are women; most are domestic workers or factory workers in countries such as Saudi Arabia, Malaysia, Hong Kong, Taiwan, and Singapore.[7] Men typically work in industrial, manufacturing, construction, and agricultural industries in Malaysia, Saudi Arabia, Korea, and to a lesser degree Japan. An increasing number of undocumented male migrants also work as seafarers for Taiwanese or Korean-registered companies and ships.[8] In 2014, the vast majority of migrants were from East, West, and Central Java. Promised wages abroad can be at least double and up to ten times local wages. For example, the minimum monthly wage for factory workers in Central Java was around 1.2 million Indonesian rupiah in 2015. Yet, domestic and plantation workers in Malaysia could earn minimally two to three million per month; domestic workers in Singapore, Hong Kong, and Taiwan could earn around four to six million; while factory workers in Taiwan and Korea could expect up to ten million. Similarly, the costs of migration vary, depending on the job, destination country, and whether or how many falsified documents are required. Migrants typically embark on journeys indebted to their brokers, kin, informal moneylenders, and/or banks. Generally, female domestic workers and an increasing number of migrant men to Korea participate in forms of "indentured mobility" (Parreñas 2011), in which they work abroad to pay off their debts to agents who withhold their passports. In contrast, migrant women and men who work in factories and plantations often borrow from kin or moneylenders to pay for their migration journeys upfront.

Nearly all of them are on what are commonly termed "guest worker" programs (Piper 2006, 142), in which migrants are allowed to work and live in destination countries for two to five years, upon which they can renew their contracts or return home. Indonesian migrants follow a pattern that may be categorized as "circular," "back-and-forth," "on and on," or "serial migration," through a hierarchy of migration destinations (Constable 2009; Liebelt 2008; Paul 2011). Whether migrants embark on one journey or many, and to one or more destination countries, can vary widely according to individual experiences, desires, and circumstances.

Religion, Gender, and Morality

The temporary transnational labor migration of women from Indonesia was first encouraged by President Suharto's militaristic New Order state in the 1980s, as part of a broader national development agenda. This promotion of women's migration, however, appeared to contradict earlier Islamically based gender discourses of *kodrat* that women should stay in the home. Kodrat refers broadly to the idea of fixed gendered destinies and duties specific to men and women (Blackburn 2004, 229). The following sections outline the ways in which religion, gender, and morality have been articulated in overlapping and contested ways by various state and non-state organizations in Indonesia. Contextualizing the historical and shifting relationship between religion and politics in Indonesia, particularly through more recent national moral debates, allows a better understanding of how and why women's contemporary transnational migration has emerged as a key site for current struggles between groups and individuals over power.

Islam in Indonesia

The nature of Islamic adherence and practices across the archipelago varies, for which Clifford Geertz's model of "Javanese religion" remains largely paradigmatic and partially useful, despite his critics.[9] His model distinguishes between the orders of *abangan, santri* and *priyayi*, in which the first can be summarized as a syncretism of Hinduist, Islamist, and animist beliefs and practices; the second as stressing Islamic orthodox practices; the third as consisting mainly of elites who stress Hinduist aspects of their religious practices (Geertz 1960). Later scholars built on these distinctions to differentiate between "nominal" and "pious" Muslims observed in Javanese contexts (Beatty 2002)—those who regularly go to the mosques and pray regularly—and the "ordinary, indifferent villager" (ibid., 475). In late post–New Order Indonesia, heterogeneous and abangan-syncretic forms of religious practice, belief, and identity, such as Javanism or Javanese animism, have been gradually rejected or downplayed by many Indonesians in favor of organized forms of (mainly Sunni) Islam or Muslim identities, consumption, and practices (Hefner 2011; Fealy and White 2008).

Nevertheless, Islamic organizations and leaders have, historically, largely had tense or delicate relationships with the Indonesian state. Contestations over the authority to define the political and moral terms of Indonesian nationalism and development marked Indonesia's independence as a nation, and these contestations have continued and been exacerbated through multiple presidencies into the twenty-first century. First President Sukarno's advocacy for a unitary, secular state was not compatible with Muslim intellectuals and the *ulama*'s focus on religion's role in nation-making. Eventually, the Jakarta Charter was drawn up in 1945 as a compromise on the part of Muslim intellectuals for national independence. Accordingly, the state was based on the belief in one God, while Muslims—who form a majority of the population—were required to follow sharia or Islamic law.[10] Sukarno also proposed and articulated the national ideology of Pancasila: five guiding principles of the nation based on the five pillars of Islam: the belief in God, humanitarianism, national unity, democracy, and social justice (Seekins 1993). Despite its unique secular-but-theist state foundations, the vast majority of Muslim voters and politicians has ensured the influence of Islamic discourse on national politics.

Islamic practices, ideologies, and local regulations in contemporary Indonesia are partially shaped by contact with Muslims abroad (such as through religious education in or temporary migration to Islamic countries) and transnational Islamic movements, ideas, and cultural products that are widely available online and through other media (Fealy 2008; Irawanto 2010; Salim 2015). Scholars have noted a shift in the meanings of Islamic identity and practice in the Indonesian public sphere following the fall of Suharto's regime in 1998, partly due to a backlash against liberal Islam in a post 9/11 (September 11) world, as well as a growing anti-Westernization discourse promoted by more extremist Muslim groups following the war in Iraq and Afghanistan, and responding to the political struggles of the Palestinians (Wieringa 2015).

The Islamic Defender's Front (FPI), which emerged in the disorder of 1998, is one example of an "extremist" group that primarily functions to attack individuals or groups which they perceive to be immoral, un-Islamic or threatening to Islamic moral values in Indonesia (Wichelen 2010, 103). Sometimes they are represented or perceived to be a paramilitary group, with close links to individual police and military officers. They are mostly associated with a concern for imposing negative sanctions on smoking, alcohol consumption, gambling, and homosexuality, as well as monitoring women's duties, rights, dress, and behavior (Hooker 2003, 140–142). The combatting of moral vices by FPI is often justified by its members through citing the Qur'anic injunction to "command right and forbid wrong." As Robert Hefner notes, "invocation of this injunction … has been a regular feature of modern Islamist politics in Muslim-majority countries. [This] allows activists to legitimate their usurpation of state authority by claiming to act on the basis of divine law, rather than that merely human" (Hefner 2008, 141). Condemning FPI's acts of violence and incitation of hate, members of various civil society groups have called for FPI to be banned or disbanded (International Crisis Group, 2008; Lazuardi 2017). Nevertheless, recent years have witnessed the expansion and increasing mainstreaming of radical groups like FPI. These trends notably occurred alongside the first formal gathering of the Indonesian female ulama in 2017, where members tackled longstanding controversial issues linked to patriarchal attitudes and laws that some Muslim groups and leaders have supported by reference to the Qur'an. The female ulama emphasized that polygamy was "not part of Islamic teachings" and issued a fatwa against early marriage, framing it as a moral obligation for Muslims to prevent such practices (Ramadhani 2017a; 2017b).

These ongoing struggles between and within religious, state, and non-state organizations over the authority to define the terms of morality and piety are often explicitly gendered and sexualized, focusing on the control or "protection" of women. Such gendered anxieties are also frequently linked to antagonism against capitalism or the state's economic development plans and processes of democratization, particularly since these processes have led to increasing socioeconomic mobility for women. Scholars have observed that radical Islamic groups and more informal Muslim "gangster" groups usually appeal to and comprise socially and economically marginalized young men from Jakarta's slums or poor neighborhoods, who use violence against women and elites to protest against their disenfranchisement and threatened masculinity (Wilson 2012, 133).

With the decentralization of the government post-Suharto, local and regional governments began to harness the support of Muslim organizations, engage with Islamic discourses publicly to regulate social behavior, and pass legislation enforcing aspects of Islamic practice or law in everyday life (Blackburn 2004; Salim 2015). Such widespread institutionalization of Islam in everyday life and politics is unprecedented in the nation's history. The prominence of Islamic discourse, identity, and regulation in contemporary Indonesia cannot be understood purely in terms of religious ideals and adherence; it is also due to worldly concerns, such as strategic ways for groups to garner political and community support, sometimes through providing economic resources to Muslim groups or receiving funding from international Muslim organizations (Salim 2015). For individuals, religious identity, faith, and expression are never only a matter of religious doctrine: they also provide ways for coping with the anxieties and ambiguities of contemporary life.

In my specific field sites, the vast majority of Central Javanese residents I spoke to identified as Muslim. They mostly aligned with Nahdlatul Ulama (NU), one of two main national Sunni Islamic organizations. Residents were also aware of specific villages and areas nearby that are comprised mainly of active practitioners of Javanese animism (*kejawen*) who did not participate in Muslim activities, such as the annual fasting season. In Cilacap, however, kejawen was practised in some households by elders, and gently criticized by their adult children who professed Islam. Several Cilacap residents, including Sita, remarked that women wearing the veil (hijab) upon leaving the house was a relatively recent (i.e., post-2000) phenomenon in the villages. In contrast, the Yogyakarta villagers, on the whole, identified their village as one that has practised Islam longer than neighboring villages, and boasted of extended families of respectable local *kyais* (an expert in Islam or local Islamic leader). I did not hear of any Yogyakarta households that practised kejawen, or of any non-kyai spiritual healers (i.e., healers who were not Muslim religious leaders). Nevertheless, the Muslim Yogyakarta villagers still attended and observed (as nonactive participants) kejawen celebrations of the Javanese New Year, *Satu Suroh*, which involves the offering of food to the South Sea Goddess. In other words, Indonesian Muslims are far from homogenous. Individuals, families, and groups disagree on the role of the state or religious groups in defining and legislating spiritual practice, social life, and public morality (Arnez 2010; Blackburn 2004; Weintraub 2008; Wichelen 2010; Wieringa 2015).

Islamicization and Javanese Gender Roles

Dynamics among Muslim organizations, leaders, adherents, and President Suharto during his military regime arguably laid the groundwork for the nature and breadth of the influence of Islam in public discussions and social life after 1998. Although Suharto's regime was initially suspicious of religion in general, in the early 1990s he began to align with particular Muslim elites, partly due to his weakening support among the military (Irawanto 2010). His initial suspicion was linked to political criticism by some Muslim intellectuals, which led to the banning of particular Muslim publications (ibid.). Thus, when Suharto gave more preachers free rein to practice, he privileged those who were inclined to literal readings of the Qur'an. These scripturalist teachings, Suharto hoped, would also encourage congregations to do away with popular syncretic practices that he viewed as an obstacle to Indonesia's development agenda (Salim 2015; Wieringa 2015). During the New Order regime, however, young Muslim women began to wear the veil (hijab) as a sign of resistance and protest to Suharto's government (Candrangingrum 2013; Wieringa 2006). The emergence of Islamic dress, expressions, and identity in the public sphere in the 1980s and 1990s were thus not only linked to religious revival, but also driven by political criticism with moralistic overtones, in protests against the moral illegitimacy of a violent government (Candrangingrum 2013).

Yet, the New Order government also drew on Islamic discourses of *kodrat* to successfully institutionalize particular gendered ideas nationally, such as through the state-controlled Family Welfare Guidance (PKK, Pembinaan Kesejahteraan Keluarga). The state thus propagated the biologically deterministic idea that women had "natural" roles, duties, and functions as obedient wives and mothers, stressing the heteronormative family structure in which men are the "breadwinners" and women are proper carers in and of the home (ibid.; Wieringa 2015). In the 1970s, under the banner of "women and development," when the state encouraged women to labor in the wage earning sphere, this was on condition that women did not neglect their domestic duties (Silvey 2004, 252–253). In other words, women were articulated as citizens primarily through their roles as nurturing mothers and wives (Martyn 2005, 206). These two examples—the hijab as protest and kodrat discourses in defining gendered obligations—articulate the ways in which gender, religion, politics, and morality are often interlinked in divergent ways.

In prescribing the "proper" economic division of labor between the sexes, the New Order, state-promoted kodrat discourses diverged from the reality of Javanese kinship and household organization. Ethnographic research conducted prior to and during the military regime (Brenner 1995; Geertz 1961; Jay 1963; Wolf 1988) showed that Javanese women played a central role in economic affairs within and outside of the household. In fact, women's activities and power were associated with the marketplace, whereas men were perceived (both by women and men) as being inept and useless in handling finances. Javanese women and men both typically worked in the rice fields together. Bilateral descent, property ownership, and inheritance marked and continue to mark Javanese kinship organization. Daughters and sons ideally inherit their parents' property and other valuables equally. Marriage and property customs and laws dictate that husbands and wives share whatever property or wealth they earn after marriage. Upon divorce, whatever they separately owned prior to marriage remains rightfully theirs (Brenner 1995; Geertz 1961; Katz and Katz 1975; White and Schweizer 1998).

Susanne Brenner wrote in the early 1990s that

> women earn as much as or more than their husbands. In fact they are often the main or even sole breadwinners for their families. This is certainly the case in (women-headed) households where men are absent, but it is also true

in households where both husband and wife are present. Women's earnings through agricultural or other wage labour in the informal sector not infrequently exceed their husbands' economic contributions to the household (1995, 24).

Yet, Brenner also observed that most people expressed the view that fathers were heads of households and "deserving of deferential behavior from every other member of the family" (ibid., 31). Men dominated the political order and served as representatives for families when dealing with state bureaucracy, a role linked to men's perceived capacity for self-control, as opposed to women, who were viewed as more "irrational" and "weaker" in controlling their base desires (ibid.; see also Hatley 1990). These two gender paradigms—one emphasizing economically capable, breadwinning women, and another highlighting spiritually potent men as leaders of households—arguably persist in Central Java today. Thus current gender roles and discourses in Java are linked to a longer history, and (adult/married) women's substantial economic roles and contributions to the family should not be taken as an entirely new phenomenon enabled by migration. Brenner contends that these two seemingly contradictory views of gender dynamics should be viewed as "alternative paradigms," which "can be called upon to legitimate and to interpret the actions of males and females in different contexts." She argues that in formal discourse (linked partially to Islamic discourse and settings), the hegemonic view of male potency and control will more likely be emphasized, while the view that men are incapable of managing money and desires will arise "in casual discourse where there is less at stake ideologically" (1995, 32).[11]

In Central Java by 2015, however, partially due to the increasing social, economic, and political influence of Muslim leaders and organizations in Indonesia, there was more at stake ideologically in public and everyday discourse in the promotion of both of Brenner's proposed gender paradigms—women or men as leaders of households. Paradoxical gender ideologies are expressed and harnessed in the ways that local leaders and governments attempt to promote *and* regulate mobility, particularly that of women. What is new in terms of gendered relations and roles in Javanese households is the exacerbation of differences in opportunities for work, higher income, and geographical mobility afforded to women and men in rural Java, alongside the decreasing economic security that agriculture and land can provide to families. The promised income and potential risks to women who can now choose to work abroad are also exponentially different in comparison to women's internal migration at the time of industrialization. How women and men should fulfill their ideal gendered responsibilities (kodrat) in relation to how families should practically sustain household livelihoods takes on different meanings and greater tensions in an era where transnational migration is variously perceived as a problem and/or solution to both of these imperatives.

Framing the Moral

The transnational migration of Indonesian women and their lives abroad regularly provoke commentary in national media and public protests, constituting an enduring and well-worn moral debate that I turn to in the next chapter. Such polemical moral debates on a national scale—especially regarding the regulation of sexuality, public behavior, dress, and mobility—are associated with the greater freedom of press and speech in the post-Suharto era, alongside greater autonomy given to local and regional governments to pass their own legislation over "local culture" (Salim 2015). These public contestations over morality often concern the cultural legitimacy of citizenship, defined as "not so much an effect of national attachment but as the effect of cultural politics in which the self negotiates its values in relation to a changing and dynamic society, [such as] how individuals or groups balance their rights *vis-a-vis* their responsibilities to the broader community" (Wichelen 2010, 116).

National moral debates of the 2000s concerned the regulation of women's bodies and sexuality, and illuminate broader struggles over meanings of national identity and citizenship, such as the so-called "antipornography bill." Apart from the regulation of production and distribution of pornographic material, the bill includes laws that regulate "immoral conduct" which was widely interpreted as targeting women's bodies, public behavior, dress and sexuality (Wichelen 2010, 99). News of this bill, which was passed in 2008, divided the nation particularly in terms of religion and "culture." On the one hand, opposing parties—including Muslim feminist and women's rights groups—argued that the bill discriminated against non-Muslims and non-Islamist values and norms. Many traditional forms of dance across Indonesia are often sensual, with costumes that do not meet the bill's "decency" requirement (ibid.). On the other hand, supporters of the bill included multiple national Muslim organizations and smaller militant groups, as well as individuals aligned to an Islamic political party (*Partai Keadilan Sejahtera*) who represented their support for the bill in terms of "the nation's declining morality, arguing that the nation had to protect its women and children against the influences of pornography and obscenity" associated with perceived Westernization and liberalization of Indonesia's economy and social norms (ibid., 102).

These debates thus generally appealed to either the "diversity" or "unity" aspect of Indonesia's national motto, respectively representing the country as either predominantly Islamic or pluralistic. Women's agency was at the center of the debate, with critics of the bill arguing that women had the right to interpret Islam for themselves, and that the bill explicitly identifies and objectifies women's bodies and sexualities as sites of control. Ironically, supporters of the bill also framed it in terms of defense of women's rights and the struggle against violence against women (ibid., 104). The difference, however, is how women's morality and piety are understood and linked to the overall moral condition of the nation. In 2005, the President Susilo Bambang Yudhoyono, along with the Democratic Party, publicly expressed disdain at the "over-exposure" of women's bodies on television channels such as MTV, regarding these images as "alien to Indonesia's norms and identity" (as quoted in Wichelen 2010, 104). Discussions over the "antipornography bill" illuminate how public discourses about morality in Indonesia are often couched in terms of national, ethnic, and religious identity and intimately linked to political and economic power in the production and consumption of images or activities. Conversely, these debates over the meanings of national identity in relation to Indonesian history, Islam, and "Western" modernity are also usually struggles over defining morality. While the following chapters focus on the moral discourses and tensions over women's transnational migration specifically, I locate these struggles to define and practice gendered morality in the broader and ongoing discussions and anxieties over identity and power.

Facilitating and Contesting Women's Transnational Mobilities

Transnational female labor migration was promoted by the Indonesian state beginning in the 1980s but really increased in popularity only after the 1997 Asian Financial Crisis. Initially, the New Order government mainly targeted rural, uneducated women for migration, whose work abroad and remittances were framed in terms of alleviating poverty and encouraging economic development. The resulting separation of low-income, rural women from their families contrasted starkly with nationalist metaphors at the time that reflected the ideal middle-class nuclear family. The promotion of rural women's labor migration as the antidote to rural poverty highlights the state's complicity in reproducing gender and class hierarchies in Indonesia (Silvey 2004). By the 1990s, with the state's promotion of labor migration to the Middle East, their "dominant vision of idealized femininity was translated into a migratory income-earning woman for the sake of the 'national family's' larger goal of economic development" (ibid., 253). Additionally, recruitment agencies and state representatives initially encouraged women's migration to Saudi Arabia rather than non-Muslim countries like Hong Kong or Singapore, because of the assumed religious-cultural proximity between the Muslim populations of the two countries. Particularly appealing for many women was the possibility of making the pilgrimage to Mecca (Silvey 2006; 2007b; Rudnyckyj 2004). Due to the rapid increase in transnational female labor migration and accompanying financial remittances in the 2000s, state authorities began representing migrant women as "heroes" of national development, or more precisely, "foreign exchange heroes" (*pahlawan devisa*). A banner welcoming these "heroes" home can be seen in the Jakarta airport (*Antara News* 2012b).

The increasing popularity of women's transnational migration provoked a backlash by religious authorities, particularly in the post–New Order era when conservative Muslim discourses notably entered into the public sphere (Wieringa 2015). Despite general state validation of female labor migration over the years and presidencies, Muslim women began to face religious-based social sanctions against their transnational mobility (Wieringa 2006). In response to media publicity of abuses against women migrants in 2005, an influential national community of religious leaders, the National Council of Ulama (MUI) declared female labor migration to be un-Islamic, alongside "liberalism," which includes feminism (Wieringa 2006, 4). Although the National Regulation of Placement and Protection for Migrant Workers (UU 39/2004, Article 51) stipulates that all migrants require written permission of a spouse or parent to migrate, in practice this is only applied to migrant women. A woman requires permission from her father or, if married, her husband. Indonesian state representatives also frequently (and hypocritically) pledge to stop sending Indonesian women abroad as domestic workers in terms of defending the "pride and dignity" of the nation (*Jakarta Post* 2015b; *Kompas* 2014). Nevertheless, these religious-based social sanctions and legal stipulations are only loosely and unevenly enforced in Central Java. Thousands of Central Javanese Muslim women not only continue to migrate annually, but are also, in many cases, publicly and privately encouraged and praised for doing so.

Transnational gendered labor migration from Indonesia is thus shaped and encouraged through changing ideas about gendered and moral duties to the family and nation, in terms of the economic and spiritual development of the individual and the nation. State endorsement and placement of migrants, alongside the relative lack of effective mechanisms of protection and redress for migrants abroad (see next chapter), must be contextualized within Indonesia's weaker economic and political bargaining position vis-à-vis migrant destination countries (Silvey 2004), and rivalry between state institutions in charge of migration (Palmer 2016). Although transnational labor migration is regulated by the state, it is largely carried out by a diverse range of commercial recruitment, training, and travel agencies. A complex and dense network of commercial, state-licensed recruitment agencies, informal recruitment agents and fieldworkers, NGOs, and migrant labor activists (Lindquist 2010; Lindquist, Xiang, and Yeoh 2012; Rudnyckyj 2004) also draw on the state's discourses about migration, development, and nationhood to criticize the industry or to justify their respective roles within the migration infrastructure.

Indeed, contemporary migration in Indonesia and elsewhere is not "determined by autonomous markets, policy logic, nor according to individual migrant agency" (Xiang and Lindquist 2014, S143), but rather is a result of "systematically interlinked technologies, institutions, and actors that facilitate and condition mobility" (Xiang and Lindquist 2014, S124). The decentralization of governance and deregulation of labor regimes in the post-Suharto era saw an overwhelming increase in recruitment agencies (also known as PPTKIS, an abbreviation in Indonesian for Privatized Agency for the Placement of Indonesian Migrant Workers). Hence, most workers now apply for jobs through middlemen and PPTKIS rather than directly to a company or employer (Lindquist 2010; Lindquist, Xiang and Yeoh 2012; Silvey 2004; Tjandraningsih 2013). While recruitment agencies were previously regulated and linked to state patronage, decentralization witnessed not only the rise of registered private agencies, but also, due to the ineffective enforcement of existing laws, informal and unregistered ones (Lindquist 2010; Silvey 2004; Tjandraningsih 2013). Practices of labor outsourcing and the centrality of "middleman" companies are trends applicable to both the domestic and international labor market for those engaged in manufacturing, construction, or domestic labor and services. These new trends and practices give workers less control over their employment and labor conditions; organized protests against an employer, recruitment agent, or the state would no longer be as effective in the context of these reformed relationships of codependence and complicity.

The contemporary transnational migration infrastructure thus includes various actors and institutions involved in processing, facilitating, or addressing any issue or practice involved in migrants' preparation for departure, training, arrival, employment, return, deportation, or post-return reintegration. I view these parts as constitutive of one another and propose these actors and institutions share and disperse social, economic, and political risks in uneven ways. For example, both NGO workers and recruitment brokers depend "on the inherently unpredictable circulation of capital that in different ways set migrants in motion" (Lindquist 2015, 171). NGOs, recruitment agencies, and state agencies are diverse in their practices and intentions, as well as the persons who work for them (Lindquist 2015; Palmer 2012; 2016). Following Johan Lindquist (2015), I do not assume that recruitment agents or NGO staff occupy particular or mutually exclusive positions in a moral spectrum, in which the former are typically associated with immorality or deception and the latter with altruism and justice. Shifting the focus away from existing scholarship on these broader political and economic structures facilitating transnational movement, this book examines instead how such broader political and economic dynamics of the migration industry are negotiated and shaped in relation to gender, morality, and faith in Central Javanese migrant-origin villages.

Moralizing Gender, Gendering Moralities

While religion and morality are closely related, they are not synonymous. Nevertheless, in the context of Indonesian politics and social life, Muslim groups and discourses often take center stage in constituting and shaping "the moral" in everyday life. This chapter has highlighted the complex dynamics of politics, religion, and gender in Indonesia broadly and Java in particular. Migration, women's migration, and Islam are not new phenomena in Indonesia. Yet, the twenty-first century has seen the institutionalization of Islam in politics and everyday life to an unprecedented extent, alongside a pluralization and transnationalization of Muslim identities, attitudes, and consumption practices.[12] In this context, the increase in demand for women's labor not only outside of the village, but abroad, sometimes in non-Islamic countries, and in the intimate spaces of foreign households, has generated a unique, organized commercialization of *and* backlash against women's migration on a national scale, a response that did not happen with women's internal migrations for factory work.

Indonesian institutions' attempts to promote or restrict women's mobilities occurred alongside other polemical national events and issues, which involve increasingly fierce and even violent contestations over what constitutes public morality, the moral legitimacy of authoritative leaders, and the role of religion in politics. Yet, framing these social tensions as a cultural war of "values" or a conflict between Muslims and non-Muslims (or different kinds of Muslims) overlooks how gender, class, and ethnic and religious identity intersect to shape the ways that politicians and religious leaders have instrumentalized these issues and anxieties in rallying for political and economic support. Central Javanese residents' attitudes towards transnational migration—especially that of women—are shaped by these broader and diverse discourses of piety, Muslim identity, and gender in moralizing terms. The following chapters, drawing on a number of ethnographic examples, will demonstrate how such dynamics importantly influence institutional, social, and individual approaches and responses to transnational migration.

Notes

1. Ninety participants identified as women, while forty identified as men. This includes sixty-nine former migrants, thirteen prospective migrants (including six who tried and failed to migrate), and thirty-three nonmigrants. I also interviewed six recruitment agents (all except one were former migrants, I interviewed four mainly in terms of their recruiting practices, while two were interviewed as former migrants as well, and are included in the previous category). Nine NGO-associated staff and activists were interviewed, one representative of BP3TKI, and one director of JasIndo insurance company, which works with

Cilacap-based recruitment agencies and migrant workers. The interviews lasted between half an hour to three hours, and for many participants, our conversations during the initial interviews carried onto multiple more informal ones in everyday life as well.

2. As such, I refer to these villages as "Central Javanese" villages. This contrasts with the official government demarcation of Cilacap as falling under the province of Central Java, while Yogyakarta is a "Special Region" of its own. While the official statistics of "Central Java" exclude Yogyakarta, including it only serves to increase the significance of this data set. I define villages in terms of the Indonesian local government unit of *desa*, which is demarcated by a village head (*lurah desa*). The villages I worked in comprised 6000–7000 people, who participated in a village-wide Muslim sermon and gathering once a month. My social networks clearly did not extend to all members of the villages, but were bounded by whom I was introduced to, often the family and social networks of the persons I stayed with, and the immediate neighborhood. However, schools provided an opportunity to meet villagers who lived slightly further away, since there are very few schools in each village.

3. Throughout the book, I use the term "migrant-centered NGO" as a shorthand for nongovernmental organizations that specifically focus on issues, advocacy, and programs related to transnational migration.

4. The region of Yogyakarta is governed by the Sultan, who strongly discourages recruitment agencies from facilitating the migration of women as domestic workers. Consequently, recruitment agencies located in Yogyakarta tend to be stricter in their migrant selection processes, and follow certain standards for migrants' predeparture training programs. Recruitment agencies located in Cilacap, however, are notorious for ignoring government regulations and guidelines such as the minimum age or training requirement for migrants. Many Cilacap-based agencies are also known for falsifying identity and medical documents, or sending migrants abroad on tourist visas, as opposed to employment visas. Contrary to my expectations, however, many Yogyakarta-based residents simply travelled to Cilacap or Wonosobo to acquire migration documents, if they did not fulfill the requirements to migrate through Yogyakarta-based recruiters.

5. I documented speeches and interactions among state representatives, commercial actors, journalists, activists, return migrants, and prospective migrants. I was a participant-observer in several national conventions and less formal meetings organized by the National Migrant Labor Union (*Serikat Buruh Migran Indonesia* or SBMI). I attended a national conference organized by *Koalisi Perempuan Indonesia*, a coalition of women's organizations involved with migrant labor issues. Additionally, I attended many conventions and events of various scales organized by BNP2TKI. These included at least two migrant entrepreneurship "fairs," where banks and insurance agencies were present (in Yogyakarta city, and in a smaller town center of Yogyakarta). I also attended one public talk on "trafficking" by state representatives from the Ministry of Foreign Affairs to another migrant-origin village in rural Yogyakarta. I was a participant-observer in two development programs. One was a cooking and entrepreneurship course funded by BP3TKI for return migrant women in Yogyakarta. The other, funded by a foreign government and facilitated by a Yogyakarta-based NGO, was a course focused on educating and socializing primarily return migrant women on effective communication and cooperation. Both programs included opening and closing ceremonies, where local and district government figures attended and commented on the effects of local migration

and development. For an examination of the impact of such development programs targeted at migrant-origin villages, see Anwar and Chan 2016.

6. The transmigration programme also meant the seizing of land from traditionally land-owning peasants of the outer islands, and "resettling" them so that such land and rainforests could be cleared for (foreign-owned) corporate agriculture and modern irrigation.

7. In the 2000s the common estimation was that 80% of all Indonesian migrants were women, while annually between 2011 and 2016, the figure has decreased to around 60%. This statistical decrease is likely due to on-and-off moratoriums on sending women as domestic workers to Saudi Arabia and Malaysia, and does not account for any changes (increase or decrease) in irregular, undocumented migration of women due to these restrictions (see BNP2TKI 2017; Xiang and Lindquist 2014, S128). In Cilacap as of 2014, 90% of its overseas migrants were women, while 80% of all who work locally were men. See Badan Pusat Statistik Kabupaten Cilacap 2015.

8. These ships travel as far as South Africa, Trinidad and Tobago, and New Zealand. See for example, Mukti 2015, Nur'aini 2015, and Palmer 2017.

9. Later scholars of Indonesia and Islam elsewhere built on Geertz's model to imply that most Indonesians are not "real" or practicing Muslims but "nominal" ones, whose conversion to Islam was deemed superficial, since they continued their previous religious practices (Woodward 1996, 17). "Indonesian Islam" emerged as an object of analysis after the 1980s among scholars, as well as the apparent Islamicization of Indonesia (Bowen 1993; Hooker 2003; Varisco 2005). This is as opposed to previous work (drawing on Geertz) which denied various local ritual practices and religious beliefs as being part of Islamic tradition, but perceived them as being syncretic, "corrupt versions" of Islam, "an essentially foreign religion" (Woodward 1996, 25–26). This results in a paradox in which if there were "real Muslims" to be found in Java, then their Javaneseness would be questionable (ibid., 33). Thus critics of Geertz' early models of Javanese socioreligious order argued for a more dynamic and contextual understanding of religious practice and Islam.

10. The *ulama* is a body of scholars trained in Islamic law and science, usually seen as authorities of interpreting Islamic doctrine and law (Hooker 2003). In Indonesia, this is usually represented by MUI or Indonesian Council of Ulama, a body comprising of the majority of Indonesia's Muslim groups with various approaches to Islam. Sharia, or *syariah* in Indonesian, is usually defined as Islamic law based on the Qur'an to guide the moral and civil conduct of Muslims. Interpretations and implementations of sharia in religious and secular contexts vary, with some arguing it only applies to Muslims. Some argue there can be no fundamental separation of religion and state (Hooker 2003).

11. The state's kodrat discourses at the time arguably contributed to reinforcing the hegemonic idea of male superiority and control, a view that can be traced to preexisting rhetoric of the elites informed by Islamic doctrine and pan-Islamic gender ideologies, in addition to the patriarchal tendencies and governance of Dutch colonial rule (which also influenced the speech and attitudes of the local elites) (Brenner 1995, 30–31).

12. This pluralization, however, is largely limited to what Robert Hefner has called a "Sunni center" (2008, 158) of Indonesian Islam, alongside arguably diminishing or less visible forms of non-Sunni practices in the public sphere.

2 Mobilizing and Moralizing Indonesia

An EMACIATED, BADLY burned, and scarred twenty-three-year-old Indonesian woman was found limping at the Hong Kong International Airport in January 2014, barely able to walk (Mam 2014). The extreme abuse and violence that this woman, Erwiana Sulistyaningsih, suffered during her employment as a domestic worker in Hong Kong came to light only after various graphic images of her scarred face, bruised body, peeling skin on her fingers, and blackened feet and hands, were circulated and went "viral" among Indonesian migrant and activist groups on Facebook. Pressure from these online communities led to an organized five-thousand-strong protest march in Hong Kong under the slogan of "Justice for Erwiana." Migrant domestic workers, sympathetic employers, and Hong Kong residents participated. These events arguably led to a widely publicized legal case against Erwiana's previous employer, Lo Wan-Tung—a case of alleged torture, which was initially classified as "miscellaneous" until the protest march (Jakarta Post 2014b). Yet, when Lo was arrested and questioned, investigators reported that "documents were also shown to our officers indicating the maid quit of her own accord" (Lo and Ngo 2013). When asked why Erwiana, in her visibly injured condition, had gone unnoticed by Hong Kong immigration officers, the Director of the Immigration Department said, "It is difficult to judge whether there were injuries because of her complexion. We cannot blame the officer" (Siu 2014).

This example highlights the processes through which forms of abuse and violence committed against migrant workers can be made publicly visible and invisible simultaneously, where issues of responsibility and blame can be elusive. Erwiana's physical wounds are literally documented via graphic images made public. Yet her abuse was undocumented and undetectable via her official migration papers or by customs officials. As one of the six million Indonesian labor migrants, Erwiana's plight is familiar, the abuse and protests unexceptional. They have instead become part of a transnational landscape of long-term, ongoing, precarious migrations of domestic workers, alongside the large presence of relevant migrant and labor activist groups. Why and how do some cases of migrant labor abuse—such as Erwiana's—garner extensive public support and state attention, while many others remain undocumented, tolerated, and apparently less relevant to public concern?

Erwiana's case points to how responsibility for migratory processes and injustices is often actively dispersed among multiple institutions and individuals, such as bureaucrats, NGOs, commercial recruitment intermediaries, employers, and migrants. In the event of fraud, unpaid wages, or work injuries, migrants and migrant activists often blame deceptive recruitment agents, exploitative employers, or governments for weak labor laws. Recruitment agents may absolve themselves of responsibility by claiming they are only facilitating the demands of employers, governments or "market mechanisms" and working within established labor laws (Lindquist 2012; 2015; Wise 2013). The Indonesian or migrant-origin state may shift the responsibility for protecting their citizens abroad onto foreign/destination states, blame recruitment agencies for not conforming to state-imposed regulatory guidelines, and/or deflect discussion from migrant injury and systemic debt to focus on ways to make "better economies" (Simoni 2016) through educating migrants to be "better" economic actors in managing their debts and finances.

Sometimes, however, discourses of responsibility and blame surrounding migration's consequences may coincide, despite apparently diverging interests of multiple actors and institutions. This chapter provides some examples in which Indonesian state representatives, journalists for national news media, and migrant labor activists, can unintentionally collude and locate ultimate responsibility for migration and both its positive and negative effects in migrant individuals—particularly women—and their families.[1] Specifically, I discuss two dominant and contradictory public representations of Indonesian female labor migrants: as national "heroes" who contribute to Indonesia's sustainable economic development, or as exploited "victims" of an unequal global labor economy.

Drawing on public discourses about migrant women, migration, and development in formal statements by Indonesian state actors, news reports, and migrant-centered NGO websites, I analyze the gendered moral assumptions underlying representations of migrants as heroes or victims. This chapter's discussion focuses mainly on migrant women, since women are often the explicit subject of moralizing migrant representations in Indonesia as elsewhere. Contrary to the apparent incompatibility of the hero/victim dichotomy, I argue that representations of migrant workers as exploited victims do not necessarily undermine representations of migrants as heroes of development, or the state-sanctioned notion that labor migration is a pathway to personal, rural, and national development. Instead, these representations of migrants as heroes and victims similarly emphasize migrants' individual responsibility in terms of gendered morality. Building on existing scholarship on this hero/victim dichotomy largely based on labor migrants from Indonesia (Ford 2002; Ford and Lyons 2012; Lindquist 2010; 2012; 2015) and the Philippines (Aguilar 1996; Oishi 2005; Parreñas 2001; 2005; Pratt 2012; Rafael 1997; Rodríguez 2010; Suzuki 2003), I focus on the less-studied category of the "immoral victim," or migrant women who may be depicted as criminals or perpetrators alongside their victimhood. Such a focus on migrants' individual morality and responsibility allows discourses of migration as a pathway to development and migration as labor exploitation to appear mutually compatible.

The Indonesian state is one among many states that actively promotes labor migration as a temporary solution to national unemployment and poverty. Current debates over the role of labor migration in post-Millennium Development Goals—the relationship between migration and development—have largely focused on the social and economic causes and consequences of labor migration on migrants' countries of origin (Faist 2008; Castles 2009). Scholars and policymakers tend to emphasize greater protection and welfare provisions for migrant workers, and/or proposed solutions and pathways to developing these countries concerned, such as increasing the range of employment options for migrants and their communities (e.g., Thieme and Ghimire 2014). This chapter takes a different approach. Instead of asking how migration can better contribute to development, or how development programs can be reformed to include "well-being" (Scott 2012), I ask how migration as a development strategy, even if a "temporary" one, is taken for granted, promoted, and maintained by international migration institutions, states, and NGOs, despite compelling evidence that the lives and labor of many migrant workers are literally unsustainable and unbearable (Brennan 2014; Ladegaard 2013a; 2013b). What kinds of lives, luxuries, forms of abuse and sacrifice are being sustained in the name of development? What is it about the promise of development in the Indonesian context that makes migration appear necessary?

The answer lies in how various Indonesian institutions and actors, in their selective representations of migrants as heroes or victims, often evoke similar moral assumptions of what makes a "good" or "bad" Indonesian woman and worker. These gendered moral assumptions serve narratives which imply what I call a *gendered moral hierarchy* of migrant workers, where some are deemed more or less deserving of their wealth, well-being, or the violence perpetrated against them. The case of Indonesia, I would argue, mirrors public discourses in other migrant-origin and destination countries, where some migrants can be heroes who deserve media attention, while some are unfairly abused and deserve state protection, and still others partly deserve their tragic fates. In attempting to distinguish between guilty and innocent victims, and between "illegitimate" or "tolerable" violence, these gendered moral hierarchies emphasize migrants' individual moral responsibility and blame. The responsibility of states and institutions for migrant safety, labor protection, and aspects of social welfare is thus downplayed in public discussions of labor migration, exploitation, and development. In other words, focusing on the gendered morality of migrants in cases of wealth or sickness obscures broader transnational relations of power, knowledge, and capital that articulate persons as particular migrant and labor subjects.

Migrants as Heroes of Development

The Indonesian state officially began regulating transnational labor migration in 2004, largely in response to the rapid increase in female labor migration after the Asian Financial Crisis and the fall of Suharto's New Order State during 1998 and 1999. I outlined in the previous chapter how the New Order government, in the 1980s and 1990s, initially promoted and legitimated the labor migration of rural women by reinterpreting women's Islamic gender roles (*kodrat*) as mothers, wives, and citizens. Subsequent Indonesian governments have continued to promote labor migration as positively contributing to the social and economic development of the nation, where migrants are commonly referred to as "foreign exchange heroes" (*pahlawan devisa*).[2]

For example, in a public speech reported in local newspapers in 2012, then-chief of BNP2TKI Jumhur Hidayat drew on a 2012 World Bank report not only to highlight the potential for migrants' remittances to contribute to the national economy, but also to emphasize that migrants' financial remittances are in fact more resilient to economic crises than foreign aid and foreign direct investment (*Antara News* 2012b). This makes migrant remittances a more "sustainable" resource for development than its alternatives.[3] To quote the report, he "expressed his gratefulness to the migrant workers for helping Indonesia bear the impact of the economic crisis.... 'If there are lay-offs during a global economic crisis, poorly paid migrant workers are usually the last ones to lose their jobs.'" Migrants who are "legal" or "formal"—who migrate through state-sanctioned regulatory channels—have also been deemed "national assets," who are noble (*perkerjaan mulia*), and represent the good image (*citra*) of the nation abroad (BNP2TKI 2014; *Edisi News* 2014).

Migrants have also been represented by the state not only in terms of contributing to the national economy, but also to "the people's economy" (*ekonomi rakyat*) (Pemerintah Kabupaten Cilacap 2011). This term evokes the sense that migrants, particularly in terms of their remittances, can directly improve the everyday lives of people at the village or district level. Following this view, Indonesian state agencies have implemented various financial education and entrepreneurship programs targeted at return migrants, their kin, and neighbors. For example, in January 2014, BNP2TKI made several press statements focusing on the aim to empower "foreign exchange earners" through these programs (*Jakarta Post* 2014a). Implicit in the idea of such "empowerment" is the expectation that such businesses will help to reduce unemployment by providing jobs to migrants' kin and neighbors, as evident in the following speech by the chief of BNP2TKI's Bandung branch: "These skill training programmes will hopefully improve the welfare of migrant workers and their families, that they will be capable of creating jobs and employment by themselves, through entre-preneurship" (Nugroho 2015).

Indonesian labor migration and higher wages overseas have indeed enabled some migrants to pay for school and medical fees, build concrete houses, start small businesses, and increase consumption (Silvey 2006; Sukamdi and Abdul 2004). However, state institutions dealing with transnational migration and labor represent such cases of "success" as normal or even guaranteed, as long as migrants work hard. While financial education and entrepreneurship skill train-ing programmes do provide individual participants with some financial, human, and physical capital, these alone do not ensure that participants eventually start their own businesses after the training sessions end, or that these enterprises are sustainable over time. In other words, these programmes operate under the opti-mistic but unfounded assumption that such entrepreneurship programmes will either lead to the success of individual enterprises or create external benefits for migrants' communities (Anwar and Chan 2016).

Rarely do these reports on "development" focus on the issue of better wages, legal rights overseas for migrant workers, or complementary strategies to address unemployment in Indonesia. Instead, low wages for migrant workers are framed and accepted as inevitable due to market forces. Thus, through the public cultural valorizing of migrant workers, Indonesian state authorities depict and justify mul-tidimensional socioeconomic inequalities as a natural state of affairs. Additionally, migrants are positioned as responsible for creating jobs in order to reduce or pre-vent future migrations from their own communities. While state representatives applaud migrants' "hard work" and self-discipline, the state is presented as primar-ily responsible in helping migrants channel their remittances productively.

In addition to the state's emphasis on individual responsibility and discipline as a factor for successful migration and development, I highlight the following examples to support scholars who note that the Indonesian state and recruitment agents promote migration not only in its economic promises and advantages, but also in terms of gendered, moral, and religious or spiritual development. For example, migration is commonly framed in terms of carrying out a patri-otic or (feminine) familial duty (Robinson 2000; Rudnyckyj 2004; Silvey 2006; 2007a). In a visit to a regional office in East Java in July 2013, Jumhur specifically addressed women who desired to become migrant domestic workers overseas (but who had not yet left):

> The lure of high wages overseas and the association with consumption indeed can encourage [the migrant] to become wasteful or extravagant.... Do not change your mobile phones frequently, buy mobile [phone] credit, smoke, or sit

happily in cafes [clubs]. The wasteful migrant reduces the possibility that one can send money to families in the homeland [*tanah air*]. Remember, if you consume too much, you will accumulate debt, and this isn't good for your future, and your family. I'm asking you not to be wasteful, be frugal, and save money. (*Waspada* 2013)

That same month, Jumhur's message to female migrant candidates in Central Java similarly called for women to save money and be wary of "flirtatious employers" (*majikan genit*). He emphasized twice, "If you are seduced by your employer, refuse, but also don't be tempted (*jangan mau*). Just say that you are only there to work. If everything is fine over there, then bring money home and start a business" (Purbaya 2013). After Jumhur was replaced by Gatot Abdullah as head of BNP2TKI in 2014, Gatot dispensed remarkably similar moralizing advice to prospective migrant workers, including "stay away from drugs" (BNP2TKI 2014).

The gender-specific exploitation and abuses confronting Indonesia's migrant domestic worker population have been widely documented (Constable 2007; Ford 2002; Ford and Lyons 2012; Huang and Yeoh 2007; Kloppenburg and Peters 2012; Ladegaard 2013a; 2013b; Silvey 2007a; Soeprobo and Wiyono 2004). While experiences of migration are variously dependent on chance, luck, and a migrant's confidence, personality and skills, many women usually risk or are entangled in relations of financial debt to informal recruiters, recruitment agencies or employers. They may also face physical, verbal or psychological violence by employers, and their work hours and conditions tend to be unregulated, since domestic workers live within their employers' households. High-profile cases of abused Indonesian migrant women overseas have contributed to national media and scholars questioning and reinforcing the state's responsibilities to its citizens abroad (see Silvey 2004). These cases shed light on the Indonesian state's role in effectively "sponsoring" precarious labor and "trafficking-like" labor migration, through the state's active promotion and regulation of such mobilities and simultaneous oversight of problematic labor and recruitment practices (Palmer 2012; 2016; Tjandraningsih 2013).

It is clear that the emphases of state representatives on migrants' financial education, responsible consumption behavior, and proper female moral discipline shift the focus away from broader structural inequalities in terms of gender, ethnicity, class, and political-economic relations between Indonesia and destination states. These discourses also eschew state complicity in exploitative recruitment and training processes: government officials and institutions openly recognize the profitability of regulating labor migrations through issuing visas and identity documents for migrant candidates, as well as licenses for recruitment agencies (Palmer 2016). However, in public discourse, state representatives instead tend to (mis)represent the failure of some migrant women to remit money and the accumulation of debt in terms of their tendency towards extravagant consumption patterns. The dangers of physical or sexual abuse of female migrant domestic workers, most of whom are required by laws in destination countries to live with their employers, are sometimes represented in terms of female promiscuity and moral weakness, in allowing themselves to be tempted and seduced. Jumhur's "pep talks" quoted above effectively represent good workers as "exploitable" women, while reinforcing a national feminine ideal of the sacrificial family-oriented citizen. Simultaneously, his speeches pathologize those who may reject such conditions of "success," or do not conform to these performances of gendered morality (see chapters 3 and 4).

These gendered and moral attitudes are usually religiously and culturally inflected; their salience and power depend on the contexts of their communication and practice. For example, female labor migration and remittances are often discussed by state representatives and recruitment agents in terms of religious piety or identity (Silvey 2007b). Representatives of state banks and migrant-related ministries also highlight the increase of remittances around the Muslim fasting month of Ramadan, thus linking migration with the fulfillment of religious and familial duties (*Antara News* 2012a; *Lensa Indonesia* 2012). In these ways, ideas linking financial flows with expected moral behavior are conveyed and sanctioned by authoritative figures in Indonesia, and, as I elaborate in subsequent chapters, enforced through village talk.

The state has responded to publicized cases of abuse and violence against migrant domestic workers in paternalistic ways, such as temporarily banning female migration to Malaysia and Saudi Arabia. Stricter bureaucratic requirements for female migration were also imposed (Silvey 2004; Quiano 2011). In 2012, the Indonesian state, under President Susilo Bambang Yudhoyono, announced plans to "stop sending domestic workers abroad by 2017" (*Jakarta Globe* 2012). This has remained a recurring state promise during Joko Widodo's presidency (*Jakarta Post* 2015b). As discussed above, there has also been a significant turn in state discourses to devolve the responsibility for safety onto women themselves.

These responses are generally met with skepticism by migrant and labor activists in Indonesia, and seen as the result of pressure from the influential national community of religious leaders, the Council of Indonesian Ulama (MUI), when MUI issued a religious decree (fatwa) that transnational female labor migration was un-Islamic (Wieringa 2006, 4). Migrant workers and activists have also argued that these negotiations and plans have not done much to reduce the rate of violations against migrants. Instead, new reports on ending moratoria or interstate negotiations have notably focused on how to increase employment quotas for "cheap Indonesian labor" in Saudi Arabia, Malaysia, and Hong Kong, specifically for Indonesian migrants in "nondomestic work" industries (BNP2TKI 2011; 2014; *Jakarta Globe* 2012; *Jakarta Post* 2011; Zubaidah 2015). While the Indonesian state has appeared to successfully resolve issues with Malaysia and Saudi Arabia on things such as migrants' rest days, salary, and the right to keep their passports, these negotiations sit uncomfortably alongside the state's active promotion of migration as a pathway to national economic development.

Migrant and labor activists, workers, and their families contribute to and critique these institutionalized moral evaluations and expectations of migrant women in diverse ways (Silvey 2004; Choo 2013). Nevertheless, these paternalistic responses from institutions of authority reinforce Indonesian perceptions of migrants who do not conform to ideal expectations—of pious, dutiful, remittance-sending daughters, mothers, and wives—as vulnerable women. Such women who "fail" in their migratory missions—who are either abused or in debt—are seen as uneducated, untrained, naïve, in need of protection and control, or even as psychologically ill, morally ambiguous, or suspect (*Detik News* 2015; *Indosuara* 2014; Faizal 2012b). The abovementioned state measures or "solutions" to the exploitative and unstable migrant work conditions have been opposed by more critical migrant labor activists and scholars, who argue that forbidding women from migrating would not actually stop their migration but only contribute to increasing the vulnerability of women to exploitation by increasing the numbers of risky and undocumented forms of migration (Killias 2010; Silvey 2004, 259). These are as opposed to changes proposed by activists that would structurally favor and enhance migrants' bargaining power (see Conclusion).

Apart from increasing regulations on migrant women's mobility, the Indonesian state has framed cases of migrant labor exploitation, fraud, and abuse, in terms of "illegal migration" or "trafficking." These terms distinguish such "bad" migration as processes not legitimated by the state, and hence different from state-sanctioned labor migration. In recent years, state agencies have regularly deported large groups of undocumented migrants from Malaysia, and represented these returns as laudable "rescue" efforts (Ardyan 2014). At an informal press interview given by then-chief of BNP2TKI, Gatot Abdullah Mansyur, at a public event about migrant entrepreneurship in Yogyakarta which I attended (September 17, 2014), I observed that journalists' concerns about the reintegration process of such forcefully repatriated migrants were dismissed and ignored. Furthermore, in 2014 and 2015, the national police, and representatives from BNP2TKI and the Ministry of Labor conducted raids in recruitment agency offices and migrant training centers, where those found violating state regulations had their licenses revoked (Fadly 2014). The "problems" Indonesian migrants face abroad are thus attributed by the state at least in part to commercial recruitment agencies that have been compared to human traffickers and "mafia rings" (*Tempo* 2014; Fadly 2015). State representatives such as BNP2TKI chiefs regularly shift discussions of "protection" mechanisms to highlight instead "formal" and "regulated" labor markets available for prospective migrants abroad (BNP2TKI 2014). As of 2017, multiple state institutions are collaborating to "prevent" and "stop" what is now termed "nonprocedural" (or "informal") migration, by educating prospective migrants and their families to avoid the risks of migration by "using . . . official channels" (KEMENPORA 2017). The dichotomies of formal/informal, regular/irregular, and official/unofficial migrations from Indonesia are, however, difficult to sustain, and put the impossible task of distinguishing accurately between "legitimate" and "illegitimate" recruitment agencies on migrant candidates themselves, who paradoxically rely on these very agencies to facilitate documentation procedures to migrate.

To illustrate the state's role in shaping both meanings and processes of "formal" and "informal" migration: in 2004, the state introduced a licensing regime for recruitment agencies (PPTKI), although this was not strictly enforced. Simply put, "formal" processes entail migrating through the use of these licensed agencies, and/or by providing all the documentations required by the state. All migrations that do not fit into the definition of "formal" are by default "informal," and associated with errant recruiters and false or improper migration or identity documents. As outlined in the Presidential Regulation 39/2004 for the Placement and Protection of Migrant Workers (UU 39/2004), recruitment agencies are positioned as responsible for almost every aspect of the migration process from recruitment, to placement, to post-employment. This includes ensuring that migrants travel with the proper documentation, adequate and relevant training and skills for their jobs abroad, the placement and employment of migrants abroad (Articles 35 to 51), as well as the overall protection of migrant workers (Article 82). The Regulation effectively legitimated and encouraged practices existing at the time of enactment, when migrant candidates and their brokers were highly mutually dependent for their economic welfare (Rudnyckyj 2004; Spaan 1995). Nevertheless, this dependency is marked by unequal risks born by migrants and brokers, in which brokers can stand to recuperate potential losses of "failed" migrants, but migrants deceived by fraudulent brokers or who face wage issues abroad have limited avenues for redress (Rudnyckyj 2004). In contrast, the Regulation stipulates the state's main responsibility as "monitoring" and governing recruitment agencies (UU 39/2004: Article 81). The state also has the authority to stop or cancel the migration journeys of any candidate not deemed suitable for work abroad (Articles 81 and 100). This official document—which was the main legal referent for migration at the time of my fieldwork—has been criticized by many Indonesian activists for its uneven emphasis on the technicalities and regulations of placement processes of migrants, over ensuring protective legal mechanisms for migrant candidates locally and migrants abroad.

Interestingly, in contrast to state ministers' effective bargaining with foreign states to increase or enable labor opportunities for Indonesian migrants, I observed on multiple occasions how ministers, foreign ambassadors, and

Indonesian Consulate staff publicly turned to prayer when faced with questions regarding improving labor laws for migrants. During a speech in Singapore on Indonesia's roadmap called "Development 2025," an Indonesian member of the audience criticized the Minister for focusing on issues facing the middle class, as opposed to underlying issues of poverty and unemployment leading to precarious labor migration. In response, the Minister said that "God willing" (*Insyallah*), these issues will be resolved. A similar tactic was employed by then-chief of BNP2TKI, Gatot Abdullah, at a speech addressing prospective migrants and return migrant entrepreneurs in Yogyakarta. In response to a question about what BNP2TKI will do about the problems facing migrants, Pak Gatot said, "*Insyallah, masalah-masalah akan berkurang*" (God willing, these problems will be reduced). These prayers are seldom followed by indications or assurances that BNP2TKI or the Indonesian state are actively taking steps to ensure better labor conditions for citizens at home and abroad.

Migrant-origin states such as Indonesia do not accidentally neglect the protection of domestic spaces and migrant workers' rights, since the lack of regulation of such spaces produces and maintains particular middle-class and elite privileges required for the further generation of social, economic and political capital (Silvey 2004, 259–260; see Palmer 2016). While the state frequently frames migrants as "heroes of development" in bringing in billions of US dollars' worth of remittances annually, they also systematically devalue domestic work, practical skills, and forms of labor associated with rural populations' lack of formal education, and migrants' safety (see Sen 1998). In a telling interview, an unnamed state official explains that migrants' lack of "skills" and "under-education" render them "more prone to exploitation and torture by unscrupulous employers and agencies" (Saragih 2014). While this may be true in a broad sense, BNP2TKI's discursive and programmatic focus on migrants' self-responsibility serves to explain labor abuse in terms of migrants' own uniquely class-based failings.

Such state discourses and responses to the exploitation and abuse of Indonesian migrant workers contribute to sustaining the precariousness of migrants' lives and labor. This is done through discursively naturalizing the unfair working conditions of workers in informal sectors domestically and abroad with uncritical references to global market inequality, in addition to partially shifting the blame for abuse and violence onto errant recruiters, "God's will," and migrants themselves. A consequence of this is that the possibility for successful and safe migration journeys is largely left to migrants' sheer perseverance, courage, luck, and personality. Discussions of development or migration's "positive" impact on migrants and their families must thus take into account the gendered and moral assumptions underlying notions of and legitimate paths toward pursuing "the good life" and a "better" future.

Migrants as Victims of Exploitation: Gendered Moral Hierarchies

Dominant media and activist accounts of violence against migrant workers often strategically focus on cases that are extreme or scandalous—whether to sell newspapers, garner Internet traffic, or draw more people to activist causes. Yet these representations and sensationalizations of extreme cases in the public sphere tend to frame these cases of abuse as exceptional, unintentionally supporting the Indonesian state's official stance that "success" is the likely achievable norm of the pious and self-responsible "good" migrant. In comparison, everyday forms of labor exploitation—such as long working hours, inadequate rest or food, poor living conditions, and delays in wage payments—appear mundane, tolerable, and normal.

When migrant workers, activists, and scholars have called for greater state accountability in the face of labor exploitation and abuse, these are usually framed in terms of human, migrants' and labor rights. However, scholars have pointed out that "rights" discourses are not abstract, universal, or value-free (Choo 2013; Lai 2011). Instead, the politics of migrants' and women's activisms are complex, and may contribute to reinforcing moral and gendered hierarchies embedded in understandings of victimhood, exploitation, violence, and protection.

Indeed, global human rights discourse broadly engages with, critiques, and reproduces the hero-victim dichotomy (Bernstein 2010; Brennan 2014; Kempadoo 2012), including discussions of Indonesia migration in terms of human trafficking (Ford 2002; Ford and Lyons 2012; Palmer 2012). These Indonesian images and tropes of victimhood and heroism linked to migrants' gendered morality find striking parallels in the case of the Philippines (Parreñas 2005; Pratt 2012; Rafael 1997; Rodriguez 2010). Elaborating on what makes a hero or victim in the contemporary Indonesian migration context, I present examples below to argue that discourses of victimhood are not simply contrasted with those of "heroic" agency. The category "victim" is not a homogenous one of the stereotypically innocent, exploited, and defenseless migrant woman. Instead, it is a category that is loaded with value judgments about what makes victims deserving or undeserving of their circumstances, or what makes some victims pitiable and others "blameable." Mainstream news media and activists in Indonesia have evoked particular, culturally salient gendered and moral assumptions in representing cases of labor abuse, violence, and illness of migrant domestic workers. These representations of blame and responsibility present challenges to discourses of rights, migration, and development by state and non-state actors.

Cases of violence and deaths of Indonesian migrant domestic workers can be distinguished in terms of how victimhood and blame are allocated in three broad categories: (1) immoral victims who are blamed for their plight; (2) innocent victims who deserve social justice; and (3) unlucky (amoral) victims of fate. I argue that the moral privileging in public discourse of the "successful" or "pitiable" migrant woman who is innocent, vulnerable, heroic, and/or selfless, produces her negative gendered subordinate: the immoral and ill-fated woman who falls short of the ideal expectations of a mother, daughter, sister and wife. I discuss and compare the following examples in order to highlight why cases of "innocent victims," such as Erwiana's (introduced at the opening of the chapter), are able to garner more public outrage, support, and media coverage. Only in these cases where the migrant is "unblameable," can recruitment agents, employers, and states become exposed to critique, and thereby held accountable.

Immoral or Morally Ambiguous Victims

Despite an estimate by Indonesian NGO Migrant Care that approximately 1249 Indonesian migrants died abroad in 2013, the Indonesian government initially prevented, and now actively discourages second autopsies of migrant workers' bodies that are sent back to Indonesia (Knight 2013).[4] While such statistics have been the subject of debate among labor ministries and migrant-centered NGOs, the state's official discouragement of autopsies leaves the "true" causes of death open to gossip and speculation, while heavily skewing public acceptance of official reports of deaths overseas as due to accidents, natural illnesses, or by capital sentences due to migrant workers' unjustified or immoral acts.[5] Highly publicized cases of violence against migrant domestic workers often involve a death sentence in Malaysia or Saudi Arabia. In 2014, at least 236 Indonesian migrants faced death sentences worldwide, mostly women who have allegedly murdered their employers or other migrant workers, who are accused of black magic, or who are accused of committing adultery with a Saudi Arabian man (KEMENPORA 2017; Sarigih 2014).

Labor activists often emphasize that harsh labor conditions, long-term physical mistreatment, low pay, or even no pay are the conditions that provoke migrants' violence in acts of self-defense or temporary insanity (Knight 2013, see chapter 5). State officials have also admitted that some cases of "adultery" were actually cases of rape (Sarigih 2014). However, some media reports and state officials tend to downplay these arguments due to a lack of evidence. Regardless of the truth, and keeping in mind the state's policy against second autopsies, blame and responsibility seem to lie mostly with the "adulterous" women, or the unskilled and uneducated naïve rural "victim" (Aslibumiayu.net 2012). The emphasis on the potential guilt or immorality of the migrant victim is evident in the following excerpt from *The Jakarta Post* (January 25, 2014) about Indonesians with death sentences:

> The [unnamed] state official acknowledged that some of the suspects were actually rape victims, but that a significant percentage of them had been

charged for having extramarital affairs with Saudi men.... According to the official, data from Indonesian representative offices in Saudi Arabia showed that about 7000 children were born from such affairs. "The identities of their fathers are unclear. This should raise a serious concern because this is about our young generation too," the official said.

The official said the government had worked to repatriate the children by providing temporary documents, though admitted that the children could have trouble obtaining official identity documents in Indonesia because they had no birth certificates and unknown fathers.

"The government has tried to establish Islamic marriages for [the women] to help them obtain documents in Saudi Arabia before returning to Indonesia, but most of them were reluctant because they had been married to Indonesian men before going abroad to work," the official added. (KEMENPORA 2017; Sarigih 2014)

In the above example, a significant part of the article focuses on the state's claims to be actively helping illegitimate stateless children "return" to Indonesia, efforts that prove difficult due to the women's apparent reluctance and the fact that their children were born outside of wedlock. The state official's narrative shifts the focus of the article away from Indonesian migrants with death sentences to the question of their morality and whether they deserve legal aid from the Indonesian government.

Another telling news report by *The Jakarta Post* (September 30, 2013) describes the "tragic fate of Indonesian workers in Malaysia" (Aritonang 2013). The report provides a list which includes detailed descriptions of extreme physical abuse of migrant women. Any mention of sexual abuse is glaringly absent. Similarly, Ford and Lyons (2012) observe that in discussions of human trafficking and labor exploitation in Indonesia, sex workers are noticeably seldom the focus. In other words, cases that are not seen as "tragic," or cases that attract less public attention and sympathy often involve more morally ambiguous or socially taboo aspects, such as sexual abuse, greed, depression, single parenthood, or divorce. These are sometimes told in the genre of a moral or cautionary tale.

A report written and published on the website of an Indonesian migrant-centered NGO begins with a Javanese folk saying: "One goes overseas in search of gold, but it rains stones instead" (Buruh Migran 2008). What follows is a case of extreme physical torture of a domestic worker in Malaysia, who had just returned to Indonesia:

This proverb is apt to describe the unfortunate events experienced by Radisem Bint Sumarjo, a female migrant worker [28 years old].... Currently lying at the Regional General Hospital ... after working in Selangor, Malaysia. There are bruises all over her body, and her legs are paralyzed after being tortured by her employer.... She requires an oxygen mask to breathe.... According to the victim's brother, Radisem only just managed to rest this morning, after babbling to herself all night long. It seems as if she is still in Malaysia, and in fear.

The narrative goes on to represent Radisem's migration experience in terms of her individual choice and aspirations for wealth:

Last July, Radisem left home with a sense of pride. She will become a maid in Malaysia and in the future, she will be able to bring home large quantities of Ringgit. However, not only did she not get any ringgit, she also encountered misfortune [*nasib buruk*].

The writer then expands on how Radisem got a "good employer" and wrote home twice. However, her family stopped receiving news after this, only to find out much later that during this period of silence,

Radisem was often abused by her employer for stealing her employer's money. Radisem received blows all over her body, from her legs, back, head and she was even strangled by her neck.... She did not get to eat much or often. Sometimes only once a day.... As a result of not bathing often, Radisem contracted a skin disease that added to her misery.

Although the report ends by ultimately referring to Radisem as a "tragic victim" and calling for the Indonesian government to "take action," the narrative is wrought with moral ambiguity, in which Radisem's "tragic" situation is variously explained in terms of her pride or greed, bad luck, and the fact that she might have stolen from her initially "good" employer. In a similar narrative vein, a human rights media platform begins a case of abuse in Taiwan by also framing the migrant woman's departure as one where she is "cheerful" in spirits, although she left against her father's wishes (Ayyubi 2009). She returned "crazy" and severely depressed, claiming her employer hit her until her teeth fell out. The report ends with police investigating "whether or not she was really mistreated." These examples illustrate a genre of victim narratives that introduces suspicion of the victim, leaves the moral of the story open to the reader's interpretation, and either implicitly or explicitly contains a warning along the lines of filial piety and modesty, and against greed.

Innocent Victims of Abuse

These morally ambiguous narratives of women who are promiscuous, greedy, or disobeyed their elders, contrast with stories of the extreme abuse of "innocent" victims. Consider the following report in *The Jakarta Post* (August 8, 2014) about seventeen-year-old Wilfrida Soik, who was charged with killing her sixty-year-old Malaysian employer in 2010:

Wilfrida was charged under the Malaysian Penal Code, which carries a death sentence upon conviction; but the court ruled on Monday that she was mentally unstable when the incident took place, therefore, found her not guilty....

Human rights activists and politicians, who have given legal assistance to Wilfrida and monitored the legal proceedings over the past four years, praised the ruling. "The court's verdict is fair because the murder was an act of self defense, which was to protect herself from torture committed by her employer," Migrant Care, an NGO that promotes the rights of migrant workers, said in a statement. Migrant Care said Wilfrida should have been acquitted because she was underage when the crime took place.

"We have always believed that Wilfrida must be freed because she was underage when the incident happened. She is a victim of human trafficking," it said.... The investigation also showed that Wilfrida was only 17 years old when she entered Malaysia on falsified documents, which, thus, would make her eligible for protection under the UN Convention on the Rights of the Child, which forbids capital punishment for minors, a convention that both Indonesia and Malaysia are signatories of....

The campaign to spare Wilfrida from the death sentence also brought together various groups, including members of the Regional Legislative Council [DPRD], the Regional Representatives Council [DPD] and the House of Representatives [DPR]; the Catholic Church in Belu; interfaith communities; singer and activist Melanie Subono. Netizens also showed their support through the #SaveWilfrida petition on Change.org, which had more than 13,000 signatures, making it one of the most popular petitions put up on the popular website (Aritonang 2014).

In comparison to cases of "immoral" or guilty victims, Wilfrida's case provoked a sense of public moral outrage, evident in the petitions collected in her name, and the wide range of groups and public figures that supported her court appeal against her death sentence. Media and activist representations of her focused on her moral innocence in framing her as a "child" and a "victim of human trafficking." Furthermore, she was "mentally unstable" (and hence, not fully responsible for her actions), and she had acted out of "self defense ... to protect herself from torture."

Another case involved a "53-year-old grandmother" who was beheaded for murder in Saudi Arabia in 2011 (Al-Alawi 2011). She claimed to have killed her employer because she was forbidden to return home to see her three children. Her death sparked public protests in Indonesia, and provoked a state moratorium on labor migration to Saudi Arabia. These examples are representative in showing how, in almost all cases inspiring extensive media coverage and state intervention, women are framed as innocent victims—and the violence against them as unjustified.

I highlight these cases to argue that they may have provoked more outrage because moral judgments are often based on the perception of one's intentions under specific circumstances (Duranti 2015). Hence, despite having committed murder, a migrant is viewed as innocent because she was trafficked against her will, or due to her sacrifices as a mother when she migrated to provide for her family. On the other hand, women's agency and intentions are depicted as morally suspect where women have professed some prior desire for adventure, pleasure, or wealth. Even in cases where women do not profess such "deviant" desires, where sexual abuse is concerned, the moral innocence of women seems suspect by default, as in the case of rape being represented as adultery. This focus on moral agency contributes to shifting the location of blame for violence onto migrants themselves. This also sanctions only a particular motive for migration—for economic reasons, and supporting one's family—as opposed to addressing cases in which women are pressured against their will by family members to migrate, or in which women migrated to escape pressures to marry, or stigmatization as single mothers or divorcées (see Chan 2017a; Constable 2014).

Unlucky Victims of Fate

Other deaths and sicknesses are represented in the media and informal discussions as "natural," morally neutral, or associated with bad luck. A prominent national news agency, Tribunnews, archives all news regarding Indonesia's migrant workers under the theme (*topik*), "The fate of migrants" (*Nasib TKI*). Former BNP2TKI chief Jumhur Hidayat, has publically referred to "victims of human trafficking" as "those who are less lucky" (*kurang beruntung*) (*Republika* 2012). These cases of bad luck or illness are often framed factually, and depoliticized by state authorities.

For example, the following report was posted on the website of an Indonesian migrant-centered NGO regarding the hospitalization of two migrant workers in Dubai (Buruh Migran 2014a). It hints at the employers' failure to provide adequate heating, but unlike other reports of migrants' deaths and abuse, this one is free of criticism or blame, and does not conclude with calls for state action or suggestions for the implementation of proper labor laws ensuring proper living conditions for workers:

> Two Indonesian migrant workers in Dubai unfortunately experienced charcoal smoke poisoning on Friday.... They were poisoned after carrying a burning charcoal into the room, due to recent cold weather conditions in Dubai.
>
> In addition, the room provided by the employer for both workers was cold, and eventually they brought a piece of burning charcoal into the room. Both Indonesian migrant workers inhaled carbon monoxide from the burning of this charcoal. Both were found lying unconscious in the room.

Another migrant death was more controversial, since the migrants' relatives demanded an autopsy of the dead body. Khodijah Dede was a migrant domestic worker, who died three months after she arrived in Jeddah. According to a news report, her family was told by state officials that she died due to illness, though

Dede's recruitment agent separately informed her family that she was poisoned (*Solopos* 2012). In response to the family's request for an official explanation, BNP2TKI released a report to confirm that Dede had died due to "drinking organic phosphoric chemicals" (BNP2TKI 2012). Despite this detail, the report concluded that upon reexamination, the cause of death was "natural," due to "a decrease in cardiac function in the respiratory tract."

Medical anthropologists argue that diseases and illness are seldom simply "natural," but also the result of improper and irregular diets, and environmental conditions that are usually social and political (Hamdy 2008). Yet, state and media accounts of these sicknesses may sometimes naturalize and uncritically frame these cases as "bad luck" and "ill fate," although some minority critical voices are calling for enforcing autopsies on all Indonesian bodies that died overseas (Knight 2013).

Dispersing Responsibility and Blame

Responsibility and blame for migrants' problems are often dispersed by and among multiple institutions and actors, often via moral discourses. The discourses in Indonesia linking gender, migration, and morality produce a double-edged view of women as, on the one hand, highly individualistic and conscious agents of their own fate; and on the other hand, highly vulnerable to worldly temptations and thus requiring protection and discipline. While these two apparently incompatible views of women as clever, rational, economic agents and overtly emotional, irrational beings has been traced by older ethnographies of gender in Java (see chapter 1), the political, economic, and sociocultural stakes of evoking both discourses by institutions on a national scale are heightened in the context of feminized transnational migration. In this contemporary manifestation of the dual gender paradigm, migrants, particularly women, bear the bulk of the blame and burden of ensuring "successful" migration outcomes, and enduring the shame associated with failing such expectations.

Indonesian migrants, particularly domestic workers, are represented in overlapping and intersecting ways by the Indonesian state, activists, and journalists. Whether (female) labor migration is represented by these actors as exploitative or a positive economic force for families and the Indonesian nation depends on how they frame the role of and relationship among the Indonesian state, the global market economy, and the gendered moral responsibility of the Indonesian citizen/worker. This chapter has argued that the precarious labor migration of Indonesian women in particular is legitimated, tolerated, and sustained by Indonesian policy-makers and the general public due to the often overlooked gendered and moralistic aspects of dominant narratives about migration and development in Indonesia. A gendered moral hierarchy of heroes and victims in these narratives renders invisible, mundane, or irrelevant to policy-makers and public attention those who might not be suffering as visibly or extremely as Erwiana and other "innocent victims," but who are not yet successful enough to return to Indonesia as "foreign exchange heroes." Furthermore, these expectations for migrants to succeed in being economic providers and good women and men mean that migrants often represent themselves and their host countries to their families and communities of origin in positive terms, in which the host countries are safe, and the migrants are achieving relative social mobility (Kankonde 2010). These pressures to represent migration in terms of success sustain the development narratives, desires, and fantasies of their nonmigrant peers: that migration may remedy local struggles for livelihood and better futures.

Whether Erwiana's case can lead to substantial changes in laws to enhance migrant workers' welfare and political positions in their countries of origin and work depends on whether the outrage and grief over her suffering can not only effectively highlight the global structural inequalities, but also the culturally specific gendered moral inequalities that contributed to her plight. In her case, migrant activists managed to provoke enough public uproar that unprecedented attention was given to the case by state actors in Hong Kong and Indonesia. The limits of such outrage and attention may lie in the fact that Erwiana fits representations of the "good" and innocent victim, as a young, fresh-faced woman whose experiences in Hong Kong reduced her to an undernourished, barely walking, heavily bruised body. Although these are crucial moments of negotiation between states and migrant-centered NGOs on a wide variety of issues, the potential for critique of broader structural inequalities is limited by the pervasive dual and narrow visions of migration as a tool for development, or migration as a form of trafficking.

Gendered moral assumptions underlying representations of violence against migrant workers have significant consequences for whether international or state policies and regulations further restrict mobility and choice for migrants, or address cultural and structural conditions of migration and violence. While state institutions articulate a vision of women who can (and should) be both good family members as well as migrants who live and work away from their families, the next chapters examine how migrants and migrant-origin villagers struggle to reconcile women's identities and responsibilities as family members and migrant workers. The following chapters will elaborate on how the stigmatization and pathologization of migrants deemed "immoral" crucially affect their access to local social support networks upon return to their hometowns, particularly for women. Nevertheless, overemphasizing women as victims overlooks migrant men's experiences of gendered risks and violence, such as the harsh working conditions of construction workers, and the malnourishment and nonpayment of irregular migrants in the international fishing industry (see Palmer 2017).

Implicit gendered moral hierarchies in institutionalized discourses about migration significantly impact how migrants, their kin, and neighbors unevenly negotiate the risks of transnational labor migration in relation to the promise of better lives.

Notes

1. I acknowledge that the Indonesian state is largely made up of agencies and institutions that may adopt contradictory policies and visions in relation to migration or gender-related issues (Ford and Lyons 2012; Palmer 2012; 2016). However, there has been remarkable rhetorical consistency (and consequentially, consistent effects on related policies and programs) regarding the placement and protection of migrant workers, from its Presidents, BNP2TKI, and the Ministry of Labor, in the twenty-first century.

2. The official state rhetoric has been remarkably consistent, although my research has seen three different persons heading BNP2TKI over three years and two presidencies. They are: Jumhur Hidayat (2007–2014) and Gatot Abdullah (April-October 2014) under the Susilo Bambang Yudhoyono presidency, and Nusron Wahid (2015-present) under the Joko Widodo presidency. The term pahlawan devisa is likely inspired by or borrowed from the Philippine state, which referred to its migrants as heroes about a decade before the Indonesian state (Rafael 1997; Rodriguez 2010).

3. This discourse or perspective has been expressed by IOM (International Organization of Migration, 2013) and UNFPA (United Nations Population Fund 2013).

4. This figure is based on estimates from Indonesian embassies abroad, BNP2TKI, Migrant Care, media reports, and families of victims; see Tables "Migrant Workers' Deaths Worldwide in Year 2013" and "Violation of Migrant Workers' Rights in Year 2013." http://migrantcare.net. Accessed on July 2, 2014. However, Migrant Care's statistics on violations against Indonesian migrants have been dismissed by the chief of BNP2TKI (See Dagur 2013; Sijabat 2013): BNP2TKI's official statistic is 186 Indonesian migrant deaths in 2013 (Databoks 2017). These differences are likely due to the fact that Migrant Care includes irregular and undocumented migrants in their estimates, which Indonesian Consulates abroad also tend to do. Thus, the number of Indonesian migrant deaths in Malaysia in 2013 were similar according to two sources: 910 according to Migrant Care, and 922 according to the Indonesian Embassy in Malaysia (Mahmudah 2013).

5. On more than one occasion, labor attaches in Indonesian Consulates overseas have claimed that abuse and violations against migrant workers are very "rare" or "few." See for example, *Jakarta Post* 2010b. For a response by activists in Hong Kong, see Grundy 2014.

3 Evaluating Migrant Success and Failure

"Here, almost everyone [who is a migrant] is successful."

>—Elderly female resident, who has never left Indonesia (Yogyakarta)

"If you ask me, in this whole village, nobody is successful yet."

>—Former migrant woman who worked in Malaysia, mid-twenties,
> married to a former migrant to Korea (Yogyakarta)

"[Success or failure] depends on our own selves and our family. For example, it depends on whether we work hard or not, but also how our children and spouses are ... if they are lazy or if they work, and if children spend a lot of money or not. Sometimes we [migrants] are just the same when we are working overseas [*sama saja*] but our families here are spending it on other things."

>—Former migrant woman who worked in Taiwan, early thirties, who
> returned to Taiwan to work after this interview
> in late 2014 (Cilacap)

IT WAS A clear, sunny November morning in Cilacap. I had been staying in a migrant-origin village there for about a week with Nurul, a woman in her forties who had worked in Malaysia and Singapore for more than twenty years before returning to Cilacap. On this day, Nurul took me to visit her close friend, Rina, who had also worked in Singapore as a domestic worker in the 1990s. Rina's house had newly painted concrete walls, a bigger than average living room with cushioned Javanese wooden chairs, and a large photo of Mecca in Saudi Arabia. This spacious abode was a stark contrast to Nurul's small and modest house, which had a mat instead of chairs for guests, and had only been tiled six months previously. Rina served us warm sweet tea, along with a generous variety of local snacks such as sour mandarins and fried corn fritters. After some small talk, Rina took out an old photo album of her time in Singapore. She had photos with and of the Chinese family she worked for, as well as of some Islamic religious activities she took part in with fellow Indonesian domestic workers on Sundays and *Idul Fitri*.[1]

Rina was a rice farmer who worked on her own land bought with her earnings from abroad. She married at fifteen, then divorced, before moving to Singapore to work. Now, her son was working in Korea with an *aspal* passport, a common Indonesian abbreviation for *asli tapi palsu* (real-but-fake) identity documents (Ford and Lyons 2011).[2] Although he had passed all the required medical and language examinations, he still could not get a job in Korea, so he paid 60 million rupiah (around USD 6,000) to "buy" a job that a neighbor had secured. This meant that at eighteen, he left the country with someone else's name and passport, but with his own photograph in it.[3] To pay for her son's migration, Rina "rented" (*disewa*) out all the agricultural land (*sawah*) that she had. "Thank God [*Alhamdulillah*]," she said, her son was able to send back enough money for them to get back their land and repay their debts.

After his first contract ended in Korea, Rina's son returned to Cilacap to get married, before leaving for Korea again. However, his wife spent most of his remittances on a new motorcycle while he was abroad. Rina also suspected that her daughter-in-law was having an affair with another man. So when her daughter-in-law suggested that she wanted to work in Singapore as well, Rina did not object. In fact, a few months prior to my conversation with Rina, her daughter-in-law had left Indonesia for Singapore to be a "live-in" domestic worker. She had only spent a week in a predeparture training center before her departure, although such training courses for first-time migrant domestic workers were—at the time of my fieldwork—legally required to last at least three months.[4]

Once Rina began telling stories about migrants and their families who lived in the area, it seemed there was no end to it. The stories kept coming. One neighbor came back pregnant after working in Malaysia, though she already had five children and a husband in Cilacap. Her husband was a farmer and took care of their children by himself. This husband, however, accepted the new child. While his wife was in Malaysia, she did not send money home, and when she returned, she did not bring much money with her either. People said (*katanya*) that she had married her Malaysian employer, who was rumored to be the father of her child.[5]

There was also a girl who returned from Singapore with big and ugly scars on her arms. People said that her employer had scalded her with a hot iron. Nurul remarked, "Maybe the girl did something wrong. Sometimes, the girls may not be well trained.... It could be that she did not know how to iron properly or something, which made the employer angry. Sometimes that happens, especially if the boss is Chinese."

Rina mentioned that another girl had returned after only five months of working in Singapore. She now had bald patches on her head, as if her hair had been torn out by someone. I asked Rina if she knew what happened, and she replied that she did not. She added that she did not even dare to ask the girl's family, because it may be hurtful (*sakit hati*), offensive (*tersinggung*), or humiliating (*malu*) for the girl's family to receive such questions, and for the neighbors to highlight these signs of injury.

At this point, I remarked there seemed to be so many tragic stories of migration (*peristiwa*). What did Rina think of such migrations, and the people who were planning to work abroad today? To further simplify my question, I asked, is it a good thing, or not (*bagus atau tidak bagus*)? To my surprise, Rina replied without hesitation, as if the answer was obvious, "*Ya bagus lah*" (Yes it's good).

"But why?" I asked.

"You can build a house, buy land ...."[6]

Perplexed by her certainty, I pushed further, "So migration is generally good ... even though some may have such terrible experiences?"

She replied, "Yes, it depends on our own selves and our family. Sometimes employers want to test us just like we want to test them, or we are being tested. It is up to us to accept [*menerima*] or refuse [*melawan*] them in cases of employer's seduction [*digoda*]...."

Rina's views of the various consequences of migration, in terms of wealth or sickness, abuse, and adultery, are typical of other residents I spoke to in Cilacap and Yogyakarta. Her statements about being "tested" also bore a striking resemblance to state representatives' warnings to migrant women not to flirt or be seduced by employers' advances (see chapter 2). Despite the fact that many villagers observed and discussed the sickness, violence, or debt that migrants and their families face, villagers generally perceived labor migration positively, in terms of the wealth and material welfare it promises. Such positive affirmations about migration highlight how residents actively produce and sustain the hope that migration will improve their lives, particularly for persons such as Rina, whose son and daughter-in-law were working overseas.

This chapter elaborates on how residents of migrant-origin villages variously define and talk about migrant success or failure in moral and temporal terms, linked to notions of obligation and intention. Kinship and neighborly relations crucially shape these contextual evaluations of migration, in which individuals' expressed views are not always consistent and may change with additional information obtained about a migrant's familial circumstances. I argue that sustaining hopeful attitudes towards migration is intimately linked to how migrant money is valued, not only in terms of an immediate and narrowly defined economic exchange value, but also in terms of the gendered moral values associated with the production and circulation of money over time (see Keane 1996, Zelizer 2000). As we shall see, ideas about migrant success and failure are messier from the perspectives of migrant-origin villagers.

Promises

In the Cilacap and Yogyakarta villages, stories of migrant-related success were ubiquitous, gendered, and at first seemed nearly homogenous. Unsurprisingly, they were also often tinged with envy, jealousy, and suspicion. These stories of what constituted success point to predictable local desires for modernity: migrant remittances that funded two-story concrete houses, former migrants who opened their own food or motorcycle repair shops or started small businesses, migrants whose children and family can afford fashionable clothes, cars, motorcycles, mobile phones, a college education, and hospital fees. There is a popular *dangdut* song about migrant women, "TKW," whose title refers to the shorthand for migrant women (*Tenaga Kerja Wanita*).[7] The song is based on stereotypes of the beautiful TKW heroine who works hard overseas, despite her limited skills. Residents told me that this stereotype of the fair and beautiful TKW is due to the fact that TKWs often work indoors, as domestic workers in private houses, as opposed to farming under the hot sun. Additionally, beauty is expensive: TKWs are viewed as able to afford expensive whitening creams or injections to achieve modern standards of Indonesian beauty. Former or potential migrants cited others' successes as evidence that they, too, could eventually achieve their material and financial goals if they worked overseas.

Some migrants are more successful than others, and return migrants in particular often cite the tensions between individual will and familial responsibilities as a key contributing factor, though in surprisingly different ways. For example, despite having worked abroad as a domestic worker for over twenty years, Nurul returned to Cilacap with relatively little to show for it. Divorced, she lived with her elderly mother and teenage daughter in a small and modest house. She had not bought land or saved enough capital to start a business. In a conversation with Nurul and her friend Lita, Nurul suggested that migrants who were unmarried were often more successful than those like her, who had children. To Nurul, migrants without parents or children who depend on them financially were better positioned to save money for themselves. Since they had few family financial burdens and responsibilities, these single persons ought to be able to save money to buy land or open shops.

Lita disagreed. A mother of two young children born before her migratory journey, Lita returned after three years in Taiwan with enough savings to open two small businesses. In contrast to Nurul, Lita said that migrants who had young children like her tend to be more successful. For Lita, since single and unmarried migrants had few familial responsibilities, they tended to spend their earnings on clothes, going out, and having fun. Instead, migrants with mouths to feed tended to think about the future, and to save money for their family's needs.

Both women's views shared the assumption that success is associated with the relative presence or absence of familial duties in relation to an individual's position in the Central Javanese life course. On the one hand, for Nurul, financially supporting her elderly mother—who was singlehandedly taking care of her children while Nurul was abroad—curtailed her ability to save or plan for her own and her children's future. On the other hand, Lita saw her children's needs as a source of motivation and self-discipline, which inspired her to be frugal and future-oriented. Yet, in their attempts to find general explanatory patterns for why some migrants are financially successful and others are not, Nurul and Lita neglected important differences in their households. Lita was married, with a husband who took care of their family businesses. In contrast, Nurul was divorced and a single mother. Lita's siblings contributed to supporting her parents. Nurul was her mother's only provider. This was partly because as a then-migrant and the only migrant among her six siblings, Nurul's (older and younger) siblings assumed she was better able to support their mother, in addition to the fact that their mother was taking care of Nurul's children. Among Javanese families discussed in earlier ethnographies, parents typically did not explicitly expect sons or daughters to give them money or support them financially, although they may have preferred to live with daughters (see White and Schweizer 1998; Wolf 1988). However, as evident in Nurul's and Lita's examples, migrant women are increasingly experiencing financial obligations towards their parents whether as unmarried or married women (see Chan 2017a). Additionally, the care of elderly parents is not dependent on sibling order, but instead is negotiated among siblings according to where they live, their livelihoods, and other financial and caring responsibilities.[8] Despite these differences, Nurul and Lita's generalizations illuminate how migrant success is linked to the ways migrants are able to align their individual aspirations and earnings with familial needs so that they can satisfy the desires of all involved.

Temporality emerged as a key feature in discussions of migrant success, in which residents distinguished between what I call migrants' short-term and long-term successes. While migrants might return home with cash and savings, many also ended up spending all of these savings quickly to build houses, buy consumer goods, or repay debts. Migrants whose successes were thus short-lived were sometimes considered "failures" (*gagal*) or "not yet successful" (*belum berhasil*). Such return migrants could be portrayed as lazy, arrogant, unfriendly, greedy, or stupid, in descriptions of their post-migration unemployment (*menganggur*), in which the dominant image of them is one of "sitting at home" (*duduk di rumah saja*), confusion, and puzzlement (*bingung*).

Tri was one such former migrant who "sat at home" post-migration. During the annual Idul Fitri celebrations in Cilacap in 2012, we were introduced by a common friend. Tri had worked in Malaysia two years prior to my visit, on a three-year contract. During small talk about her circumstances, she remarked that she had been trying to stay at home these days, despite the festivities, since she did not have the extra money to shop or buy many snacks for this special period. She told us that she was just waiting for her young children to grow up, so that she could apply to work in Singapore. Her situation illuminates how migrants' earnings abroad mainly finance the daily expenses of families at home, or the building of houses. Migrants often return with little or no alternative means to generate or earn income beyond fulfilling basic necessities (Khoo et al. 2014).

This local stereotype of the confused migrant who returned with nothing to do but "sit at home" and wait for a future opportunity contrasts with perceptions of migrants who have achieved long-term success. The latter refers to those who either continue to stay abroad and send money home, or those who have returned with enough money to start profitable or sustainable businesses. Migrants who managed to save a lot—who returned with larger consumption capacities—were viewed as more hardworking and pious while abroad. Those who started businesses were commonly referred to as being smart (*pintar*) with managing money. They were typically contrasted against their selfish, hedonistic, and less wealthy peers, who were assumed to have spent their earnings lavishly on themselves and consumer items. Other migrants perceived as having long-term success were circular migrants, or those who "come and go multiple times" (*pulang pergi berkali-kali*). The majority of circular migrants were women. This term describes their specific pattern of mobility, in which migrants embark on multiple consecutive trips, each consisting of two- or three-year contracts with employers and companies. These comings and goings can be sustained for five or ten to twenty years, if not longer. Their success as circular, continuous migrants is often associated by residents with migrants' good luck or fate, in being able to secure good employers, and in their ability to adapt to a foreign land and feel at home (*betah*). Success is also attributed to their ability to endure and persevere for the sake of their families at home despite harsh living and working conditions.

At the time of my fieldwork between 2014 and 2015, the majority of the people I spoke to—including NGO activists, an insurance agent for migrants, state representatives, return migrants, and residents of migrant-origin villages—consistently highlighted the ideal that migrants should aim to accumulate capital (*modal*) to start businesses when they return.[9] It was not enough or practical to simply migrate in order to have money to build a nice house, or for children to go to school. While these were certainly good and expected consequences of migration, many people I spoke to focused on the necessity for migrants to have the discipline and diligence to save while abroad, and not send all their money home. This nearly ubiquitous focus on accumulating capital contrasted with my visit to Cilacap in 2012. Then, residents talked about migration mainly as a way for people to build houses and earn a little "extra" (*tambahan/lebihan*) beyond what was required for daily basic necessities. My observations in 2014, however, complemented similar research findings among Indonesian female domestic workers in Singapore. Women who wished to return home, or who were asked to return home by their family, cited the lack of savings and capital to start a business as a barrier to their return (Platt et al. 2013, 34).

This increasing emphasis on migrants' need for capital and savings coincides with the time period (2012–2013) when the Indonesian state started to explicitly draw on international migration-for-development discourses to talk about migrant remittances. During this time, institutions such as USAid (U.S. government), AusAID (Australian government), and the International Monetary Fund (IMF) actively implemented and encouraged entrepreneurship programs in Indonesia as a pathway to sustainable development (Kevin 2012; Koo 2013; Lagarde 2015; May 2012; University of Sydney Business School 2015). I mention these to suggest that villagers' temporally oriented perceptions about the ideal situation of return migrants, or ideal motivations and aims for prospective or current migrants, were likely influenced by these state and international discourses and projects of migration and development.

The Limits of Success

Superficially, these dominant narratives and definitions of migrant success appear predictable and standard: success is typically linked to migrant money and status-linked indicators of being modern, such as fashion, the latest motorbike, car, or concrete houses. However, I found that even when migrants do fulfill the checklist of what a typically successful migrant should be, they may still perceive themselves, or be evaluated by resident neighbors and peers, to be "failures" or "not yet successful." This is especially true for women's self-evaluations. My point is that narratives and standards of migrant success often do not refer only to financial, physical, or educational welfare of migrants and their families. Such standards often illuminate gendered and moral ideas associated with money and success as well (see Keane 2007).[10]

To illustrate: migrants, particularly women, who had been abroad for more than five years were usually either seen as very successful or very immoral. On the one hand, villagers might suggest that some migrants managed to stay abroad for so long because they had successfully adapted to a foreign country, or had the good fortune to work for good employers who are "like family." On the other hand, long-term migrants could also be perceived as having "forgotten" or "left behind" their spouses, children, parents, or their "Javanese culture," and were just selfishly having fun overseas. These opposing interpretations meant that migrants had to prove their filial attachments to their families by sending money often (Constable 2014; McKay 2007; Parreñas 2005), and by being attentive to their reputations as good daughters, sons, wives and husbands overseas. Maintaining their gendered moral reputation entailed performing transnational emotional care-work such as regular phone calls or text messages home (Lai 2011; Madianou 2012), not being seen in places deemed inappropriate overseas (e.g., bars), spending frugally on material items for oneself, sending or bringing gifts home, or remitting more money during religious holidays such as Idul

Fitri and Idul Adha. Such acts of sending dollars or bringing gifts are typically interpreted as expressions and acts of care from migrants to their kin (McKay 2007; McKenzie and Menjivar 2011; Parreñas 2005).

Women were subjected to harsher moral judgments and standards of success. If men did not regularly send money home, they were sometimes excused for having to pay their own debts, or for needing the money for expenses such as cigarettes, food, or lodging. On the other hand, women were expected to be frugal, nonsocial, and to save almost all their earnings for their family at home. These high expectations for migrant women to regularly send money home was evident in how residents were quicker to accuse women of sexual promiscuity in the absence of remittances. For example, one male community-based leader put it starkly, "My analysis is this. In cases where [women] migrants return without bringing any money, it is definitely because they had affairs there, *hoorah-hoorah*, with Pakistani people or whatever." Such a viewpoint was expressed to me more than once, by residents, return migrants, activists, and state representatives, of both genders and various age groups. This view of some women as hypersexual beings who cannot control their desires echoes dominant ideas that migrants are ultimately responsible for migratory outcomes, such as in this chapter's introduction, where Rina said that success ultimately "depends on our own selves and our family."

Even in cases where migrant women sent large sums of money home, returned with enough money to buy a car, build a big house, or start a business, such financial success typically raised suspicion or doubt about women's sources of wealth. Villagers may gossip that some women's remittances were "not halal" (religiously forbidden), or "hot money" (*uang panas*), implying or explicitly saying that these women probably earned extra money from sex work or received it from rich foreign boyfriends (which suggested extramarital sexual relations). These stories were often circulated by return migrants who worked in the same countries as the women being gossiped about (see chapter 4), or else by resident nonmigrants who made such judgments based on the way migrant women dressed when they returned, or the photos they posted on social media platforms such as Facebook. Scandalous stories in national media, or through informal Facebook posts online, which "exposed" stories of Indonesians "trafficked" into sex work, or Indonesian sex workers in Hong Kong or Macau, encourage and perpetuate such views and stereotypes. Nonmigrant villagers often asked me incredulously if it was actually possible for "proper" migrant women to earn so much in a month or in a year.

Once, a middle-aged woman wondered aloud if her female migrant neighbor was "really just a domestic worker," since she reportedly returned home with savings of about 60 million rupiah (approximately USD 6,000) over the course of a year. Based on my interviews, as well as other research on migrant women's labor in Taiwan (Lan 2002; Wang 2007), foreign domestic workers and factory workers typically earn between six to ten million rupiah a month, or between USD 500 to nearly USD 1,000. In this light, it is possible and reasonable to expect that a migrant worker who has already paid off her recruitment fees and debts could save around 60 million rupiah a year. It would be difficult, but not impossible. Nevertheless, the sources of migrant women's financial success were often suspect and associated with immoral means, unless they managed to maintain good reputations as respectful family members in the village.

Migrant women who appeared financially successful were also sometimes accused of secretly being in debt in order to appear successful, and to avoid the shame of being seen as a migrant failure. An example of such suspicious attitudes towards successful migrant women was gossip about one migrant woman who worked in Taiwan. While some villagers said she only managed to build a big and beautiful house for her elderly parents from her "non-halal" work, others said that she was in fact deeply in debt. Some migrant women were also criticized for their perceived beauty, that they spent too much money on clothes and makeup instead of sending their earnings home to their families.

Evidently, evaluations of migrant women's successes are highly moralizing— through explicitly framing women's work, money, and beauty in terms of the potential desired or undesired social impact on the religiously-inflected organization of gender and the heteronormative family in the villages. This contrasts starkly with villagers' responses to financially successful migrant men. I never heard anyone doubt the source of men's wealth overseas. Instead, it was considered common knowledge that men's wages in Korea, Japan, or Taiwan were typically higher than that those for women. Some villagers told me that married men, as rightful breadwinners of the household, would naturally save and remit more of their earnings for their wives and children. Women, however, ostensibly would not have the same sense of responsibility to financially support the household. Similarly, while not all villagers approved of men spending their earnings on cigarettes, alcohol, or commercial sex, many villagers tacitly accepted that these were "natural" or "biological necessities," or else beneficial expenses for men to adapt to foreign cultural norms and pressures associated with living and working overseas.

These double standards of gendered morality and infidelity, specifically higher tolerance for and tacit social acceptance of male infidelity, are also dominant in other parts of Indonesia, such as East Lombok (Bennett 2005a, 153). Such tacit acceptance of male infidelity is linked to the fact that women are often blamed for their husband's infidelity. Women are said to have not remained attractive enough, or to have not fulfilled their spouses' sexual needs (see Bennett et al. 2011, 154). Such double standards are arguably linked to influential patriarchal ideas locally, sanctioned by prominent national Islamic organizations and the Indonesian Marriage Law for Muslims. According to the Marriage Law, husbands are obliged to be the main breadwinners of households, while wives' main duties are caring for the household and children (Katz and Katz 1975). In this light, male infidelity may be viewed as more excusable as long as husbands are able to provide financially for their families, while female infidelity directly violates her proper legal and religious duties to her husband.

In general, when acknowledging the potential financial rewards of migration, nonmigrant villagers and NGO workers also discussed the moral "trade-offs" of migration. Two men who never left their villages spoke at length about filial piety and "Javanese culture," according to which children should live or be physically close to their ageing parents. One man said sharply that nothing would ever justify being so far away from family and for such long periods of time. He negatively judged his siblings-in-law for deciding to migrate for perceived "economic" reasons. This sentiment echoes others that I heard repeatedly, where migrants were judged for being bad parents, children, or unfaithful spouses who "abandon" their families (Constable 2014; Gamburd 2000; Parreñas 2001), even if they may be working overseas precisely to provide for their families. Thus some residents—though a minority—may be doubtful of and even dismiss the economic rewards of migrants' journeys as evidence of their success as devoted family members.[11]

In light of this discussion, it may seem nearly impossible for migrant individuals, especially women, to be considered successful by their kin and neighbors. After lengthy discussions of definitions or examples of "successful" migrants, I realized that most conversations followed a template of "s/he is successful ... but ..." In other words, the rewards of migration were frequently understood in terms of what migrants and their families risk or lose in the process of migration and return. In some cases, the trade-offs are perceived as never justified by the financial rewards of migration, while in most cases, residents were less sure, and more ambivalent (see chapter 6). Clear and unequivocal statements of "s/he is successful," which were not followed up with a piece of gossip or a "but," were very rare during the course of my fieldwork, even in one special case where I knew the "successful" migrant in question. This migrant appeared to epitomize locals' standards of fulfilling her familial and gendered duties, sending money home often, and returning to start a profitable, sustainable business. To my surprise, a fellow villager told me that this migrant was probably in debt but just hiding it. She was also said to be "exploited" by her family, for whom she worked so hard overseas. Frustrated at what I felt were extremely harsh and elusive local standards of migrant success in Yogyakarta, I asked, "Then who in this village can be said to be successful?" The response was simply, "If you ask me, in this whole village, nobody is successful yet."

Risks

In contrast to the material reality of migrant wealth (*kaya*) such as hard cash and houses, stories of migrant failure—marked by mysterious injuries, death, or the absence of material indicators of success—were often based on hearsay and gossip. Such associations of failure with rumor and secrecy are partially due to the anticipation and experience of shame for migrants and their kin (chapter 4).

The most common example of migrant failure was one who does not send any or enough money home. Migrant men were accused of spending too much of their money on gambling, drinking, or commercial sex overseas—activities considered by most Central Javanese Muslims as associated with male vice and sin. As mentioned, these activities were seldom explicitly condoned by migrant-origin villagers in Yogyakarta and Cilacap, though they might be tolerated to varying degrees. Migrant women were typically accused of spending their earnings on consumer luxury items, foreign boyfriends, cafes, or nightclubs. In these scenarios, I sometimes offered an alternative explanation for why migrants may not be sending much money home. Migrants might be paying off their debts to recruitment agents, particularly in their first year of migration (Platt et al. 2013, 27–29).[12] Some employers, especially in the case of domestic workers, might choose to illegally withhold migrants' wages, or in the worst cases, not pay them at all (Constable 2007; Ford 2002; Ladegaard 2013b). People often either shrugged off my suggestions dismissively, or reluctantly agreed that this may be the case. Migrants' kin and neighbors, especially for those who have never migrated or attempted to migrate overseas, tended to downplay or not consider the financial costs of migration. Most people were aware that migrant domestic workers and some migrant men embark on migration journeys indebted financially to recruitment agents (Killias 2010; Lindquist 2010; Spaan 1994; Palmer 2012), and others might pay—prior to their journeys—between thirty to forty million rupiah (USD 3,000–4,000) to work in factories abroad. Yet, migrants' kin and neighbors typically expected that these costs would be quickly and rather easily paid off by the comparatively high wages abroad.

Bodies and houses are generally—in Indonesia and elsewhere—expected to embody the consequences of healthy lives and families. In the case of Central Java, migrants' bodies and houses are thus taken as indicators of their migration outcomes. Houses in disrepair and wounded bodies are often the subject of rumor about failed migratory projects or journeys. One recurring example was a bamboo house in the Yogyakarta village, where most residents, regardless of whether they had migrated or not, had at least renovated their houses to include some form of concrete or wood. On different occasions, residents recounted versions of the same story about this house. An elderly couple lived there, and their daughter had been working in Hong Kong for more than ten years. Despite this, her elderly parents still had to sell fermented soybean (*tempe*)—a common and cheap food—in order to get by. This indicated to many locals that their migrant daughter hardly sent any money home to help her parents. To many villagers, the only reasonable explanation for this phenomenon of the migrant's "ugly house" (*rumah jelek*) was that she had abandoned her parents, was content with her new life overseas, and had no desire to return to the village.

While a simple bamboo house may indicate a migrant's intersecting financial and moral failure to provide care for her family, there were also several stories involving large concrete houses built with migrant money that were empty or abandoned. Such houses stood out as stories of migrant success *and* failure. For example, on the road where I lived with Nurul in Cilacap, there was an abandoned brick house in mid-construction. Nurul and her neighbors told me that the plot of land and house belonged to a migrant who was in Malaysia. Initially, he had sent money home to build this house for his wife and children. However, during the construction of the house, the couple got a divorce. One interpretation of why the house remained half-built and neglected was that the owner no longer had the heart to complete it, since it would now remind him of the divorce and his ex-wife.

Another migrant house in Cilacap was said to be empty after a migrant returned from Saudi Arabia to divorce her husband. Her husband subsequently chose to move away from the village and work elsewhere, while their young child was placed in the care of a grandparent. Yet a third migrant house in Cilacap was abandoned, then demolished. A migrant woman had returned to find that her husband had not only taken a mistress, but he had also run away with all the money she had sent from abroad.

Other abandoned houses were attributed to conflict and distrust among siblings, or between migrant parents and their children. When I was in Singapore, two migrant women from Central Java respectively told me about their "empty" houses in their home villages. Both had funded the building of these houses from their earnings abroad. In one case, the migrant's siblings moved out of her "humble" house because they were too "ashamed" of it. In the second case, a divorced migrant's daughter chose to move out due to the increasing emotional distance from her mother, who was continuously working overseas.

Success and failure were thus often evaluated in relation to the other. Migrants may be perceived as successful in financial and material terms, but failed to keep their families together in the process or as a result of migration. These abandoned, demolished, or half-built migrant houses in migrant-origin villages were symbolic and material reminders of what I call "collateral damage" of migration. Village talk about the presence of these houses and their abandonment form significant social commentaries on the fragmentation of broader kinship ties, in a context where village neighborhoods are largely conceptualized as extended families, and neighborly obligations can on particular occasions be equivalent to those between kin (Carsten 1991; Retsikas 2014).[13] Nevertheless, these commentaries on the damages of migration tend to cast gendered and moral blame on migrants. Villagers fault migrants for being negligent and uncaring spouses, siblings, parents, or children. Stories of migrants who committed *zina* (forbidden sexual relations) abroad were so pervasive to the point that when migrant women returned pregnant, villagers were quick to attribute this to adultery with other Indonesian or foreign migrant workers abroad, or migrants' employers. This interpretation of migrants' pregnancy was particularly convenient in the case of female domestic workers, who lived and worked in their employers' households.

Villagers also circulated stories of migrants who returned very tired or sick, or of the dead bodies or ashes of migrant workers that were sent back to the village. There were stories of migrants who returned very tired (*capai*), with various health problems such as asthma, diabetes, cancer, high blood pressure, heart problems, and who died within a year or two. These cases of sickness were typically taken as "normal" (*biasa*) and/or due to working overseas. A neighbor of a then-recently deceased migrant said to me, "Of course [the sickness] is because working overseas was really hard.... His death was not sudden, he was already weak since he returned from abroad." In other cases of migrants who returned temporarily or permanently disabled or dead, people perceived the causes to be "accidents" (*kecelakaan*) such as motorbike or car accidents, or falling out of high apartment windows, or slipping in bathrooms (usually simply referred to as *jatuh*, meaning "to fall" in English). While some of these cases of sickness or death were attributed to harsh-but-normal working conditions abroad, they were sometimes also understood as due to migrants' bad luck or fate (*nasib buruk*), especially in cases of accidents.

In almost all cases of death, however, villagers, regardless of their migratory or educational background, typically said that death was due to God's will, or destiny (*takdir*) (see chapter 5). Villagers' narratives of migrant-related sickness also typically included an intersection of physical, social, and moral reasons for the deterioration of health. According to Nurul,

> There was a woman here who went to Saudi Arabia. Her husband was a very decent man, a tailor. He worked for himself and took care of their child ever since his wife left. But once his migrant wife returned, she wasn't like a wife. I mean, she didn't do what wives were supposed to do.... You cannot hide it. So the family found out that she had a boyfriend overseas in Saudi. Her father was so ashamed [*malu*], you know, imagine how terrible it was for the parents, so extremely shameful [*malu tinggi sekali*]. His health got weaker and weaker, and finally he passed away.

Sicknesses or deaths of migrants' kin were thus typically explained as consequences of migrants' actions or behavior as a result of working or having worked abroad. Although other narratives of sickness in Java may frequently include supernatural and social causes, what is notable is how centrally migration figured in many local sickness narratives, alongside previously discussed narratives of money and wealth.

Due to the typically unverifiable sources and "true" reasons behind migrant failures, migrants' own stories of why they returned unwell, pregnant, divorced, or with little savings, were frequently dismissed and doubted. Thus sustained patterns of migrant failures were evaluated as individual and exceptional cases, where migrants were largely to blame for their less than ideal circumstances.[14] In contrast, migrant success was—paradoxically—perceived as more common and normative than migrant failures. This tendency to individualize migrant experiences is not unique to Central Java. Kankonde (2010), in his research among Congolese migrants and their origin communities, found that migrant failure was not only associated with misfortune, but also migrants' intrinsic lack of character or desirable traits. Similarly, in villages of Central Java where I worked, stories of migrant failure were typically explained by either migrants' own lack of self-discipline, luck, morality, filial or religious piety, or problems and dysfunctions in migrants' families. Even in cases where foreign employers had clearly physically abused migrants, as I described at the beginning of this chapter, neighbors may take on employers' perspectives by suggesting that such abuse occurred because of the Indonesian worker's incapability or wrongdoing: "Maybe the girl did something wrong ..." These so-called failures, such as migrants' injuries, debts, and deaths, could also be explained in terms of "nature" (for illnesses), or due to wicked or unlawful recruitment agents or employers. With the exception of cases where return migrants had participated in migrant or labor activism with nongovernmental organizations abroad or in Indonesia, rarely did prospective migrants, return migrants, or residents attribute failed migration projects to national, foreign, or international labor and migration policies or laws.

Shameful or Sympathetic Failures

Migrant failures are often perceived and experienced by migrants and other villagers as a source of shame for migrants and their families. Shame is experienced in gendered ways, according to how individuals are perceived or perceive themselves to have failed or violated gendered expectations and norms (see chapter 4). Shame is also temporal, such as "temporary" or "life-long" shame.

The former president of a national migrant labor union (*Serikat Buruh Migran Indonesia*) once told me about a migrant woman who got pregnant while she was working in Jordan. A stranger on the street had raped her. She gave birth to the child when she returned to her home village in Indonesia. I asked if some migrants who were rape survivors would choose not to return home, and why, and if there were alternative options for them. The reply was that some forms of shame were short-lived, like debt, or not finishing one's employment contract. Other forms of shame, like rape, especially in cases that resulted in a child, were life-long (*sepanjang umur*). This former union president then elaborated that the mother would not only have to suffer shame for surviving rape, and bearing the child of a rapist; when the child grows up, the mother would also have to suffer questions from her child and grandchildren. These children would also likely receive questions about their absent fathers, and be bullied or humiliated among their peers. These examples were used to explain and describe such shame as gendered (only women would experience such shame), and long-term, a shame that would span across generations.

Long-term shame or deep humiliation (*aib*) is often associated with familial or personal dishonor, in contrast to short-term shame (*malu*), which typically refers to milder or harsher forms of embarrassment. I elaborate on these terms in the next chapter, and how migrant money and forms of gendered behavior can mediate the effects and durations of such shame. I find that long-term shame is typically experienced by and acted upon individuals who transgress sexual norms. Despite the prevalence of sexualized speeches and jokes in daily rural life in Central Java, sexuality is still a taboo topic (Wieringa 2012). Divorce for men and women is such an example of long-term shame if persons involved do not remarry (Mahy et al .2016; Parker 2015).

In contrast, short-term shame is shame that can be erased, forgotten, or eventually overcome if individuals take actions regarding the sources of shame. For example, those in financial debt may eventually find work, earn an income, and pay it back. Individuals who violate gender norms, but not in terms of sexuality or sexual practices, may eventually overcome such shame if they compensate these violations with financial support, or by performing other gendered duties. Women who leave the village or country without a male relative's permission may experience such short-term shame. Divorced men and women may partially overcome shame if they remarry within an acceptable period of time.

While these are broad categories to distinguish between how shame may be experienced in lasting or transient ways, it is important to note that individuals experience, negotiate, or find ways to cope with shame differently. This will be the focus of next chapter. Such transgressions and violations of gender and sexual norms are not uncommon in Cilacap and Yogyakarta, even in cases of nonmigrant individuals and kin. However, cases involving migrants are often highlighted and circulated, and those transgressions are perceived to be consequences of migration. Such transgressions might provoke harsh negative social sanctions or threats against individuals by local leaders and villagers, to reinforce local norms (see chapter 6). They can also provoke reflexive discussions on the nature or inequality of gender norms themselves among some villagers. This was particularly true in cases where male authority was perceived as being weakened or threatened, such as when women leave the country without male relatives' permission. Increasing rates of female-initiated divorce might also contribute to a sense that Javanese-Muslim ideals of gender and marriage are less stable than before.[15]

Not all residents were equally harsh in their judgments of migrants' "failures." In some cases, villagers might blame migrants' *kin* for the migrants' failure to save enough money, build nice houses, or even to return home. Long-term migrants were sometimes pitied for working so hard overseas only to finance their father or husband's gambling or drinking habits at home, or to finance their nonmigrant spouses' adulteries and conspicuous consumption. Rina, described, for example, how her daughter-in-law had taken on a lover, and bought luxury items for herself, while her son was working abroad in Korea. Some women also privately expressed pity or sympathy for migrant women who have children out of wedlock, since they would have to raise children as single mothers. Nevertheless, such expressions of sympathy rarely translated into providing emotional or social support for stigmatized women. This might be particularly crucial during the first few months upon return when women, their foreign-born children, and other family members needed time to adapt to the women's presence and the new circumstances.

However, not all stories of migration-related failure resulted in negative moral judgments about migrants or their families, particularly if migrants appeared to fulfill gendered familial roles and duties. In response to some cases where locally respectable prospective migrants were cheated of savings by recruitment agents, or where long-term migrants seemed to be endlessly funding elderly parents' medical fees, onlookers simply expressed sympathy for the burdens that migrants and their families have to bear. Thus, despite the circulation of dominant public opinions and discourses about "good" and "bad" migrants, attending to the subtle dynamics of everyday life in Central Javanese migrant-origin villages reveals their moral pluralism (chapters 4, 6). As we shall see, villagers, even those who are the subject of gossip, may, in order to gain social acceptance and fend off further suspicion about their moral character, outwardly reproduce heteronormative moral discourses and gendered double standards in blaming (other) migrants or kin for migrant failures.

Other (Im)mobilities: In Between Leaving and Staying Behind

Some people inhabit an ambiguous position in between leaving and staying in Indonesia, and in between being "migrants" and "nonmigrants." During my initial visits to Cilacap in 2012 and 2013, I was introduced to dozens of *ex-migran*, an Indonesian term referring to former transnational labor migrants (as opposed to those who have moved for work within Indonesia). To my surprise, however, when I asked them which countries they had worked in, some responded that they never left Indonesia. Their processes of becoming "migrants" yet remaining "nonmigrants" highlight the inadequacy of viewing migration in terms of individual rational choice and agency, or a coherent commercial and/or legal migration industry. Instead, a multifaceted migration infrastructure—comprised of interrelated commercial recruitment intermediaries, bureaucrats, NGOs, social networks, and technologies (Xiang and Lindquist 2014)—*move* people, and shape the (im)mobilities and migrant subjectivities of persons. Looking at why such individuals (typically considered nonmigrants) are perceived as former migrants and/or migrant failures illuminates the extent of normative and gendered expectations of migrant success by migrant-origin villagers, which in turn shape future migration patterns.

When I first went to Cilacap in 2012, I met Hazam, who had volunteered for a year in Jakarta with a migrant labor union, SBMI. He referred to himself as a "failed" (*gagal*) and "ex" (*mantan*) migrant, although he had never left the country. Hazam said that initially he never considered working abroad. He had some land, and enough to live on (*cukup*). His neighbor's son, however, wanted to work abroad in Taiwan. He had everything required for him to leave (i.e., a passport and other identity and medical documents), except for a "certificate of guarantee" to serve as collateral, in order to finance his migration via loans. Feeling sorry for him, Hazam took a risk and loaned the neighbor his land certificate. Before the boy left, Hazam reminded him to work hard, make his parents proud, and importantly, return to the village.

After several months in Taiwan, the boy called Hazam to thank him for his generosity. He was happy in Taiwan, and the job paid well. To repay Hazam's kindness (*balas putih*), he encouraged Hazam to apply for the same job in Taiwan as there were vacancies. Hazam "didn't know what came over" him, and soon paid three million Indonesian rupiah in cash to a recruitment agent (approximately USD 300 or three months of an average factory worker's wages). When Hazam arrived at the Jakarta airport, ready to leave for Taiwan, he was informed, along with a group of other men, that the recruitment agency had shut down. The owner had run away. Hazam lost all of his three million rupiah, and was outraged. Instead of returning to the village, he decided to stay in Jakarta with SBMI, who had a shelter for victims (*korban*) of migration-related problems.

The experiences of many other nonmigrants who identified themselves as former migrants were very similar to that of Hazam. Men and women might share experiences such as failing medical checkups or being unable to produce convincing false identity documents. The vast majority of men were victims of fraud, and as a result, were heavily indebted to banks, loan sharks, relatives, or neighbors (to the tune of up to forty million rupiah or USD 4,000). When I returned to Cilacap in 2014, a close friend and former migrant domestic worker told me that men in neighboring villages had recently paid between USD 500 and USD 600 to fraudulent migrant brokers. Due to their debts, these men were living on the streets. Some were too ashamed to return home, while others had been thrown out of the house by their parents or siblings. Most of these men never left Indonesia. Nevertheless, as a Cilacap resident said, "We can call them failed migrants too, because they are also victims of migration."

Unlike in English, in which "failed migrants" might imply and include "the failure *to* migrate" which is not incompatible with the category "nonmigrant," in the Indonesian language it is more accurately translated as "a (transnational) migrant who has failed" (*migran yang gagal*). Such people are thus described as if they had already migrated overseas (*mantan tapi gagal*) and are thus distinct from nonmigrants. Thus, "former migrant" is a broad category referring to all individuals who have embarked on a migration process, and who are commonly categorized as someone who failed or succeeded (*gagal/sukses*). As mentioned earlier, migrants are generally viewed as failures if they did not complete contracts, sent little money home, were deported or injured, or additionally, if they did not manage to leave the country. Only upon elaboration was I able to distinguish between "former" or "failed" migrants who had worked or lived abroad, and those who had never been outside Indonesia. These counterintuitive and surprising uses of the term "ex-migrant" or former migrant suggest a need to examine the processes and meanings of becoming migrant and nonmigrant.

Nearly all women who failed to migrate had either run away from a predeparture training center, or paid substantial fees (between two and thirteen million rupiah) to leave it. These centers are notorious for their poor living conditions, food and facilities, their harsh and exploitative training regimes, and the many restrictions on women's mobility and entitlement to communicate with their families or friends. This explains why so many women run away or pay to leave the centers.

Desi, for example, failed to migrate twice. Given that she was twenty-five years old and unmarried, her presence in the Yogyakarta village was unusual, since others like her were typically not found in the villages, but instead working in urban Indonesian cities or overseas (see Elmhirst 2007). When I first asked her why she was not working abroad, her male friend who was with us teased her and answered, "Because she's not capable (*tidak mampu*), she failed her language exams!" Appearing upset and defensive, Desi immediately shouted that he was a liar. When I later interviewed her alone, she said that she had first tried to work abroad when she was sixteen (though the official legal migration age for men and women is eighteen) because going to university was too expensive as an option. Her sister was making a lot of money as a migrant in Taiwan at the time and seemed happy (*senang*) there. When a recruitment agent approached her family, Desi agreed to have the agent declare her age in her passport as twenty-two. However, when she was about to leave from the airport in Jakarta, a police officer who suspected that she looked younger than her (falsely) documented age, singled her out and sent her home. Fortunately, her recruitment agent refunded her fees.

After this experience, she did not give up. Less than a year later (still technically underage), Desi signed up with a recruitment agency in another city known for being "less strict" with official regulations. She thought it would be easier this time to leave the country. While staying at the training center for a few months, supervisors and staff made sexual advances towards her. She observed that women in the training center who accepted these propositions were sent abroad more quickly. Unwilling to do the same, Desi phoned her father and told him of the situation. He advised her to lie that her grandfather had died, so she could request to return home for the funeral. With the agency's permission, she left all her belongings behind, promised to return the next day, and made her escape. She never recovered her belongings nor identity documents.

Migration Infrastructure and Migrant Subjectivities

The common categories of migrant and nonmigrant are mutually exclusive in migration studies, in which the crossing of national borders importantly distinguishes migrants from nonmigrants. However, as the cases of Hazam and Desi reveal, in Central Java, in an important sense, migratory journeys are perceived and experienced as beginning as soon as someone decides to work abroad.[16] These people inhabit an ambiguous space in between leaving and staying. They are (former) migrants because they are perceived to have embarked on transnationally oriented journeys as candidates who have applied to leave the country. These active (though failed) attempts to migrate overseas differentiate them from other residents or typical "nonmigrants" who never left the village, domestic (internal) migrants, and others who decided to stay and never thought about migrating abroad. Yet, they are also nonmigrants, because even in their locally legible status as failed or former migrants, their experiences of the migration processes are incomplete and distinct from persons who have worked and lived in foreign countries.

Scholars have examined the forms of discipline and governance that turn prospective migrants into productive and ideal workers both prior to their journeys (Guevarra 2006; 2010; Hugo and Stahl 2004; Rodriguez 2010; Rodriguez and Schwenken 2013; Rudnyckyj 2004) and in the destination countries (Constable 2007; Lan 2006). I argue, however, that other factors also shape migrant subjectivity. These include the ways in which prospective migrants imagine and construct the spatial boundaries of the village, the recruitment agent's house or office, the training center, and the airport as particular spaces "in-between" national boundaries or gateways to other countries. In Central Java, individuals who identified as former migrants tend to emphasize the migration application process (*daftar*)—paying recruitment fees, preparing the relevant documents, undergoing medical tests, living and working in training centers, or arriving at the airport ready to leave the country. These are processes, spaces, and forms of knowledge that mark them as candidates for migration (*calon*), as distinct from other nonmigrants who would have never seen what lay beyond the training center gates (Rudnyckyj 2004). Being at the airport, especially the one in Jakarta, were important elements of Hazam and Desi's experiences as former migrants (Silvey 2007a). Even if they never actually boarded a plane, or passed through immigration, the airport is a space most nonmigrant kin and neighbors would have seldom inhabited. At the time of my research, obtaining or applying for a passport or identity documents such as the Overseas Worker Card (KTKLN) was also part of being formally identified and identifying as a migrant, even if the documents were never used (Killias 2010; Lindquist 2010; 2012). Finally, before people left home for the center or airport, it was customary to bid a formal farewell to their neighbors and relatives. Villagers usually wished them safe journeys and expected them to return only upon finishing their contracts overseas (Allerton 2013, chapter 6). Thus when Hazam and Desi returned home, they were received as former migrants—people who had already embarked on their journeys abroad, whether or not they had actually left the country.

The sites, processes, and networks that facilitate transnational journeys and that determine how migrants are documented, the nature of their work, and to which destination country they are sent, can also simultaneously lead or discourage others from eventual migration or returning home. In the cases of Hazam and Desi, social networks such as the ties of friends and families to migrant brokers or representations of life abroad played an important part in shaping their decisions and attitudes—including uncertainty, curiosity, and a sense of adventure (Bélanger and Wang 2013; Lindquist 2012; Spaan 1994; Stoll 2013). The commercial agents who facilitated the predeparture processes (and negotiated the regulatory mechanisms) whereby women like Desi are moved to and confined in training centers (Lindquist et al. 2012) are a powerful factor. The eventual nondeparture of prospective migrants can also be provoked by restrictions to their movement, agency, and communications in the training centers or by actual acts of prevention—for example, when Hazam's agent ran away or when the police sent Desi home. Women's departures or escapes from the training centers are usually facilitated—as in the case of Desi—by the intervention or advice of family members (see also Chan 2017b; Lindquist 2010). Desi's return to her home-village marked her departure from the path of achieving migration, and thus her transition to being a former migrant who failed. The new and ambiguous social identities of such former migrants are often accompanied by actual shifts in their mobility or immobility. These can occur through fear of running into recruitment agents (to whom they might owe money), debt or the loss of nearly all their savings, and/or the absence of the national identity documents needed to obtain jobs in cities or to buy a vehicle.

In these ways, it becomes clear that the migration infrastructure not only facilitates mobility but also shapes "non-cases of mobility, those ... stopped before they start" (Salter 2013, 10). Those who fall between migrant categories often experience deep ambivalence about what to do after their failed migration attempts.

The social stigma or negative perceptions of failed migrants also shape their experiences of "return" and perceptions of future paths and options (Kankonde 2010; Long and Oxfeld 2004; Xiang et al. 2013). In some migrant-origin contexts, such as Senegalese boat migrations (Hernández-Carretero and Carling 2012), failed journeys may still gain the admiration of others, where migration attempts, regardless of their outcomes, are perceived as courageous and heroic.[17] In contrast, negative social and moral perceptions surround "failed migrants" in migrant-origin villages of Central Java. In this context, individuals may be more averse to claiming victimhood or identifying as failures.

Hazam, for example, was financially broke and unemployed in a sociocultural context in which he experienced pressures as a man to be the family's primary breadwinner. As such, he felt he could not immediately return home, and he aimed to gain skills as a volunteer and migrant activist in SBMI before he felt he could face his family and neighbors again. For Desi, taboos against speaking about personal sexual violence or sexual harassment, coupled with the fact that she had failed to migrate twice, deterred her from sharing her experiences. Partially because of her silence, she was sometimes the subject of gossip in the village. As I witnessed, even four years after her escape from the training center, Desi still faced half-serious joking or questioning about her inability to migrate. Half a dozen other women I met who had run away from training centers were variously perceived as lazy, mentally or emotionally weak, or insincere in their efforts to work abroad. On multiple occasions, these runaway women and male and female victims of fraud were openly called "failures" whether or not they were present to hear it, in the guise of joking and teasing among family and friends.

Thus, the categories "nonmigrant" and "migrant" sometimes overlap. These ambiguous situations critically affect the way in which migrant/nonmigrant categories and subjectivities are reproduced and refracted. On the one hand, they support locally salient discourses pertaining to "bad" migrants perceived as failures—individuals lacking the mental and emotional strength to overcome migration-related obstacles, who frivolously change their minds about migrating, or who are stupid to trust the wrong agents with their money.[18] These ideas reproduce notions of "model migrants" who may have also endured harsh predeparture procedures and, presumably, even tougher conditions of work and life abroad, yet completed their work contracts to return with money and gifts (Aguilar 1999; Liebelt 2008; Silvey 2006). On the other hand, in failing to migrate, these nonmigrants serve as the opposites of the "good" nonmigrant (Fioratta 2015; Hannaford 2015). Unlike pious Muslim daughters who stay or who work in nearby cities, women like Desi are perceived as potentially exposing themselves as sexual prey for recruitment agents, foreign employers, and foreign men (see Elmhirst 2007; Lindquist 2004; Suzuki 2005). Unlike humble residents who are content with a simple life, they are impulsive and greedy about the prospect of acquiring riches from abroad (chapter 2). Such moral evaluations of migrants and nonmigrants emerge at the intersections between state, commercial, and humanitarian discourses and programs (Choo 2013; Fassin 2012; Ford 2002).

These situations and subjectivities in between leaving and staying highlight their marginalization and exclusion from national, international, or nongovernmental development programs that typically target either "victims of trafficking" or "former migrants" who are assumed to have returned to Indonesia with new skills and experiences. Banks, state representative, and NGOs encourage "model migrants" to invest their remittances and skills in their places of origin (Anwar and Chan 2016; Faist 2008). Rehabilitation programs provide aid, shelter, and skills to those identified as legitimate victims of trafficking (Chan 2014; Ford and Lyons 2012; McNevin et al. 2016). Policy-oriented research examines the vulnerabilities and well-being of nonmigrant children, their foster caregivers, and the elderly who are "left behind" (e.g., Graham and Jordan 2011). In contrast, these failures to migrate constitute different kinds of (im)mobilities and subjectivities, demonstrating how increasingly regulated migration processes create more uncertainty not only for migrants (Constable 2014; Huijsmans 2012; Killias 2010), but also for migrant candidates, and for those considered nonmigrants, due to the multiple ways that migration infrastructure constrains or (re)directs their agency and mobilities (Nail 2016; Xiang and Lindquist 2014).

Such processes of subjectivization—becoming migrants and nonmigrants—further produce, order, and value migrant and nonmigrant identities in relation to each other. Individuals in between migrant categories bear the brunt of negative social and political attitudes that disparage aspects of transnational migration, where migrants are criticized for abandoning families or nonmigrants are shamed or pressured into leaving to achieve social status equivalence with their neighbors (see Bélanger and Wang 2013; Kankonde 2010). By neither having decided to stay, nor being able to leave the country, it is difficult for people like Hazam and Desi—at least upon return—to stake claims to "good" migrant or nonmigrant identities. The ways in which their attempts and failures to migrate are valued importantly shape their subsequent possibilities and attempts to migrate, delay returns, or affect their decision to stay at home.

Given the increasingly sophisticated forms of migration regulation and intervention in countries of migrant origin and destination (Guevarra 2010; Koslowski 2011; Rodriguez 2010; Kloppenburg and Peters 2012; Xiang and Lindquist 2014), the number of those who attempt and fail to migrate in Indonesia and globally is likely significant. As Daniele Bélanger and Hong-zhou Wang (2013) have noted on predeparture processes to "becoming a migrant" in Vietnam, "The route to migration is not a linear process, since it can be interrupted at any stage and then must be restarted from the beginning." Persons who attempted to but failed to migrate challenge popular assumptions that most "nonmigrants" are passively "left behind" or less advantaged as compared to their migrant counterparts.[19] The liminal positions and dual subjectivities of those who have failed to migrate illuminate the infra-structural conditions that both enable and constrain transnational mobilities.

Valuing Migrants and Money

Residents of migrant-origin villages define and talk about migrant success or failure in moral and temporal terms. Financial contributions of migrants to their families are only one potential indicator of success. Instead, migrants' gendered performances and social positions give value and meaning to their money and gifts. The gendered and moral nature of such evaluations illuminates how local narratives and standards of migrant failure and success are mutually contrasting and complementary. Harsh gendered assessments of migrant morality alongside high normative expectations for migrants to succeed financially illuminate why residents may often say that most migrants are successful, yet some may also remark that "nobody is successful yet."

Those considered to be failed migrants also experience shame in gendered and temporal ways. In the next chapter, I elaborate on how migrants and their kin experience and cope with gendered shame upon return to Indonesia or their home villages. Some such coping strategies have been highlighted through the examples of Hazam and Desi, persons who attempted to but failed to migrate. To avoid the teasing, shame, or stigma associated with failed migration, people like Hazam may choose not to return to the village immediately, and others like Desi may choose not to talk about their experiences. This can reinforce dominant per-ceptions that all migrants can succeed as long as they work hard, are religiously pious persons, and responsible family members. The examples of those who fail to migrate—who are always identified upon return to home villages as failed for-mer migrants—demonstrate the normative and gendered expectations of suc-cess that all prospective migrants face from the time they take concrete action towards leaving the village to work abroad.

While a body of work on mobilities acknowledges the ambiguity and flu-idity in migratory decisions, processes, and identities (Hannam et al. 2006), the dichotomy between migrants and nonmigrants is an enduring one, likely due to its methodological, analytical, and political convenience. Current stud-ies on "nonmigrants" have considered those who choose to stay (e.g., Bylander 2014; Fioratta 2015; Reese 2011) and those who are deciding or ambivalent about whether to migrate (e.g., Paul 2015). I have shown instead that migrant-origin vil-lagers may also understand "moving" or "staying" in multiple ways beyond the common dichotomy. Instead, they negotiate the conditions structuring their rel-ative social and geographical mobilities, partially through discourses of migrant success and failure, and by employing the categories of shame and duty associ-ated with leaving and staying.

Seeing migration and mobility from the perspective of those considered "nonmigrants" raises important questions about the entire practice of migration. Bodies, labor, and finance associated with migration may be valued differently by migrant-origin villagers, NGOs, and state representatives, according to their positionalities. Prospective migrants or migrant candidates experience fraud or exploitation prior to leaving the country as well, not simply in destination countries where they seek work. Considering the ways in which nonmigrants partially share experiences and identities with migrants can shed light on the ways that migration infrastructure shapes the relative (im)mobilities of persons and groups who encounter shared kinds of precarious circumstances and possibilities, without privileging and reproducing ideas about the vulnerability or "mobility" of any group of persons (cf. Butler 2006; Fassin 2005; 2007). A focus on such liminal spaces and subjectivities in migration infrastructure can also help us to understand the expansive and expanding ways in which transnational and domestic mobilities, immobilities, and uncertainties are mutually constituted and mediated.

Institutional oversight of persons who are neither/nor and both/and migrants and nonmigrants, coupled with dominant public discourses in migrant-origin villages blaming and shaming "failed" migrants, reinforce the chapter's argument that self-responsibility emerges as a fundamental and limiting condition for migrant success or failure. The next chapter examines how "failed" migrants and their kin experience and negotiate shame. I argue that the mobilization and cultivation of gendered shame are crucial to understanding how villagers negotiate the risks of migration and justify decisions to move or stay.

Notes

1. Sunday is usually the day off for domestic workers in Singapore and Hong Kong. According to the current laws of destination countries such as Hong Kong, Singapore, and Taiwan, domestic workers are entitled to a weekly or monthly day off. However, this is not strictly enforced due to the fact that domestic workers also live with their employers, and the laws allow room for workers to work on their days off for additional pay. Thus the practice of giving domestic workers a weekly or monthly day off varies among employers. Idul Fitri marks the end of the Muslim fasting season of Ramadan. It is the most important Muslim festive season in Indonesia, usually lasting between three days to a week. During this time, some migrants might return to Indonesia to celebrate this event with their family. In Indonesia, this celebratory period is also known as *Lebaran*.

2. Falsified documents, such as passports, refer to any documents in which personal information or data has been altered by recruiters and/or migrant candidates, with the help of bureaucrats, to deliberately mislead persons of authority, such as immigration officers.

3. Some migrants agree explicitly to such falsified documents. In this case, the neighbor and recruitment agent had told Rina's son that he could "buy" someone else's job. However,

Rina's son was not aware that this entailed traveling on someone else's passport; he only found out when he received his passport at the airport before departure.

4. These courses typically include how to use modern household equipment such as washing machines, as well as language courses for the dominant language of the destination country (typically Arabic, English, Mandarin, or Cantonese).

5. Cilacap residents often spoke about migrant women who got married abroad, despite being legally married in Indonesia. In most cases, this was seen as possible if the women's partners abroad, foreign governments, or religious leaders who agreed to and conducted the marriage rituals did not know of the women's existing marriages in Indonesia.

6. Shifting dynamics of land ownership were also factors in residents' search for nonagricultural and higher income work. Although historically the Central Javanese are rice-farming landowners, the division of land among children and grandchildren across generations means that today, most residents either have enough residential land to build a small house, or have to share agricultural land with many siblings. Furthermore, wealthier siblings, cousins, or other villagers may buy land from families willing to sell in times of hardship, or in order to afford important rituals such as weddings. Remittances from transnational migrants exacerbated this inequality in Central Javanese villages: many residents complained that due to the higher purchasing capacity of migrants, nonmigrant residents (or less successful migrants) would either be very tempted to sell their land, or never be able to afford to buy their own.

7. *Dangdut* is a genre of Indonesian popular music that is hybrid, "blending Indonesian lyrics with instruments, rhythms, melodies, and electronic production techniques from Indian film music, Malay and middle-Eastern popular music, American disco, English pop and rock, and Latin dance music" (Weintraub 2008, 370). Dangdut's lyrics tend to express "themes of everyday life, love, social criticism against class inequality, and Islamic messages" (ibid.).

8. Additionally, although Nurul's siblings had moved from Cilacap to different parts of West and East Java with their respective partners, they often turned to Nurul to fund their weddings and even their children's education. Siblingship in Central Java is important as in other parts of Java and Southeast Asia (Carsten 1991; Errington 1987; Retsikas 2014; White and Schweizer 1998). The negotiation of one's financial obligations to siblings depends highly on emotional manipulation and relationships between siblings, in which a sibling who is perceived to be doing well may be obligated to partly provide for (or offer loans to) multiple other siblings, and even cousins, including sometimes their children. How sibling obligations affect individuals' financial situations depends on how persons find ways to refuse, reduce, or delay financial requests, as well as how siblings recruit other family members and neighbors into pressurising or even shaming the sibling who is perceived as "better off."

9. Migrants are legally obliged to sign up for private health and life insurance to cover their medical expenses from the time they begin training in Indonesian recruitment centers, till the time they return to the country. Recruitment agents usually are linked to a few licensed insurance companies who monopolize the provision of migrant-specific insurance packages. Recruiters are often solely responsible for arranging for the relevant documents for migrants, and keeping their policy documents and reference numbers as well, rather than giving this information to the migrants.

10. Indeed, perceptions of migrant success resonate with earlier ethnographies on social status in Java, in which prestige may not be neatly related to wealth. Status instead is "measured on less tangible qualities such as cultural refinement, linguistic etiquette, social skills, and spiritual strength" (Brenner 1995, 25; Geertz 1961).

11. Some such nonmigrant residents were not able to leave due to the lack of alternative caregiving options, and thus may emphasize familial relations and in-person caring over the possibility of earning more money abroad (Khoo et al. 2015, 23).

12. Indonesian migrant women employed as domestic workers in Singapore may pay up to eight months' worth of salary for brokerage fees (Platt et al. 2013).

13. In one sense, neighbors are usually in fact extended kin due to the division of inherited land, and new houses built can be seen as expansions of older existing houses (Carsten 1991). However, the rituals conducted among neighbors also actively create kinship ties among fellow villagers, including the sharing of local cemetery compounds. As Kostas Retsikas writes about Javanese siblingship, "during ritual exchanges, food, ancestors and prayers are assembled in new configurations which make possible for the characterization of neighbours as siblings" (2014, 104).

14. Research on Filipino migrants has found similar discourses blaming migrants for their failures (Aguilar 1999, 115–16; Tadiar 2004, 118).

15. While residents often lamented the increase in divorce rates locally and attributed this phenomenon to migration, several ethnographies of Java have observed that divorce was not that rare (Hatley 1990). Furthermore, I came across multiple cases of divorced men and women where neither spouse was a migrant. Nevertheless, some scholars have noted that divorce rates among the Javanese declined drastically after the 1960s, likely associated with self-selection of spouses as opposed to arranged marriages (Malhotra 1997) and the cultural desirability of "durable unions" due to an "increase in Islamic consciousness and modern ideas about romantic love propagated in popular culture" (Retsikas 2014, 74; see also Arijaya 2011).

16. For more examples, see Chan 2017b.

17. For example, in a study of Senegalese (male) boat migration, such an attempt is perceived "as a courageous action to fulfill the duty to one's family and protect one's dignity as a man," where "the possibility of death becomes, for many of our informants, framed in a narrative of honor and sacrifice" (Hernández-Carretero and Carling 2012, 412).

18. Ellen Prusinski, in her research among Indonesian women preparing for transnational migration journeys, also observed that being "*siap mental* (mentally ready) is the most important element of becoming educated and prepared for migration." For these women this means being "personally resilient, independent, and brave. For others, being *siap mental* specifically meant adopting certain attitudes associated with domestic workers, particularly deference and agreeability, in order to keep an employer happy" (2016b, 11).

19. Despite substantial empirical evidence that some nonmigrants do not attempt or desire to migrate, due to their relatively stable or secure socioeconomic situations (e.g., Khoo et al. 2014, 15–19; 27–29; Massey et al. 2005), labor migrants in general are still represented and perceived in international and national media in Indonesia as more ambitious, more resourceful, skilled or capable than their peers at home, and often returning wealthier than nonmigrant peers. Despite the obvious fact that this is not always true, such perceptions persist. While some studies have emphasized how migrants are not necessarily the "poorest of the poor" due to the costs required to migrate, the cost of migration from Indonesia is increasingly perceived by residents in migrant-origin villages as less relevant. This is because many women, and progressively men, can migrate without up-front capital, by borrowing from recruiters, and repaying their debts through salary deductions (Lindquist 2010; Palmer 2010). Thus in Indonesia, value judgments about migrants' inherently "better" characteristics might be stronger than other contexts with higher financial barriers to migration.

4 Shame

"Take care of yourself with faith and piety/ Maintain the dignity of the nation/ Above all be honest/ Remember you are a foreign exchange hero."

—Lyrics from a popular song titled "TKW" (Female Migrant Worker)

"To become 'irregular'/ Year after year/ Wishing to go home/ But I bring no money/ Return in shame/ [Or] don't return, [and] my heart yearns"

—Song created by unnamed Indonesian migrants in Saudi Arabia, to the tune of popular Bollywood song *"Bole Chudiyan."*[1]

Sвмı (*Serikat Buruh Migran Indonesia*) ıs an NGO that provides temporary housing for migrants who return with various legal or personal problems. In an interview, its then-president explained that some return migrants choose not to immediately rejoin their families in their villages of origin or hometowns because of shame, or *malu*:

> There will be stigma ... when [migrants] return without money, and there will be malu. Even if it's not about money, it may be about family problems. I think families often don't want to understand the conditions abroad. People like to promote everything good [*bagus-bagus, apik-apik*], the successes, like advertisements.... When migrants encounter problems and they return, they are too malu to talk about it anyway. It is also important for families to be prepared. Because they usually have little information about migration and processes, they cannot imagine the risks their family members take. If they really knew, maybe they won't even allow people to migrate. Or migrants wouldn't even decide to go themselves if they knew.... People who return [to Indonesia] can sometimes also not be ready to return, and be malu, so they migrate again to erase their footsteps [*menghilangkan jejak*].

During interviews and conversations with migrants, their kin and peers, activists, state bureaucrats, and recruitment and associated insurance agents, many talked about the role of shame, fate, and destiny in shaping not just migratory experiences and outcomes, but also in motivating migration, remigration, or return. The above suggestion that families promote migration and shame migrant failures due to a lack of information about risks is representative of how well-intentioned NGO workers or state officials tend to justify some of their programs in migrant-origin communities. Many of these programs typically educate migrants to follow proper legal procedure, despite acknowledging that such procedures offer little guarantee against exploitation or fraud (see Prusinski 2016a).

It is clear that although migrants' kin and prospective migrants may not know the specific risks they may face, most of them have had firsthand experiences of migration-related loss. Many have lost relationships, reputations, money, and the lives of migrant kin, friends, and neighbors. Instead of asking why Central Javanese risk the things and relations they value in order to migrate or help another to migrate, this chapter explores how migration-related knowledge and risk are situationally and relationally constituted through circulating and embodying shame.

Everyday gossip, acts of shaming, and negotiating threats of shame generate specific forms of knowledge about risk, particularly in villagers' self-awareness that their knowledge is always partial and incomplete (see Elyachar 2012). Furthermore, gossip—or the everyday production of social knowledge—about migration also generates, shapes, and renews social relationships among migrant-origin villagers. Gossip and stories about migrants and migration create moral and social boundaries by establishing trust, respect, friendship, and kinship, or by distributing mistrust and skepticism. This approach to knowledge and risk contrasts with dominant attitudes of well-intentioned NGO workers, policymakers, and scholars, in assuming that migrants' relatives and prospective migrants simply "lack" adequate information or knowledge to avoid apparently preventable phenomena such as fraud or irregular and undocumented migrations (Aradou 2013; Hernández-Carretero and Carling 2012; Prusinski 2016a; 2016b). Instead, prospective migrants may relate differently to sources of information about risk and thus evaluate the likelihood of risk differently in their individual cases, or question the veracity of the information. Rather than being ignorant about risks, persons may simply downplay the dangers they hear about, or treat the information as irrelevant (e.g., because they are braver or smarter than other migrants), or treat the source of information as unreliable, such as news media outlets, or embrace perceptions that NGO and state-issued educational brochures may have vested interests to prevent or redirect their migration plans (Hernández-Carretero and Carling 2012). I agree with the observation that "training and awareness-raising campaigns assume that knowledge changes what people do. Yet, these campaigns do nothing to transform the material conditions in which people live. Without an understanding of the conditions of action, learning and educational practices will continue to fail" (Aradou 2013, 3).

Migrant-origin villagers participate in shaming others, respond to feelings of shame, or help others mitigate the threat of shame. While the production and mobilization of malu—by shaming others such as through circulating gossip—are often associated with negative emotions such as contempt and jealousy, individuals are also encouraged to cultivate and possess malu. This second sense of malu roughly refers to a sense of dignity that is gendered. Thus to cultivate appropriate shame, or in response to the threat of shame, return migrants may strategically employ more common everyday approaches such as silence, publicly conforming to ideal gendered expectations, or spreading rumors about other migrants. They may also enact risky or apparently incomprehensible behavior such as running away from employers or recruitment centers, embarking on irregular migratory journeys, enduring unreasonable and harsh working conditions overseas, or, in extreme cases, murdering employers or attempting suicide. Attending to these situations and practices from former migrants' perspectives—in relation to how they negotiate fellow villagers' views about migration, its processes, and consequences—gives us a different view of migration-related risk, knowledge, and moralities.

Villagers' stories about migration—such as the ones presented in chapter 3—may appear to harshly judge and shame migrants and their kin. However, they do not simply reflect a lack of human sympathy for failed or unsuccessful migrants, or a lack of knowledge about the risks of migration. This chapter considers how malu operates and is experienced by migrants and their families in gendered ways. I argue that shame, or the threat of shame, strongly shapes the motility and mobility of villagers; it conditions their decisions to stay, migrate, or return. Narratives and circulations of shame reflect and respond to migration-related as well as broader socioeconomic anxieties in migrant-sending communities.

Malu

Malu, an Indonesian word with Malay origins, is commonly translated into the English term "shame." In Indonesia, "to be accused of having no shame [*tak tahu malu*] is one of the worst insults" (Davis 2014, 32). As a lecturer in a university in Yogyakarta told me, "If one does wrong, but still feels malu, this is good enough [*cukup baik*]." In other words, malu is perceived as an appropriate embodied response to wrongful behavior, in the acknowledgment of transgression. Conversely, to know shame or to have shame can be positively associated with those who successfully perform or fulfill "gendered and status-oriented expectations of behavior" (Munro 2015, 169; Boellstorff and Lindquist 2004). It is in this sense that malu is also closely related to a gendered sense of dignity and self-worth.

Malu is relational and implies a moral hierarchy between the one who ought to feel shame and those affected by the shameful actions of another. It distinguishes those who acted out of step from those who have better managed to achieve expectations and standards (at least temporarily). Learning to cultivate malu is an important part of Javanese children's emotional development, and involves the acquiring of particular social norms: how to behave and respond appropriately to others in terms of their gender, age, and social status (Keeler 1983). Closely intertwined with the performance or transgression of gender and sexual norms, in urban as well as rural Indonesia (Lindquist 2004; Bennett 2005a; Nilan et al. 2013), malu is thus a powerful regulator of gendered performance and sexuality, because it does not only affect people who "acted out of step, but also the entire extended family" (Davies 2014, 33). Sharyn Davies calls such extensive shaming "kinships of shame" (ibid., 33), in which female chastity is equivalent to family honor and its good name. Extended families can act to repair or renew disrupted social ties, such as by forcing couples caught having illicit sex to marry (ibid., 33–34), or forcing rapists and their victims to marry.

Specific urban and rural contexts shape the local varieties and norms of femininities, masculinities, and sexualities. Nevertheless, I follow other scholars who adopt a generalized approach to Indonesian malu in relation to normative gender and sexuality, particularly because I find that descriptions and understandings of malu do not vary much despite the wide variety of research locations such as Sumatra (Parker 2009; Collins and Bahar 2000), Java (Nilan et al. 2013), Lombok (Bennett 2005a), Batam (Lindquist 2004), Papua (Munro 2015), and parts of Malaysia (Peletz 1996). For example, malu is found to have the same self-regulatory effects on women in West and South Sumatra and Java. This is despite the fact that Western and Southern Sumatran ethnic groups are typically matrilineal, where women are self-represented as strong and aggressive, in contrast to the Javanese emphasis on feminine submissiveness (Parker 2009). Similarly, studies of malu and masculinities found commonalities across ethnicities and geographic location. Men express feeling malu when they are viewed as incapable (*tidak mampu*) of fulfilling gendered familial duties, particularly when they are unemployed or not earning as much income as their female peers (Elmhirst 2007; Nilan et al. 2013). Studies also have found that men tended to explain male violence and aggression as a response to feelings of malu associated with lower socioeconomic status (Nilan et al. 2013; Wilson 2012).

Social class and status also influence experiences of malu. Daniel Fessler's (2004) comparative fieldwork and linguistic surveys in Southwest Sumatra and California found that the Malay-speaking Bengkulu in Sumatra linked malu to feelings of inadequacy, subordinate status, and social rejection. Many participants in Fessler's research linked malu to being "reluctant to approach someone of higher status," "embarrassed by others' importance," "feeling inferior," and "feeling stained or dirty" (Fessler 2004, 232–233). In contrast, the culturally diverse and urban respondents in California did not associate the English term shame to social status or shyness, but with the terms "guilt," "remorse," "feel[ing] bad for," "sorrowful," and "apologetic" (ibid., 228). While Californian English speakers tended to link shame to empathic feelings for other individuals, Bengkulu Malay and dialect speakers linked malu to terms for shaming actions of others that cause feelings of malu, such as "sneer," "verbally abuse," "despise," "ridicule," and "swear in disapproval" (ibid., 232–233). How gender and class positions intersect to influence malu is evident in Ayu Saraswati's (2012) analysis of why skin-whitening products were popular amongst working-class and professional women in the cities of Jakarta and Balikbapan. Rather than using these products in order to be more attractive, she argues that women's skin-whitening routines are motivated by desires to avoid feelings of shame and embarrassment linked to a sense of inferiority to others in public (Saraswati 2012, 115–116). These women also linked malu to a fear of mockery, anxiety, and feelings of inadequacy, including morally unacceptable gendered performances. In this context, women's skin-whitening practices can be understood as a way to deal with malu, which reflects their desires to be treated with dignity, or as an equal to those with whom they interact daily (ibid., 119).

While Saraswati and others have argued that Indonesian women tend to be more passive or withdrawn in coping with shame, in order to avoid unwanted attention (Collins and Bahar 2000, 48), others have emphasized the creative ways women manage their reputations while engaging in "illicit" affairs. For example, Lindquist (2004) argues that malu was a reason for (internal) migrant Muslim women in Batam to practice veiling. To ensure productivity in Batam's factories, employers tried to control female workers' sexuality through the rationale that women's work would be affected if they were having sex or "fun" during nonwork hours. In order to manage women's sexuality, the company encouraged religious activities, and provided premarital counselling targeted at preventing premarital sex and pregnancy out of wedlock. Women who were caught having illicit sex could be fired and sent home, thus bringing shame to themselves and their families. Women had to work to manage their appearances and reputations as sexually virtuous women, or women who "know shame" or "have shame." One way to do so was through veiling, which both enabled women to control their desires, and enabled them to divert employers' attentions away from their sexually transgressive behaviors. Linda Bennett's (2005a) work among young single women in Lombok also shows how women may perform malu and piety to hide clandestine relations with boyfriends.

The fear of malu, however, also significantly deters many other women from engaging in such relations or premarital sex. Malu can act as a "'brake' on 'passion' and its expression or realization in social action" (Peletz 1996, 226). As Bennett puts it, "A constant, embodied sense of personal shame is thought to be essential for a woman to behave in a socially appropriate manner" (2005a, 25). In this sense, malu can be understood as "a necessary emotion that enables the self-regulation of female sexuality, yet is also threatening when it derives from public exposure of female sexual impropriety" (ibid.).[2]

In comparing the gendered ways that shame informs individual behavior and motivations, Davies argues that "women may follow prescriptions about femininity in order to avoid causing shame, while men must follow prescriptions about masculinity to defend and restore shame violations relating to sexuality" (2014, 35). Pam Nilan, Argyo Demartoto, and Alex Broom argue that "compensatory aggressive behaviour" of Indonesian men is shaped historically by factors including the "residual effects of 300 years of Dutch colonization, resistance against the Japanese invasion, the subsequent war against the Dutch for independence, and the late twentieth-century struggle for democracy" (2013, 5). In other words, while malu or the threat of malu may provoke women to preserve their honor, these may provoke men instead to perform in ways that restore their honor and sense of masculinity.

The gendered associations of malu as positive and necessary are significant in maintaining social and political hierarchies in Indonesia in relation to class and national identity (Collins and Bahar 2000; Wieringa 2003; Wichelen 2010). Recent analyses of malu describe how individuals may experience it in relation to particular gendered national values and expectations, or threats to perceived national values (Munro 2015, 169). For example, the malu that men experience in relation to their failures to live up to breadwinner roles can be related to late New Order state discourses for Indonesian men to be "'strong males' as an expression of national character," as fathers, husbands, and providers (Nilan et al. 2013, 6). Similarly, the New Order state explicitly built on Islamic discourses of kodrat to articulate women, nationalism, and development in terms of women's primarily domestic roles. This idealized notion of femininity that naturalized women as "devoted to the maintenance of a stable, nurturing, domestic environment were central to the state's vision of an orderly and morally controlled nation" (Silvey 2004, 252; Wichelen 2010). These ideologies were produced and reinforced in institutions established by the New Order state that still exist today, in which the family is taken as a metaphor for the nation.[3] In the post–New Order era, these gendered ideas about the family were "deployed by nationalist and [liberal] feminist, as well as Muslim and Islamist groups" for their own respective political ends (Wichelen 2010, 111).

In other words, Indonesian citizenship is communitarian and explicitly gendered and heteronormative. Thus scholars have linked gendered experiences of malu to evaluations of the self or dangerous others against the state's gendered ideals. For example, Boellstorff (2004) argues that male perpetrators of public violence against gay men typically act upon strong feelings of malu. As Munro puts it, "Malu in this case arises because a particular kind of nationalised masculinity is at stake, and the nation is perceived to be in imminent danger of being represented by non-normative men" (2015, 170). Similarly, Davies shows how the controversial conviction of a male celebrity found distributing pornography in 2011 caused feelings of malu among the general public for the nation: "People expressed feeling 'ashamed of Indonesia and no longer wanted to call themselves Indonesian'" (2014, 40). Thus she argues that kinships of shame "align people throughout the archipelago in feelings of shame against the state" (ibid.; see also Tadiar 2004, 127). Such feelings of shame may also lead to situations where religious leaders or vocal individuals publicly attack or disparage "sources" of shame, such as transgressive persons or the state as an entity, in order to influence politicians' decisions on other issues of gender and sexuality, such as pornography (Hoestery 2013; Weintraub 2008).

While state policies and discourses may have practical and affective impact on the everyday and structural organization of gender and sexuality in Indonesia, I build on the work of scholars who argue that malu also works "through subaltern networks of village biopower, effectively regulating behaviour" (Davies 2014, 47). Shame may pressure or coerce individuals into conforming to gender and social norms, but it may also inspire creative or violent responses to such gendered surveillance and expectations. Similarly, migrants, their relatives, friends, and neighbors negotiate mobilities and reputations by regulating, responding to, or managing malu.

Mobilizing and Gendering Shame

Malu in Central Java is often closely linked to failing or aspiring to fulfill familial duties and obligations in gendered ways. In the context of migration, this applies to migrants' obligations to their families, and vice versa, where families may feel ashamed that a member has to migrate due to parental or spousal failure to provide financial security. As discussed above, many of the New Order state's influential Islamic-based kodrat discourses are not only still salient in Indonesian politics and everyday life, but also even more pronounced at local and regional levels. Biologically deterministic ideas about gender roles now not only emphasize the performance of such domestic or economic duties, but include a further emphasis on the outward performance of religious piety (Wieringa 2015; see chapter 1).

In Central Java, these gendered and familial expectations and duties are often referred to and semi-codified in terms of local customary law, or *adat*. Adat can be defined as informal sets of moral regulations governing a community (Parker 2009; Platt 2012), which, in Java, eclectically draws on Islamic discourses of *kodrat pria* and *kodrat wanita* (natural gender roles). An example of adat in Central Java is that unmarried couples must not cohabit. This section outlines the various sources of gendered shame in relation to talk about migrants' work abroad, the debt, fraud, or conspicuous consumptions of migrants and their families, marital conflict and divorce in migrant families, and the sex lives and sexuality of migrants and their spouses who stayed.

Gender and Work

In the Central Javanese villages where I worked, residents evaluated migrants' labor differently according to the gendered nature of work, as well as the countries associated with such work. These are linked to assumptions that although men may migrate to seek experience and knowledge, the majority migrate in order to fulfill their duties as breadwinners and provide financially for their families. Indeed, in the common Indonesian concept of mobility, *merantau*, men could simultaneously migrate to seek adventure and fortune. In contrast to such "necessary" migrations, women are assumed to migrate to "supplement" her husband or father's income, or to provide for her children, particularly in cases of divorce and single motherhood (see Platt 2017; Wolf 1988).

Although migrants' work was often considered dangerous, dirty, demeaning, and low-paid by citizens of destination countries, such jobs were not always perceived as "bad" jobs by migrants or their kin at home. Jobs for men such as chauffeuring (in Saudi Arabia) and factory work (in Korea and Japan) were perceived as "modern" and comfortable jobs, compared to laboring in the fields under the hot sun in Indonesia or Malaysia. Similarly, when women worked in Taiwan, Singapore, or Hong Kong to care for children or the elderly, residents often downplayed or dismissed the difficult emotional and physical labor required, and perceived care work as "light" work, since women were viewed as "naturally" nurturing. Construction work was usually seen as neutral work. Despite the usually irregular and precarious nature of construction work, it was neither degrading nor prestigious, but relatively respectable in terms of associations of working-class masculinity—most nonmigrant local men do similar work in Cilacap, Yogyakarta, and other parts of Indonesia (see Khoo et al. 2015). In contrast, certain forms of domestic work can be perceived as potentially shameful, partially due to a general devaluation of the domestic work that women perform daily in their own households, as well as media representations of domestic workers as "slaves" (*budak*) and victims (chapter 2). A young unmarried woman in Yogyakarta who failed to migrate said of a return migrant neighbor whom she thought was arrogant, "Who does she think she is? She is *only* a domestic helper [PRT or *pembantu rumah tangga*]." Similarly, a nonmigrant middle-aged woman in Cilacap said of a return migrant neighbor, "This woman came back with blonde hair, short skirts, flaunting her new lifestyle and attitude. But over there, she is only a domestic helper."

While some domestic workers take pride in the type of work they do, others experience malu too. Women's status as mothers or not, married or unmarried, impact their evaluation of others' migration and their work. An unmarried Central Javanese migrant domestic worker in her mid-thirties in Singapore surprised me once by her harsh evaluation of fellow Indonesian migrant women who were married and with kids. She said, "If you ask TKWs' children, 'Would you wish for your mother to work overseas or stay?' There will be two kinds of responses. Some will say, 'I don't care what she's doing as long as there is money.' Others—who still have hearts—will say, 'I'd rather she is home, at least she has malu.'" When I returned to Indonesia, this woman's friend remarked that the unmarried migrant was not particularly close to the other TKWs in Singapore, saying, "People say she is ashamed to be a maid. She thinks she is too good for this job."

Explicitly feminized migrant labor may therefore be experienced and perceived as a source of shame, such as domestic and sex work. This is unsurprising, due to the ways that, across cultural contexts, foreign households and overseas urban cities are often viewed as potentially dangerous sites for women as independent sexual subjects (Abu-Lughod 2008; Dannecker 2009; Dreby 2009; Lai 2010; Yeoh and Huang 2010). As the quotes above suggest, domestic work (and sex work) were also linked to lower socioeconomic status, and might provoke shame in contexts where middle-class aspirations or performances of middle-class lifestyles and sensibilities dominate both in the villages and migrants' destination countries. Despite the obviously higher wages for migrant domestic workers, women in these Central Javanese sites generally viewed factory work in Indonesia as more respectable than paid domestic work in Indonesia or abroad.

Work was thus evaluated in terms of stereotypical gender traits. During my fieldwork, men's work was never associated with malu, although unemployment potentially caused malu. In a group discussion with recently returned migrant women in Yogyakarta, the women agreed that although malu was often associated with women's sexual transgressions, men suffered "*malu besar*" (great shame) if they did not financially support their families according to Javanese adat. In sometimes being viewed as "failed" men, unemployed men were potential sources of embarrassment for siblings, parents, or wives. Male unemployment was typically attributed to drinking, gambling, or sheer laziness.[4] One local nonmigrant youth in Cilacap could never hold a job for long, and was out of work for long periods. His mother frequently complained about her son's laziness to the neighbors, and a few relatives referred to him harshly as "that bastard." Everyone knew that he slept till noon, and never helped with domestic or manual labor at home. Although he was married to a woman in Cilacap city, his father-in-law refused to let him visit his wife and child unless he found a job and contributed to household expenses. To my surprise, neighbors found this forced and conditional separation reasonable. After more than a year without a stable job, this man's wife formally filed for a divorce. Despite significant difficulties for women to file for divorce as compared to men in Indonesia (see chapter 6), this wife in particular could now legally do so, since her husband had not fulfilled his end of the formal marriage contract as a "breadwinner" (Katz and Katz 1975). For some men, the potential shame associated with not fulfilling these masculine duties might propel them to seek jobs abroad (see Bylander 2015).[5]

However, male unemployment and its associated vices did not always have such real consequences for men. Many parents and wives continued to support and house unemployed husbands and sons out of a sense of parental obligation or due to the stigma associated with divorce. In contrast, gossip about women as doing undignified work or being neglectful family members nearly always affected their social standing and relationships with their immediate families and in-laws. Women's transgressions were seldom allowed the room for negotiation or tacit tolerance that could be granted to the vices of men.

Debt, Fraud, and Conspicuous Consumption

Debt or *hutang* in Indonesian, typically referring to financial debt, is often used as a dirty, negative, and shameful word. Whenever the term was mentioned in casual conversations or interviews, Central Javanese residents lowered their voices or whispered it. This remains true despite the long history of microcredit institutions in rural Central Java, beginning from 1895 (Steinwand 2013, 95). The majority of migrants from Central Java embark on their journeys with large financial debts. Yet the uncertainties surrounding migration journeys and consequences are at odds with the predictability and pressures of their loan repayments. The opportunities and risks for obtaining credit and forms of repayment are also gendered. Female domestic workers are usually indebted to migrant brokers who pay for their journeys up front, before docking their pay for seven months to a year (Constable 2007; Lindquist 2012; Rudnyckyj 2004; Platt et al. 2013; Silvey 2004). This practice has also been applied to an increasing number of male migrants heading for Korea. In other cases where migrants take on factory, hospitality, construction, or fishing work, they have to pay recruitment agents and agencies prior to leaving the country. Such fees include inflated costs of travel, food and accommodation in migrant training centers, medical fees, and unspecified administrative fees for multiple actors and institutions involved. In these cases, prospective migrants may borrow money from ostensibly reliable sources, including extensive kinship networks, neighbors, banks, or informal loan sharks to finance their journeys (Lindquist 2012; Spaan 1994).

Financial debt in my field sites was intricately linked to forms of social and moral indebtedness (Thai 2014; Han 2012), even when financial loans were given by banks or recruitment agents. This was clear when considering how migrants may use the property of neighbors and relatives—such as land and vehicles—as collateral for bank loans. As scholars have noted in cases of labor migration from Indonesia (Killias 2010; Lindquist 2012; Spaan 1994) as well as trafficking-like practices elsewhere (Brennan 2014), migrants' financial debts tie them to their brokers, thus creating complex ties of obligation and reciprocity. Prospective migrants may also take on financial loans and embark on journeys in order to repay moral, social, and financial debts to their parents, grandparents, or neighbors. As mentioned in the beginning of this chapter, some migrants move in order to "erase their footsteps" or "sins." These can be seen as moral-religious debts that other current and return migrants alluded to during my fieldwork.

Sometimes things go wrong for migrants before they are able to repay their debts and loans, as with Hazam, whose case of fraud I described in chapter 3. Many return migrants also spoke of how they ran away from employers due to dissatisfaction with coworkers or bosses, or overstayed their visas. Such incidents happened in every destination country without exception (for examples, see Constable 2014; Killias 2010; Mahdavi 2013). From the viewpoint of migrants and former migrants, overstaying was sometimes seen as less risky than returning home with financial debt, unless the migrant got caught and deported. I asked a male former migrant to Korea what he thought of such forced deportations from Korea. He replied, "We must first ask, does he have money? If he doesn't have money, *malu pulang* [he is ashamed to return]. If he has enough money for a big house, then it's okay, [he can] just return." Thus the social-moral ties and obligations that enable migrants' financial debts shed light on some material and practical motivations for harsh judgements against migrant failures. Migrants who return without money might remain indebted to kin, friends, and neighbors, reinforcing their mutual social and economic vulnerability, rather than alleviating these uncertainties through migration.

A staff member at a Yogyakarta-based migrant labor NGO, Yuna, also recounted her experiences staying at SBMI's migrant shelter in Jakarta. There, she met many men from West Nusa Tenggara who were formerly working as seamen (ABK, *anak buah kapal*) on Taiwanese-owned ships docked in South Africa. Many of them were reluctantly repatriated to Indonesia with the aid of the International Organization of Migration (IOM). They usually arrived in Jakarta without money because they had not been paid, and were unfairly dismissed before their contracts were completed (Buruh Migran 2014b). Upon their arrival in the port of Jakarta, many of them told Yuna that they were too malu to return without money, and feared the mocking that they anticipated from friends and neighbors. When I visited and stayed at this same migrant shelter in early 2015, I met return migrant seafarers from Central Java and West Java who echoed these sentiments. Rather than returning to their villages and families empty-handed, where chances of finding a decent-paying job were slim, these men preferred to stay in the shelter. There, they spent months assisting and waiting for SBMI to file their cases with BNP2TKI or the National Police Headquarters. Delaying their return home meant working toward the hope for financial compensation and a sense of justice.

Women also experienced malu if they returned from abroad before their contracts were completed. Like their male counterparts, this often meant that they had not repaid their debts or had not worked long enough for savings to matter. During an interview, a male nonmigrant community organizer in Cilacap offered an anecdote. In 2013, about ten migrants from the local area filed complaints about their migration experiences. He summarized migrants' issues as primarily caused by recruitment brokers, who inflated migration fees, and did not guarantee job security or physical safety. He had helped these return migrants file their complaints against these recruitment agencies to BNP2TKI. However, of the return migrants he had helped, only one migrant returned to her home village, while the others returned to various recruitment agencies and training centers. "Why?" I asked. "*Malu pulang ke rumah*," was his blunt reply. They were malu to return home. "It is Cilacap culture," he continued. "Once a woman has left the country [*sudah terbang*], there is *sukuran*, where everyone prays together. If after only nine months, she returns [to the village] … *Kok pulang*? [Why are you back?]" His response and his mimicked tone of bewilderment and disappointment of "*Kok pulang?*" implied that in cases of such premature migrant return, the migrant would be constantly asked what went wrong, thus repeatedly reminding her of her failure to meet intersecting financial, moral, and social obligations associated with her migratory journey.

While migrant men or migrants' male relatives may be accused of borrowing money to drink or gamble, migrant women or migrants' female relatives may be accused of borrowing money for conspicuous consumption such as nice clothes or makeup. While both gendered consumption practices are generally frowned upon, women's appearances and consumption practices tend to be more closely inspected in relation to their moral character and religiosity (Jones 2010; Smith-Hefner 2007). Furthermore, women might be blamed for male relatives' inappropriate or excessive spending, while men were rarely blamed for women's consumption practices. Importantly, while men commonly acknowledged that drinking and gambling were vices, women did not always recognize or agree with judgements of inappropriate or excessive "feminized" consumption. Thus as Carla Jones (2010) argues, women are often caught in the middle of such public censure and pressures to perform gendered propriety and religiosity. An act such as wearing the veil (hijab) may thus be deemed appropriate or excessively stylish.

Nevertheless, in two cases I knew of in which nonmigrant men were in debt, their financial situation severely strained their relationships with their spouses and parents-in-law, whereas I encountered one exceptional case where a woman's debt significantly affected her relationships with kin (see below). For example, a married young man, Rizal, worked many casual jobs in Cilacap, and was recognized by neighbors as a hardworking man and caring father. He lived with his son and his wife's parents and siblings, since his wife worked in a factory during the weekdays and only returned on weekends.[6] However, he fell into depression for a few months when his wife complained that he was not giving her money, buying her gifts, or giving her mother a monthly allowance. He explained to her that he was still repaying the family's loans on their new motorbike. His wife and mother-in-law rejected his justification. To them, that debt was his personal responsibility, one that should not interfere with his breadwinning duties. Neighbors noticed as Rizal gradually grew quiet and withdrawn. His feelings of malu and male inadequacy were made public only when he finally broke down at a neighbor's house during Idul Fitri. He complained that his wife and mother-in-law were actively ignoring him. Rizal found it unfair that they derided him for not financially contributing to the family, since from his perspective, the motor-bike loans were a family investment (for work-related transportation and family trips), not an individual luxury.

In a second example, a man in Rizal's village (also his relative) committed suicide by hanging himself by a rope from a tree. Although there was specula-tion as to whether his suicide was due to spirit possession or his own free will (see chapter 5), his family agreed that it was likely due to financial distress over his several million rupiah loan. His financial anxieties were also perceived to be the cause of his marital conflict, which was public knowledge and a source of malu for him and his family.

Other forms of debt-related malu are not necessarily gendered, but still linked to the struggles of individuals and their kin to live up to social expectations. For example, in Puspito's (2014) research on suicide among farmers in Yogyakarta, he argued that people needed and borrowed money not only for food and basic ame-nities, but also for necessary social expenses. During auspicious months, villagers in Puspito's sites, as well as in my field sites, may be invited to up to ten weddings, which likely cost in total between 200,000 to 500,000 rupiah—the equivalent of an average resident's monthly or half a month's income. Those who do not have enough money to attend these important social events may feel extreme malu, and villagers often talked about how migration had inflated the value of land as well as increased expectations of monetary and nonmonetary gifting for wed-dings. As Han (2012) argued in her ethnography among the contemporary urban poor in Chile, people living under precarious socioeconomic conditions tend to accumulate financial debt in order to renew and maintain social relations. They do so not only to meet social obligations, but also to create the mutual social indebt-edness necessary for social membership in support networks. Such pressures to be able to participate in expensive social events, including births, circumcisions, and funerals, contribute to people's experiences of social and economic anxiety, while reaffirming these necessary ties of interdependence. Although Rizal viewed his motorbike loans as a means to reinvigorate familial ties, such as being able to take on jobs further away from the village, or to take his wife and son to the beach, this financial debt also strained the very ties he sought to strengthen.

Yet, as Han points out, "the possibility of denial or disconnection is already within relations themselves," including indebtedness (2012, 234). The fact that Central Javanese villagers persist, despite increasing difficulty, in renewing their social relationships (Das 2007, 217; Schuster 2015) highlights the ways in which transnational labor migration can be seen as providing new obstacles or oppor-tunities for residents to meet, fail, or exceed these obligations. In other words, migration is always a spectre and possibility haunting nonmigrants' or return migrants' struggles to meet everyday obligations. Migration contributes to shaping residents' internalized and imposed expectations and abilities to meet these social obligations in unequal and frustrating ways.

Marital Conflict and Divorce

Several married women in Cilacap and Yogyakarta told me that "in Islam, women are not allowed to divorce men," or that "Islam does not permit divorce, and people who divorce are just less pious Muslims." These statements often refer to local interpretations of the Qur'an's position on divorce: that it is sinful, wrong, and should be a source of personal and familial malu (see chapter 6). Although divorce or marital conflict was not uncommon regardless of a family's migration history or status, migration was often perceived as the cause of divorces in Cilacap and Yogyakarta. Migrants whose marriages were at risk of dissolution were highlighted over other similar nonmigrant cases. This was possibly due to the heightened anxieties villagers had regarding spousal and parental separation in migrants' families.

During my fieldwork, marital or household arguments often became public knowledge. Houses were typically built close to one another: extended families built houses on a large shared plot of inherited ancestral land. Windows or doors were also usually open due to the tropical heat, such that neighbors were often within hearing distance of the next household when voices were raised. Such public fights were sources of shame and disgrace for families, particularly in a context in which Central Javanese villagers placed symbolic importance on maintaining "appearances" (*tampak*) of order. In contrast, a "quiet house" was referred to as a "peaceful" house, where neighbors assumed that no marital or familial conflict occurred.

These villages were also often full of gossip about adultery between villagers or with residents of neighboring villages, particularly when a spouse was a current migrant, or a recently returned migrant. When Nurul recounted tales of adultery in Cilacap, I asked, "If locals disapprove, why don't people say anything? Why doesn't anyone tell the spouse [about the other's infidelity], or stop the cheating spouse?" Nurul lowered her voice and replied that people often felt it was not their place to interfere, that it is "not their business.... They don't want to open a closed box. The important thing is that the marriage appears okay and fine and normal." When I asked if the adulterers would feel ashamed, Nurul replied hesitantly, "Of course, of course they feel malu, there must still be that [feeling]." (*Pasti mereka rasa malu, pasti masih ada.*)

Migrant women were often blamed for divorce or the breakdown of their marriages, regardless of whether villagers perceived financial conflict or infidelity to be the cause. When women were rumored to have affairs abroad, they were condemned for sinning, either in having forbidden sexual relations (*zina*, a broad term where both partners involved are not married to each other but are also not necessarily married to other people), or adultery (*selingkuh*, where at least one person involved is married). In contrast, their husbands who stayed in the village were often jokingly referred to, or might self-identify as, bachelors and "single" men. Such ubiquitous joking was directly related to the double standards applied to men in relation to monogamy and adultery, while migrant wives were blamed for not fulfilling their husband's sexual desires, so that he had to look for satisfaction elsewhere (see Bennett 2005a, 153; Brenner 1998; Rinaldo 2008).[7] Faithful wives whose husbands were found cheating were thus seldom explicitly praised for their fidelity, while "good husband" narratives were a popular genre that accompanied stories of cheating wives. These husbands might be praised and pitied for how they had been good men and model husbands in providing for the family as migrants overseas or staying to care for the children while their mother was away. The relative absence of such praise for dutiful wives and mothers—whether as migrants or migrants' spouses—further highlights how women's fidelity and piety are naturalized and taken for granted.

When women cheat on their husbands, men may experience this shame to different degrees. Instances of male suicide, of which official rates are much higher than female suicide, are usually linked either to financial debt or being cuckolded, both phenomena that challenge normative masculinity in Java and Indonesia more broadly. In Puspito's research (2014), a rural-urban migrant from Yogyakarta committed suicide after learning that his wife had a lover while he was away. Close friends said that he felt very malu because his neighbors no longer respected him, such that it was unbearable for him to go on. Although female infidelity was often attributed to deviant female hypersexuality, in some cases female infidelity could also be attributed to a husband's inability to financially support his wife. In two conversations with two women in their late thirties—a nonmigrant and a former migrant from Cilacap—these women expressed sympathy and a suspension of moral judgement on married women who were suspected of adultery. One woman highlighted that a neighbor *had* to have an affair because her husband was not financially supporting her (compare Hannaford and Foley 2015). The other explained, "Sometimes these relationships are not just for love, but for economic issues" (*persoaloan eckonomi*). In relation to extramarital relationships, she added, "You know, people can get something extra to get by in these cases." She explained that the finances flow both ways: extramarital relationships can be a source of extra financial support for both women and men.

In short, some cuckolded spouses could also be blamed for failing their gendered marital duties. Gossip or knowledge about adulterous relationships did not only cause shame for the adulterer. However, with the exception of these few private expressions of sympathy for adulterous women, women were typically blamed for marital conflict or failure, whether as adulterers or wives of adulterous husbands.

Sex and Sexuality

The sexualities of women in general and of unmarried young women in particular were considered taboo topics in the context of idealized Central Javanese femininity as daughters, mothers, and wives. In contrast, men of all ages and marital status were treated as persons with "biological needs," a euphemism for sexual desires, which were almost never publicly associated with women's needs. Returned migrants from Korea or Taiwan in Yogyakarta sometimes gathered informally to show off the photos they took abroad, including photos of fair-skinned foreign women. Former migrants to these countries would show me (and their peers) photos taken with their mobile phones, where they posed with female secretaries of their factories, or female friends of their foreign male colleagues. During one such photo sharing incident, a male former migrant to Korea joked to another, "Is that your girlfriend?" The returned migrant who was sharing his photo only smiled slightly, while his friend said to me, "Ah, he had many girlfriends there." These public exchanges often hinted at returned migrant men's romantic or sexual encounters with foreign women abroad, regardless of migrants' actual experiences. These conversations served as public performances of migrants' masculinities, suggesting that they were able to attract fair-skinned women, who are associated with beauty, higher class, education, and status in Indonesia (Saraswati 2012).

Such public displays of men's sexual encounters abroad contrast starkly with how villagers, including returned migrants, talked about migrant women's sexualities abroad. Earlier, I discussed how villagers and returned migrants may attribute failed female migration to their immoral sexual relationships with foreign men. In many group discussions and individual interviews, Javanese or Indonesian migrant women who were assumed to have had romantic relationships abroad were linked to foreign men from countries such as Bangladesh, Nepal, or Pakistan. These men were usually also precarious laborers in construction or hospitality sectors in places such as Hong Kong, Taiwan, Singapore, and Saudi Arabia. Villagers and returned migrants referred to migrant women's foreign boyfriends in racialized terms such as "dark" or "black" people (*orang hitam*), almost always in a derogatory way. Such stereotypes and representations served to publicly shame or frame migrant women's sexual encounters abroad as laughable, or shameful, in comparison to the admirable "conquest" of foreign beauties by migrant men. Notably, although some migrant women did have romantic relations with and even marry "light skinned" foreign men from Saudi Arabia, Britain, Australia, or the United States, these relationships were rarely mentioned either positively or negatively in public stereotypes. On Indonesian migrants' Facebook groups, members and participants explicitly and sometimes cruelly mock such migrant women, such as in Internet memes which reference Indonesian women and suggest they are "fools" to like Bangladeshi men.[8]

In Indonesian migrant-based Facebook groups, as well as during field-work, the stereotype of the hypersexual, promiscuous migrant woman who goes abroad *in order to* engage in adultery, sex work, or nonmarital sexual relations was popularly circulated (mainly by apparently male account users). The caption of one meme in particular reproduced and mocked the stereotype of Indonesian women who migrate to Jeddah only so they can "run away to the driver's room" (*mau kabur ke kamar supir*)—a reference to the prospect of intimate relations with a man.[9] It was a common assumption that domestic workers in the Middle East worked for rich families who also hired male chauffeurs from Indonesia or similar "developing" countries. The double meaning of the term kabur—which literally means "something vague"—refers in this meme both to the couple's potentially "obscure" and thus improper relations as well as the common association of presumably promiscuous women's undocumented or irregular migration status, where "kabur" is the common Indonesian term for undocumented or "runaway" migrants. Such representations of sexually promiscuous migrant women are accompanied by captions or comment threads which accuse women of bringing great shame to their families, children, or the Indonesian nation. Despite public bragging and gossip about migrant men's sexual encounters abroad, including visits to brothels, I did not encounter any reference or suggestion—either online or during fieldwork—that men migrate to fulfill their sexual needs or to embark on sexual adventures abroad.

While female sexuality was only deemed legitimate within the context of a marriage, male sexuality was recognized as independent of marriage, and indeed, intrinsic to a sense of masculinity. However, such standards of hypersexual masculinity stood alongside expectations for men to be good and responsible husbands, fathers, and breadwinners. In Farjado's study of Filipino male migrant seafarers, he also found similar tensions in expectations of masculinity (2011, 99; cf. Gamburd 2000; Margold 1995). On one such occasion where villagers jokingly referred to an elderly man as a "bachelor" because his wife and adult daughters were working in Taiwan, I observed that the man in question seemed uncomfortable. Such teasing and response were not uncommon, and when I commented on this to a nonmigrant woman in Yogyakarta, she said, "People are just joking and they mean no harm. But sometimes I think also that they should not do that.... Those jokes about men being single makes them feel even lonelier [*sepi*]. It is pitiful for them [*kasihan*]." While such jokes about male sexual needs may seem to encourage or excuse male adultery in the absence of his migrant wife, such adultery is only tacitly but not explicitly accepted. An effect of such jokes is that migrants' husbands may feel embarrassed or ashamed about being alone (and presumably not sexually active) for long periods of time despite being married. In some cases, husbands might demand their migrant wives to return home immediately, sometimes against their will (chapter 6).

Shame or embarrassment that men face regarding their sexual lives, however, seldom results in or amounts to stigma. Stigma, in comparison to shame, can be understood as irreversible social markers, attached to individuals' perceived and unchanging moral character (Kankonde 2010, 231). Sexual transgressions for women in these Central Javanese villages almost certainly put them at risk for stigmatization or familial dishonor, such as in cases of adultery and other nonmarital sexual relations, including rape. The public shaming and representations of sexually transgressive Indonesian migrant women in national media has arguably contributed to the predominance of a generally unforgiving and unsympathetic attitude towards women who return to Indonesia as single mothers or victims of rape or sexual abuse. There are hopeful signs, nonetheless, that attitudes may be changing very slowly (see chapter 6). In other parts of Indonesia as in my field sites, for example, a minority of women and families have found creative ways to legitimate the social belonging of migrants' children born out of wedlock (see Butt et al. 2016).

Biased representations of "immoral" or "shameless" Indonesian migrant women by official state and media reports provoke similarly judgmental comments on Facebook. For example, there was an official report by the Indonesian Embassy in Riyadh about a migrant woman who left her newborn child at a local hospital.[10] This report unforgivingly represented the migrant as "without a sense of guilt," but "maybe a sense of fear." The report further included the fact that the child was the result of an illicit relationship with an Indian citizen. This report was shared on a migrant-based Facebook group. It elicited harsh comments where the migrant was referred to as a prostitute (*pelacur*), "with morals no less than that of an animal, a person without humanity," and "faithless" (*gak punya imanan*). Online commenters further made generalizations about all female Indonesian migrants in general: "That's the ugliness of our TKW.... Their hearts are closed and they only know their desires." Several male commenters were quick to add that "most inhabitants in hell are women," or that "Not all [Indonesian migrant women] are like this, just 90% of them." Other commenters were less explicit, but added moralizing lines such as "Remember that worldly life is temporary, and there will be reckoning in your afterlife." One commentator remarked that not all Indonesian migrant women are to blame, but not all employers are morally "depraved" (*bejat*) either. This same commenter linked potentially morally "cheap" Indonesian women to their low cost as labor commodities: "Don't be so cheap. Foreigners already value Indonesians like the price of mobile phone credit. It really brings shame to our nation."

While migrant women's sexuality was commonly framed in terms of national shame, migrant men's sexuality was linked to ethno-nationalistic pride in their ability to attract fair-skinned foreign women, in opposition to less desirable dark-skinned foreign men.

Negotiating and Cultivating Shame

Despite such experiences of shame and the circulation of shaming discourses, residents, including migrants, nonmigrants, return migrants, and their kin, negotiate or cope in diverse ways with the anticipation or fear of shame and stigma. I outline in the following sections such everyday intersubjective practices, which include forms of joking, and carefully managing one's gendered reputation through or deflecting attention onto others' transgressions. Local leaders or family members may emphasize the regulation of women's mobilities, while those being shamed may opt for silence as a strategy to avoid attention. Additionally, the emotional support of kin, the arts of perseverance (*tahan*) and patience (*sabar*), and acts of violence encapsulate the range of ways people cope with shame, with varying consequences.

Joking

I was first introduced to Diah in Yogyakarta village by a mutual friend, Minah, a woman who had never migrated from Indonesia, though she had temporarily lived in a nearby city. Minah referred to Diah as a former migrant who had worked in Malaysia, and returned a failure. At first, Diah denied being a migrant. She laughed and said that she was "only a tourist" (*hanya turis*), and that she did "*jalan-jalan*" in Malaysia. Jalan-jalan literally means to walk or to take a walk, but many Indonesian and Malay language speakers use it to refer to unplanned and casual leisure activities. This may include going on a short trip, or sightseeing. For example, both going to the market or to a beach can be jalan-jalan, as long as it connotes that the speaker is not doing work or chores, but doing something for leisure or pleasure, usually to relax or see something new. When Diah first said that she was a "tourist," I was confused. To clarify, I asked if she worked in Malaysia. Diah replied that she worked in a factory in Malaysia for almost two years. Yet, she returned with no money to show for it. After working for a year to pay off the debts to her recruitment agency, Diah's father was diagnosed with a severe illness. Her wages went to pay his medical bills and her younger brothers' education fees. Before her contract was up, however, the factory went bankrupt, and Diah lost her job. She recalled even having to borrow money from friends to buy a plane ticket home.

Many other self-identified "failed migrants" I met were quick to jokingly refer to their time abroad in terms of "tourism" or "jalan-jalan." Their self-identification as tourists was often accompanied by laughter. By representing negative experiences of failure in such positive terms associated with pleasure and leisure, they drew attention to the fact that, despite failing to be successful migrants, they had at least seen other countries and places. Such everyday joking and laughing can be seen as a way to cope with a potentially shameful or embarrassing situation, memory, or encounter (Giles and Oxford 1970, in Ladegaard 2013a). By calling themselves tourists, they create situations in which they and others like them laugh about their failure to conform to expectations of successful migrants. Such joking introduces feelings of relief or humor rather than anxiety, nervousness, or embarrassment, and sets the tone of the ensuing conversation and encounter (see Ladegaard 2013a).[11]

By reframing labor migration in terms of tourism, these jokes also build on the unequal and stark contrast between the leisure and privilege associated with tourism, and these migrants' positions of "comparative disadvantage" (Constable 2009, 152–153), in which their transnational movements are mainly due to the global demand for low-wage laborers. In other words, by unexpectedly and ironically referring to themselves as tourists, they highlight to potentially judgmental and gossiping neighbors that their failed journeys were not selfish or "for fun" (as jalan-jalan implies), but instead carried financial, gendered, and moral expectations that they were well aware of. On another level, a few of these former migrants did literally mean that they travelled abroad on a tourist visa, that is, without proper documentation. However, among those I met who did travel on tourist visas for work, only those who identified as "failures" tended to refer to themselves jokingly as "tourists" in the sense described here.

While such jokes might have diffused tension in these encounters between former migrants and their nonmigrant neighbors, they also unintentionally reinforced stereotypes and perceptions that some migrants fail because of their own selfish pursuits of pleasure and leisure. When Diah joked that all she did in Malaysia was "jalan-jalan," our mutual friend Minah shot me a look and said aloud, "You see, like what I said." With this remark, Minah was reminding me of our conversation earlier that morning when she explained to me why many migrants fail. To her, this was because migrants—especially women—spent their wages on new clothes, makeup, or going out and partying. All these leisurely activities could fall under the category of "jalan-jalan." In this case, although Diah may have used the term ironically, Minah seemed to take it as Diah's confession that she did indeed spend time and money having fun in Malaysia.

Nevertheless, when former migrants got together and shared their experiences, I noticed that some easily introduced one another to me in terms of who were "tourists" or "workers" in which countries. Many spoke casually about which airports they had been to, before being "turned back," deported, or repatriated. These exchanges were, in contrast to the initially awkward conversation between Minah and Diah, full of mutual laughter, where everyone present arguably understood that "tourism" was used ironically.

Managing Gendered Reputations

When it became clear that Minah was fixated on the details of how Diah spent her free time outside of factory work hours, Diah carefully described the circumstances of her nights out in the city where she worked in Malaysia. Minah's responses to and questions about her statements concerning "jalan-jalan" were unabashed attempts to elicit gossip-worthy tales. In response, Diah started what seemed like defensive narrating. She spoke about eating new foods like Korean *ramen* and going to karaoke bars with her colleagues from the factory, who were also from Indonesia. However, she insisted that her friends would often treat her so she never spent too much money on going out. She emphasized that if her colleagues and peers had not offered to pay for her, she would not have otherwise indulged in such expensive leisure activities. Regardless of the truth, it became clear to me that Diah knew which aspects of her life and activities overseas were central to managing her reputation as a good, young, and unmarried woman, daughter, and elder sister. More than once, Diah reminded us that her migration was mainly for her family through describing how she tried to fulfill various family-related financial obligations.

How migrant women spent their earnings and free time was often the subject of close inspection and gossip by migrants' peers and kin in the villages. Ideally, women should be perceived to have suffered at least a little, in order that their migration could be framed as a form of sacrifice for their families' welfare. Recounting fun and pleasurable experiences might risk being judged as less dedicated to their families' needs at home.[12] Certainly, some migrants were perceived as women with new experiences and insights into foreign cultures, but only when their accounts were framed within culturally acceptable and legitimate social or work-related scenarios.

Since Minah continued to express doubt about Diah's self-representation, Diah began to share scandalous gossip and stories of what *other* migrant women would do, thus creating a contrast and distance between herself and "immoral" migrants. She spoke about how some migrant women would have foreign boyfriends in order to receive expensive gifts, such as branded watches. Others did sex work outside of official factory work hours. Many undocumented migrants from Indonesia and the Philippines also did such sex work, she added, and suggested that a neighbor and fellow villager was one such migrant whose earnings came from "non-halal" sources. Through the telling of these scandalous tales, Diah not only diverted Minah's questions and attention away from her own experiences, but also discursively distanced herself from these "other" women. Significantly, these selected stories of immoral migrant others were all women who were perceived as financially successful, unlike Diah, who returned with debt and as a self-identified failure. Thus Diah's stories also served to produce an image of herself as one who, though she failed in financial terms, maintained her honor and self-worth, in comparison to relatively wealthy migrants who partook in sinful work.

Ming-Yan Lai's analysis of representations of "sexy maid" stereotypes by migrant activists in Hong Kong is useful to think about in terms of the ways return migrants manage their own gendered reputations at home. Lai looked at public dances and performances by Indonesian migrant domestic workers, some of whom are labor activists, and observed that the "sexy maid" emerged as an immoral stereotype (2010, 27–28). The image of the sexy maid, who in some cases was also portrayed as eventually becoming a pregnant body, served to condemn affairs of migrant domestic workers with fellow Indonesian migrants and other marginalized non-Indonesian foreign workers (ibid.). Analyzing these performances and audience reception to these dances, Lai argues that these stereotypes produced and reinforced conservative gendered attitudes that denied migrant domestic workers legitimacy as desiring and sexual subjects (29). In other words, performances of sexy maid stereotypes elicited audience laughter through the production of the sexy maid and the pregnant migrant as an immoral "other." The sexy maid is always deviant and subject to public humiliation among migrants as well as citizens in countries where they work. Although Lai recognizes that the migrant organizations intended for these stereotypical representations to "caution [women] against sexual indulgence and to encourage them to join organizations as an alternative way to fulfilling their desires for companionship" (29), she argues that such representations reveal "a contradictory othering in the discourse of union activism" (30), where only specific kinds of female subjects were desirable or targeted for membership.

Such a strategy for the production of an immoral other is similar to Diah's management of her own reputation as a migrant female domestic worker. As a single and unmarried woman at the time of her migration, Diah also produced and reinforced stereotypes of sexual and desiring migrant women who were interchangeable with "non-halal" or immoral activities. This effectively reproduced standards of the ideal migrant woman as one whose family's needs were the same as and interchangeable with her own proper desires as a woman. Such gossip can be read as "domesticating" sexualities that are deemed out of place, by rendering such deviant behavior intelligible in particular ways (see Rafael 1997).

Marriage, or the appearance of a harmonious marriage, was crucial to mediating the impact of shame on the reputation and honor of migrants or their kin, particularly in the face of more severe threats of and experiences of long-term shame (chapter 3). For example, in one of my field sites, a migrant woman returned from Hong Kong pregnant, and the child was of visibly mixed ethnicity. She eventually married a man from a neighboring village. During group conversations with fellow villagers about her situation, a few women commented that the fact that she got married reduced the element of shame in the eyes of others. No longer a single mother, she was not a sexual threat. To my knowledge, many divorced migrants or their spouses typically remarried within six months of their divorce, especially if the migrant returned to live in the village, or if the migrant's spouse intended to stay in the village. Remarriage was usually encouraged in the event of divorce (even if not always approved by the divorced person's children), sometimes to another divorced person. As a few villagers explained to me, although marriage in Islam is not compulsory (*wajib*), it is "highly recommended" in the Sunnah, or the verbal sayings of the Prophet. Being married would gain an individual favor and merit with God.

Many people took pains to resolve their marital conflicts or stay with abusive partners to avoid divorce and the shame associated with it. One former migrant woman stayed with and repeatedly forgave her cheating, gambling, and abusive second husband. When I asked her why she did not just ask for a divorce, she said honestly, "You know I was divorced before. I had already failed and I did not want to fail again. No matter what, I just had to try to make it work."

That man eventually left her and found another woman, and at the time I met her, she was hoping to marry her current partner. Although the stigma she carried of being divorced might never really leave her, the effects could be significantly mitigated if she married again (Mahy et al. 2016). Her divorced and single status was not just a matter of her own reputation. It also affected her son's marriage prospects, as her son's prospective in-laws forbade their daughter to marry him unless his mother got remarried. The in-laws apparently did not want their daughter to marry into an "incomplete" family. This example illustrates how some forms of shame are lifelong, even extending to one's kin, and that marriage is often perceived as an important solution to apparent disruptions of a heteronormative family and social order.

Some men also actively managed their reputations as breadwinners or responsible fathers and husbands, particularly in cases where their wives were working abroad. In these scenarios, men were vulnerable to accusations that their wives had to work abroad because they were lazy, incapable of financially supporting the family, or that in addition to leeching off their wives' hard labor, they were having and financing illicit affairs (or second wives) with women's remittances. Although these things did happen, some men did not seem to pay much attention to what neighbors thought, since such behavior seldom resulted in violent confrontation between the men and their family or neighbors. However, other men may have experienced such gossip as hurtful to their sense of pride, dignity, and masculinity (see below). Consequently, I witnessed as well as heard many stories of migrants' husbands in the villages who cooked and cared for their children (Graham et al. 2012; Hoang et al. 2012; Yeoh and Lam 2013), did the laundry in public for all to see, and were seen working daily in the vicinity. It was important for neighbors and kin to witness these domestic and caring activities performed by men, or the fact that they were working in the fields, or selling their homemade products such as palm sugar. Such witnessing warded off gossip that a man may just be sitting at home doing nothing, smoking, drinking, or gambling his days and wife's pennies away.

Regulating Women's Mobility

Men whose wives or daughters were migrants may have experienced malu, as described in the previous section. This is sometimes partially attributed to their financial dependence on women, and thus failing to conform to gendered norms of masculinity. They may also experience or face malu by association, such as if a female member of their family is publically shamed or known to be promiscuous or to engage in other "immoral" activities. In several interviews with male activists and local leaders, men expressed potentially feeling *more* ashamed if a female relative—as compared to a male relative—were to commit adultery or have non-marital sexual relations. The following excerpt is from an interview with Hari, a Cilacap-based, married nonmigrant and NGO staff member in his mid-20s, who facilitated local development programs.

CAROL: When [Indonesian migrants] have problems with their family, is it more common in cases of male or female migration? Or there is no difference?

HARI: There is no difference. Both have the potential [for problems], but the cases I usually encounter are women.

C: You mean when women go abroad?

H: But it's the same, whoever contributes to breaking up the family. For example, when a woman goes overseas, and the husband here is doing whatever pleases him. Or the reverse, when the husband is at home, and the woman is doing something else overseas. But it is the same, whether or not the woman is the one abroad, or the man.... But the cases I deal with are usually migrant women.

C: When men go overseas, there are less problems?

H: There is a tendency yes, [that the problem is] more muted. Because [in male migration], men are the ones obliged to be breadwinners for their families. And when women stay behind, when they are at home, they can be watched and taken care of [*dijaga*] by the family. But if the man stays behind, it is difficult for the family to intervene [in his affairs].... In the case of women who stay at home, in houses there are norms that bind her. There are norms among the people who can control [*kontrol*] them.... The family can watch [*jaga*] her.

C: [Comparing men and women who commit adultery], are consequences harsher for men or women? Maybe in terms of malu?

H: Yes. For me, as part of a family, I will definitely feel more ashamed. I will be more ashamed if my older sister commits adultery with another man, while her husband is working overseas looking for ways to support the family.

C: Oh. But what if it is the reverse? If the husband cheats, will you feel less shame?

H: If it's the reverse . . . yes. . . . Not as ashamed as if the wife cheats. In my opinion, if the man leaves to work abroad, or even in another city, it is indeed his obligation to do so. And it is the woman's obligation to take care of the family, and whatever has been left behind by the husband. So many things are wrong now. Women are all going overseas, and husbands are staying at home. In my opinion, this is also wrong. It is wrong because men are obliged to be breadwinners, but why are women leaving instead?

As the above discussion shows, familial shame and honor is closely associated with women's reputation and moral behavior. One way that migrants' relatives attempt to mediate the effects or potentiality of such shame is to increase regulation of women's mobility in their families, or in the village. This may include the enforcement of local norms (adat) and familial surveillance, as pointed out by Hari.

During a nationwide conference for an Indonesian national migrant labor union that I attended, there was a question and answer session after a participatory activity. All members (who were former migrants or migrants' immediate kin) made a list of potential problems with migrants' recruitment and return processes. Two men raised similar questions. They highlighted a "problem" (*masalah*) that some women were migrating without permissions from their husbands or fathers, and asked the organizers and other members present what action or regulation could help to prevent such cases in future. The men's questions show how women's apparently unchecked or "free" mobility was sometimes perceived as a problem by villagers and community leaders.[13] The men framed this problem as a source of potential embarrassment for their families, which needed urgent remedy. While the organizer in charge of that session did not dismiss the men's concerns, he reframed the issue as one not of deviant women but of recruitment agents who were violating or bypassing bureaucratic guidelines for labor migrants. The 2004 Presidential Regulation on the Placement and Protection of Migrant Workers (which was the referential law at the time and at the time of writing was still undergoing revisions) stipulates that a migrant applicant has to have formal written permission (*izin*) of a husband or wife (*suami atau istri*), parent (*orang tua*), or kin representative (*wali*) (Article 51, Paragraph 5). Significantly, whenever the issue of kinship permission was raised during the course of my fieldwork, this Article was mainly associated with how women required the permission of a male kin in order to migrate. Nobody ever mentioned that men required their wives or parents' permissions in order to leave.

These regulations, however, appeared to be nonstandardized and arbitrarily enforced by local government officials as well as district level officials. For example, in Yogyakarta, there were no official records of migrants leaving or returning to the village. Residents told me that migrants typically only reported their migration or residential statuses to the district-level government in the nearest city (instead of the village government). In contrast, one of the two Cilacap villages kept poor records. According to their official books, only twenty people migrated in the year 2014, and fifteen in 2015 by the month of May. These numbers clearly did not reflect villagers' anecdotal reports and knowledge of who left in the last year, or even in recent months. Everyone in that village with whom I consulted agreed that many more than twenty people migrated in 2014. The village secretary of this field site told me that they kept records because recruitment agencies required a letter from the village head to "permit" and acknowledge that a local resident was applying to migrate. In fact, this was not strictly the case, since many migrants did leave through informal methods, without ever informing the village government in Cilacap or in Yogyakarta. There was also no stipulation in the 2004 Regulation that required a letter from the local government, although it did require that the applicant possess an identity card that could be processed at the village office. In any case, I asked this secretary if he typically signed and agreed to every request, or if there were situations in which he would withhold permission as a local government official. The reply was that in some cases he had not "dared to consent" (*tidak berani setuju*) if a migrant's husband's signature was missing from the document. Such a statement reflects many villagers' explicitly patriarchal attitudes, in which fathers and husbands were largely seen to be in charge of, and did exert control over, the movements of daughters and wives.

Silence

One morning in Cilacap, while visiting an acquaintance, Bu Heru, I met several middle-aged men who had dropped by her house to chat. I introduced myself and my research, and as usual, asked them what they thought of labor migration in general. An older man responded vaguely, "All persons have their own individual fate, migrants or nonmigrants" (*Nasib-nasiban sendiri-sendiri, TKI atau orang sini juga*). One man said that his sister had been working in Singapore for two years. I asked him how she was doing, and he said that he did not know. At first I wondered if he really did not know, or that he just did not want to tell me—a stranger—about it, or that he did not want to share such information with his peers who were present. I asked the others present, including Bu Heru, if they could share stories of female migrant neighbors and kin. Bu Heru's husband, Pak Heru, explained that people did not usually ask about other migrants, and that migrants themselves or their families usually did not want to talk about it either. When I asked why this was the case, Pak Heru replied, "Because of shame. [Migrants are] usually just maids overseas. But if they work in factories, yes, they will share stories."

As I noted earlier, gendered jobs such as domestic work can be viewed as degrading or shameful. Thus migrants and their kin may be less inclined to talk publicly about their experiences abroad performing such work, particularly if it involved harsh working or living conditions, or negative treatment by their employers. Such silence has the effect of reinforcing local perceptions that migrant domestic workers are indeed ashamed of the work they do, thus maintaining existing perceptions and stereotypes of them. Migrant domestic workers' silence might include not disputing gossip about the immoral activities of other migrant women abroad. However, as we shall see in chapter 6, migrant women who had more positive experiences in domestic work, or who formed close relationships with their employers, were more inclined to openly share their experiences to counter stereotypes of domestic work as undignified. Nevertheless, such positive accounts were less common, and had limited impact on challenging local perceptions of domestic work as shameful and lowly.

In cases where migrants had experienced physical and sexual violence by their employers, acquaintances, or partners abroad, migrants and kin might also remain silent in order to cope with the threat of shame and stigma. A female return migrant in Cilacap told me of how a relative's wife had returned from Saudi Arabia after finishing a three-year contract there. On return, this woman always stayed at home, and was very withdrawn and quiet. Her husband observed that it often seemed as if she wanted to say something, yet did not want to talk about it. He did not know what was wrong with their marriage. After three months, she finally confessed to her family, including her husband, that her employer had repeatedly raped and physically abused her. Even though this treatment began early on when she started work with this employer, she decided to stay on, because she knew that if she asked to go back to Indonesia, she would receive even harsher treatment. When she returned to Indonesia, she tried her best to pretend that things were okay. She was too ashamed to face her husband in particular because she did not know how he would react to the news. When she finally told her family what had really happened abroad, everyone present broke down and cried for how she had suffered on her own. They appreciated how difficult it was for her to confess what had happened. In this scenario, even though the return migrant gathered the courage to confess to her family, it was very likely that neighbors would not find out if the family chose not to publicize it, due to the stigma surrounding rape.

Serious public discussion of rape or sexual abuse is largely taboo in Central Javanese villages as is the case elsewhere, particularly because it is associated with long-term shame. Although villagers acknowledged that migrant neighbors and peers may have had these experiences, very few residents spoke about it in detail except to euphemistically refer to these incidents as accidents (*kecelakaan*), sickness (*sakit*), or, sometimes, broadly as violence (*kekerasaan*). This applied to other "shameful" cases such as pregnancy out of wedlock. A few local leaders attributed this taboo to the "Javanese mindset," for which such issues were sources of familial dishonour. One man described sexual abuse as "something to just keep inside, don't publicise it, don't talk about it."

Sustained discussion might, however, take place among women as close confidantes, in reflexive awareness that their views run counter to dominant public opinions. Two former migrant women told me that they felt sympathy for some women who returned pregnant from Saudi Arabia. Without suggesting reasons for these pregnancies, they simply said that they found these women pitiful, especially if the women were unmarried and had to care for the children as single mothers. These moments of silent empathy provide significant though narrow glimpses of how some residents may "witness" and testify to unspeakable violence (Marsland and Prince 2012, 463). Although rare, such silent witnessing points to future possibilities for social transformation. Remaining silent could be a way that migrants and kin cope with shame or the threat of shame, or a way to allow others to endure shame rather than bear explicit stigma and gossip (Brown 2005, 86).

Tragically, however, migrants in these cases were more often blamed for their own plight, and suspected of immoral behavior. This occurred even in the rare cases where migrants made the brave decision to speak out about their ordeals overseas. As one male former migrant dismissively remarked,

> Many migrants, when abroad, do things they would never do here because there is so much freedom, especially in Hong Kong and Taiwan. Some women who return pregnant may say they have been raped.... They say, 'I was raped....' [*Aku diperkosa*] Sometimes by their employers ... but we can never know the truth. Maybe and most likely it was a mutual relationship [*saling suka*]. But of course when things go wrong, they can say anything they want about what happened, but who knows [*siapa tahu*]?

His harsh judgment was most likely influenced by his own experiences in Korea, where he recounted how many Indonesian migrant men visited the red light district regularly, and engaged in extramarital relationships with other Indonesian migrant women in Korea too.

Such a culture of silence and shame arguably makes it difficult for those who have similar negative experiences to exchange information or seek emotional and moral support. One example made it clear to me that some people might in fact want to talk about their "shameful" experiences, but their peers or kin might not want to hear about it or confront these issues. In one field site, neighbors and relatives of a woman I knew relatively well asked me if I knew anything about her marital situation. They assumed I was well positioned to know (and thus inform them). She was said to be divorced or at least separated from her husband, since they did not live together anymore. I was surprised that even friends whom I considered to be close to her did not dare to ask about her husband and marriage. When I asked her close friend why she did not ever try to talk to this woman about her apparent divorce, her friend said, "I'm ashamed to ask. It could hurt her feelings. Anyway, I don't think I can help her or give good advice. In these situations, it is best not to talk about it. Sometimes I felt strongly that she wanted to tell me what happened. She really wanted to talk, and gave me many hints. But I quickly changed the topic."

In other words, silence can also be a way for friends and relatives of persons who are the target of shame to cope with "shame by association," or what Davies (2014) referred to as kinships of shame. By not directly confronting the experiences or issues behind or provoking malu, villagers diffuse the potential of such shame by remaining silent, and/or silencing the experiences of others. How silence can diffuse the threat of shame is also evident in Han's fieldwork among urban poor Chilean women. In remaining silent about rumors of their own transgressive behavior such as abortion or adultery, Han suggests that women's silence can be seen as a need to keep their worlds "intact" (2012, 161). This view contrasts with others who might be tempted to read silence as resistance or acquiescence to male dominance. Similarly, although migrant domestic workers may experience abuses, harassment, and hardship abroad, their desires not to speak about these experiences upon return may be a response to their heightened awareness of the precariousness of their reputations, and "relations that [their] existence [are] staked upon" (ibid.). As Wendy Brown provocatively asks, "What if to speak incessantly of one's suffering is to silence the possibility of overcoming it, living beyond it, and of identifying with something other than it?" (2005, 92).

Emotional Support of Kin and Peers

While there were countless cases in which family members and neighbors appeared or were said to be very judgmental and conservative regarding migrant failures, there were also a few cases in which familial acceptance and neighborly support were crucial in helping individuals to endure and negotiate threats of social stigma and moral judgment. Minah, an active community organizer in Yogyakarta, was also a member of a local state-run microcredit union. I regularly attended their meetings for a month, which took place once or twice a week in offices in the nearest town, or in neighboring villages, or at the facilitators' homes. Staff members, including Minah, served as fieldworkers for their own villages. They did surveys, follow-ups, and collected loan repayments from their fellow villagers. I was allowed to sit in on these meetings, and afterwards, I often asked Minah or other staff from nearby villages about who usually borrowed money, as well as the rate and nature of loan repayment. One staff member told me that most people repaid their loans. In the case of those who could not repay, due to extreme poverty, the microcredit union waived their loans. This was possible because the organization was guided by Islamic principles, over formal and impersonal economic ones (Prawiranta 2013, 134). However, she noted that in many cases, it was unnecessary to waive the loans, since the borrower's family nearly always tried to repay such loans. Because the organization functioned as a community-based lending system, those who could not return their loans faced the threat of being ashamed or shamed by their fellow community members (typically neighbors). In a few cases, neighbors might even help to repay others' loans anonymously to save borrowers from embarrassment. A staff member explained that this kind of behavior of helping another in need is encouraged in "Javanese culture," where it is often referred to as *musyawara* (mutual obligation/assistance). Indeed, as Silvey observed, in rural Java it is "not uncommon for neighbors to collaborate on the fulfillment of one another's basic needs," such as contributing to ritual food preparation for religious festivities, births, weddings, funerals, and in the building of houses (Silvey 2003b, 136; see also Retsikas 2014).

Migrants' spouses or siblings might also take the initiative to seek justice or redress for their kin. While this was not very common, I observed that husbands or sisters who actively sought help or information from NGOs or BNP2TKI usually knew about these NGOs only because they were also prospective or former migrants themselves. For example, upon her premature return from Singapore to Jakarta, Ayu managed to find and stay at SBMI's migrant shelter with her older sister's help. Her older sister had actively and aggressively sought help and information by calling the police, recruitment agencies, BNP2TKI, and NGO staff. Ayu's sister was a former migrant, who had strongly advised her against migrating. This older sister felt that their father was pressuring Ayu to do so, and he had in fact signed the paperwork. He did so despite knowing that Ayu was legally underage to work in Singapore. Her documents had been falsified to say that she was twenty-three instead of nineteen. Ayu's case illustrates how various family members can have conflicting interests or attitudes towards a return migrant who "failed." Her older sister sought legal and economic justice for her in terms of filing criminal reports against the recruitment agency, and refusing to repay the loans which she felt were unfair and exploitative. In stark contrast, upon learning that Ayu had returned and that the recruitment agency demanded money for her "release," Ayu's father told her on the phone that she was "no longer his daughter." The night Ayu received this phone call, I found her crying alone in our shared room in the migrant shelter. I could only remind her that she still had a sister who was doing everything she could to help. On hearing this, Ayu said, "Yes, I'm still lucky to have her. Since we were little, she was there for me."

Another example shows the difference that a family's emotional, moral, and financial support can make for a migrant who is ashamed and who faces potential shaming from her neighbors. Lestari was a former migrant, whose foreign boyfriend raped and impregnated her while she was working abroad. Despite thoughts and attempts of suicide, she eventually kept the child and returned to her village of origin. These were both radical decisions in light of harsh local views against rape, premarital sex, and pregnancy, especially with foreign dark-skinned men (see chapter 5). Yet, Lestari was able to do so in large part due to her mother's fierce support. Her mother was a practical and vocal woman who persuaded her that they would, as a family, find alternatives to suicide and abortion, both of which are generally considered sinful in Islam. In invoking abortion and suicide as immoral acts, Lestari's mother thus reframed the decision to keep a child out-of-wedlock as the appropriate moral response as a Muslim. In keeping the baby and returning to reside in the village as a single mother, Lestari's situation was unique and the exception to other stories of migrant pregnancy abroad. Women were rumored to have had abortions, put their babies up for adoption abroad, or leave children behind in Indonesia in order to migrate again. Many others also tried to pass these children off as legitimately fathered by migrants' husbands in Indonesia (see also Constable 2014; Butt et al. 2016).

Perseverance or Running Away

Pak Gunadi was a fisherman in Yogyakarta, who also owned a small shrimp farm. Minah had introduced us, because his wife was currently working in Taiwan. Resting by the river with a cigarette, he told me that his wife's remittances helped them to buy land and establish the shrimp farm. She had been in Taiwan for eight years, and it had been difficult for her. Her employers were not kind, but she told herself to endure (*tahan*) the hard work and her employers' behavior, so that she could finish her work contract. I asked Pak Gunadi why she repeatedly renewed her contract in Taiwan, and why she did not consider returning after her first three-year contract ended. He explained that if she came back with "nothing," they would be ashamed in front of their neighbors (*malu sama tertangga*).

Only after eight years of working and saving, Pak Gunadi said that his wife had just recently started to feel secure (*enak*), specifically because they now had the shrimp farm to show for her years of working abroad. This narrative of enduring and persevering through harsh working and living conditions abroad was common for many return and current migrants that I spoke to (see also Prusinski 2016b). Many former migrants recounted how familial obligations and expectations for them to return successful helped them to endure homesickness, physical discomfort and ailments, and long working hours. In other words, returning as failures was not a viable option for many, even though the threat of failure was real, particularly for these migrants who could choose to run away, return in debt, or return without finishing their contracts. In his ethnography on the Vietnamese diaspora in the United States, Hung Cam Thai (2014) similarly found that Vietnamese migrants may take up degrading jobs or endure poverty in the U.S. in order to fund and fulfill their families' middle-class aspirations in Vietnam.

While some Javanese migrants may cope with the threat of shame associated with failure by persevering in undesirable working and living conditions abroad, other migrants or potential migrants may instead run away from training centers in Indonesia, or recruitment agencies, employers' houses, factories or plantations overseas. As mentioned earlier, the Indonesian term for the act of running away and those who run away is "kabur," which literally refers to a sense of ambiguity or blurred boundaries. Such blurred lines point to the mainly legal violations entailed in the act of running away, and the mainstream media, NGO workers, and villagers refer to these migrants abroad as those who "kabur"—undocumented migrants. Closely associated with these runaway or undocumented migrants are those who are considered missing, lost, or disappeared. These terms refer to the fact that they have lost contact with their family, and no fellow villager in the migrants' destination country, recruitment agent, or government data can trace their whereabouts (Kelley and Thompson 2015). According to official data from BNP2TKI, such "missing" and uncontactable migrants were the third most commonly reported problem between the years 2011 and 2013.[14]

Missing or irregular migrants were typically perceived as failures, in not being able to keep their jobs, in having bad luck with finding good employers, or in presumably trading their familial obligations for a life of decadence and hedonism abroad. National migrant-centered NGO Seruni published on their website a list of "reasons why [female] migrants run away," and the list includes "unhealthy" relationships with men (*pergaulan "tidak sehat" dengan laki-laki lain*) (Seruni 2014).[15] Other reasons include escaping from physical and sexual abuse at their places of work, and Seruni emphasizes that not all runaway stories are negative or for "illegitimate" reasons. Migrants may also perceive irregular journeys or forms of work as more desirable in increasing their chances of economic success (Killias 2010). Certainly, many return migrants acknowledged that becoming undocumented typically guaranteed a worker higher wages, fewer restrictions on mobility, and safety from physical and sexual abuse within the household or workplace for domestic workers (see also Mahdavi 2013).

These examples of either enduring or running away from harsh working environments support more recent emphasis by scholars that migrants' economic objectives can be subordinate or are intimately linked to migrants' desires to become socially legitimate and respected individuals within their communities. In his work among Congolese migrants, Kankonde (2010) argues that many migrants may deprive themselves of basic necessities, or delay their own individual and initial migration aims (such as saving to start a business), not simply in order to provide for their families. In Kankonde's analysis, providing for one's family is also a near mandatory moral and social obligation, if migrants wished to someday return to their communities of origin. Transgressing socio-cultural norms by not sending enough money home would likely lead to individuals' social exclusion and marginalization from the community upon return. His point is that migrants are remitting for their families not only out of altruism or the pursuit of prestige, but also to maintain their own social membership and prevent shameful social categorization as incapable persons. Indeed, the circulation of shame can be read as central to the necessary violence of social obligations in ensuring the fulfillment of unequal forms of exchange in social life. Migrants do not only give money to kin of their own "free" volition; money and gifts are often also solicited or taken by kin through the framing of migrants' obligations to give to nonmigrant others (see Retsikas 2016).

In a similar vein, in her research in Fouta Djallon, Susanna Fioratta found that transnational labor migration as well as small business start-ups remain popular, despite the fact that both rarely result in economic success. Fioratta highlights how such risky and seemingly irrational decisions should be understood as attempts "to achieve a semblance of respectful personhood" (2015, 306) under hostile structural conditions. Locals perceived alternatives to migration and businesses as mainly unproductive activities, such as sitting and drinking tea. In this context, the act of striving for success, rather than achieving success itself, helps to "prevent—or at least postpone—not only economic failure but also a future of being considered an incapable, useless person" (ibid.).[16]

These analyses are useful to understand seemingly irrational acts by Central Javanese who apparently try to avoid or cope with shame and stigma (or its threat) by making decisions or engaging in activities that are commonly associated with failure or shame, such as running away, or working in sex and entertainment industries. In situations where migrants already face the threat of harm, unpaid wages, more debt, or unwanted deportation, many may perceive that although certain decisions may in the short-term be degrading or extremely risky, they at least offer the possibility for eventual moral redemption, economic success, and social respect.

The case of Bu Sumi illustrates this sense of desperation and radical faith in future redemption. Bu Sumi was a domestic worker in Taiwan, who, after a year and a half, had changed employers twice. Due to complex visa issues concerning a falling out with her first employer, she found herself faced with the threat of deportation and explicit rape threats by her recruitment agent. When she was taken one night, by force, to the recruitment agency, ready to be sent back to Indonesia, Bu Sumi decided to steal her passport and run away. For five years, she had overstayed her visa and lived as an undocumented worker in Taiwan. During this time, she did not contact her family even once. To them, she was another story of a "missing" or "disappeared" migrant, who had either abandoned her family, or worse, had died abroad. When I asked Bu Sumi why she had not tried to contact her family, she said that she felt too ashamed to let them know she had run away, and that she had not made any money in Taiwan. Instead, she was simply surviving from day to day, trying to repay her debts. Going home was not seen as an option for Bu Sumi—her endurance was fueled simply by the hope that she would eventually make enough money to return and explain everything to her family.

Migrants who are deported against their will sometimes turn to SBMI and seek shelter. There, SBMI staff train them to be advocates for migrant and labor rights, and help to build their self-confidence, so that they will not feel too ashamed or afraid to return home. Instead of returning to their families and home villages, some of these shelter residents may choose to migrate again, whether through legal, irregular, or "grey" processes (Ford and Lyons 2011). Nicole Constable (2014) terms this form of re-migration the "migratory cycle of atonement," referring to processes where migrants choose to migrate again and again, in order to escape gendered shame and stigma, and to make up for their past failures by sending money home to support their children, parents and other kin. Constable's ethnography of Filipina and Indonesian migrant mothers in Hong Kong includes cases in which women had committed adultery or engaged in premarital or nonmarital sexual relations, sometimes resulting in pregnancy, babies, or abortions. "Migratory cycles of atonement" draw attention to the fact that many women migrate to escape shame and stigma at home, but as Platt (2017) shows, their decisions to migrate may also generate more gossip and judgment.

A male former migrant I interviewed in Yogyakarta even went so far as to suggest that *all* women who migrate do so out of shame; since if they had a sense of shame (in the above discussed sense of dignity and honor), they would not need to migrate in the first place. A commonly given example of those who migrate out of shame is divorced women. They often endure double judgments not only as failed wives but also bad mothers when they leave their children to work overseas (Parreñas 2005; Pratt 2012; Rodriguez 2010). While their independent migrations may temporarily contribute to judgements against them, they still embark on such journeys in the hopes of eventual redemption, if they are able to give their children better lives that single women's incomes in Indonesia cannot provide.

While some may cope with shame and endure harsh conditions in the hopes of eventually finding success, others deliberately cut off ties with their family in order to escape or reject normative standards of success and failure at home. These can be seen as acts of creating alternative futures for themselves. A female staff member with the migration division of the women's NGO *Solidaritas Perempuan* told me of a case in early 2014, in which a migrant's older brother came to their office to report that his younger sister had been missing in Malaysia for many years. The organization eventually located the woman migrant in Malaysia, through migrants' social networks. She appeared to be happy and fine (*baik saja*), and was planning to get married (although it was unclear to whom). Although she was "found," she told the NGO staff that she did not want to be contacted by her family. She explained that she had deliberately cut off ties with her family because she was disappointed in them. When she had first arrived in Malaysia, she regularly sent her parents money, but her older brother spent it all and demanded more. Over time, she felt "traumatized" by the experience, and exploited by her family, since her parents did little to protest her older brother's behavior. Such stories of voluntarily "missing" migrants were not uncommon, and in fact, make up a genre of stories among many NGO activists (some of whom are migrants too) in Singapore and Indonesia about migrants who do not want to be found, and who do not plan on ever reconciling with their families.

Migrants may be willing to bear temporary shame in the hope of eventual moral and social redemption. Others may reject such normative moral standards altogether by cutting off contact with their family (chapter 6). Both are ways that migrants cope with the threat or experience of stigma or shame, and suggest some ways that migrants try to articulate alternative moralities or risk short-term moral judgment for long-term socioeconomic security and respect.

Acts of Violence

National and international news reports on informal labor migrants from Southeast Asia sometimes include portrayals of women as "murderous maids" and men as aggressive, violent, and potential rapists. Through my interviews with migrant and female NGO staff and former migrants, I found that many former migrants and migrant labor activists interpret such acts of violence in terms of migrants' desperation or extreme attempts to reclaim their sense of dignity. In a widely publicized case in 2014, a male Indonesian worker on board a cruise ship was arrested for the alleged rape and attempted murder of a female U.S. citizen in her room (McMahon 2015). The Balinese worker, Ketut Pujayasa, claimed that he had attacked her to defend himself and his mother's honor. The U.S. citizen had insulted him and his mother by calling him a "son of a bitch." During the trial, his defense counsel argued that his violent act was provoked by a deep sense of humiliation and anger (*Liputan6* 2014). He was deeply apologetic during the sentencing, and framed his act as only "human." Begging for forgiveness, he said, "I'm fully aware that whatever punishment goes to me will not ever pay for the mistake that I made." This example supports scholarship on how a man might respond to *malu* with acts of violence, in an attempt to defend his honor and sense of masculinity (Nilan et al. 2013).

In another tragic case of male violence in response to feelings of humiliation, a migrant woman from Central Java was murdered by her husband in their home ten days after her return from working in Taiwan (Sudibyo 2015). The husband, Musriyani, claimed that he had attacked her because she had offended him (*tersinggung*) with her "crude words and refusal" (*berkata-kata kasar dan menolak*) when he asked her for sex. Marital rape in Indonesia is an impossible category, given the legal understanding of a wife's duties, which includes fulfilling her husband's sexual needs. Islamic scholars who support this legal definition typically quote a hadith which states that it is a sin for women to reject their husbands' desires (van Doorn-Harder 2008, 1036). A female former minister for women's empowerment went further to consider "raising the issue to go against Indonesian culture" (Blackburn 2004, 203). Such hegemonic understandings of women's wifely duties and men's entitlements as husbands provide a context for how, in this example, Musriyani may have felt humiliated and dishonored enough to turn violent when his wife rejected his advances and insulted him.

Such impulsive acts of violence by men contrast with those of women. The majority of cases of migrant women found guilty of murder involve the murder of their employers or employers' family members. These migrants are typically diagnosed with depression and mental instability linked to physical or verbal abuse, or overwork, over a long period. Sunardi Supriyanto was found guilty of murdering her Singaporean employer, Angie Ng, and Ng's three-year-old daughter in 2002. She was accused of stabbing them to death, before setting them on fire. According to a news report, although the judge presiding over the case found her guilty, he rejected accusations that she was a "cold-blooded" and "mindless" killer (Agence France Presse 2004). Instead, he emphasized that her actions were likely motivated by long-term ill-treatment Sunardi had suffered from Angie Ng. Such ill-treatment included depriving her of proper food, feeding her with three-day-old stale noodles, and asking her to "eat [the] child's shit" (Susilo 2004). The judge added, "In my view, the cord of reason suddenly snapped when the accused could no longer control her emotions of feeling and despair." Despite her extreme response, Sunardi's case—in the broader sense of her experiences—is not rare in the world of migrant domestic workers and employers. These stories of murder frequently reveal a pattern of women from rural backgrounds with little education or experience outside their hometowns, who, prior to their violent acts of homicide, endured mistreatment and degradation over long periods of time by wealthier, privileged employers. One female former migrant who worked in Saudi Arabia defended "migrant murderers" to me, and explained,

> Murder is wrong, of course.... But sometimes you just can't imagine how employers can be so fussy, so insulting, so demanding, that one day you just can't endure it [*tidak boleh tahan*] anymore. I have seen how it drives people crazy. Not everyone can be so patient or tolerant. You have to be very, very strong.

Suicide can also be a desperate means to restore one's honor in such cases of failures or perceived wrongs. In one field site, a former migrant's husband committed suicide days after she accused him of not spending her remittances wisely. After his death, his close male friend disclosed to select neighbors that the husband had been feeling depressed that his wife did not trust him with the family's finances. He had been accused of mishandling her money, which he claimed was untrue. Suicide can also be a desperate measure to escape the threat of failure, shame, or stigma. I previously discussed the example of Lestari, who contemplated suicide as an escape from her difficult dilemma of either raising her child alone abroad, aborting her child and thus committing a grave sin, or returning pregnant and bringing dishonor to herself and her family (see Constable 2014; Ladegaard 2013a). During my stay at a migrant shelter in Jakarta, a former migrant threatened to jump out of BNP2TKI's office building when it seemed to him that he was unlikely to receive justice and compensation for his specific case of unfair dismissal and nonpayment. In 2012, a migrant worker in Singapore hung herself after having failed the mandatory English language test thrice (Singh 2012). The news report suggested that she did so because she faced substantial debt upon her likely return to Indonesia. Given that she had "reportedly borrowed seven million rupiah from relatives to work" in Singapore, it was likely that her return would disappoint many in her home village.

In short, these acts of violence to self or others are responses to extreme distress, when individuals experience the limits of their abilities to respond to their multiple obligations and circumstances. These acts expose individuals' inabilities to imagine possible futures, and ways to live in dignity.

Shame Mediating Mobilities

Migrant-origin villagers' experiences and practices of shame reveal the multiple sources of shared anxieties and uncertainties, whether or not they choose to migrate, return, or stay. While migrants are often blamed for their own failures, their kin and neighbors can also be blamed or associated with migration-related shame. Migrants also participate in shaming and blaming others, sometimes in an effort to redirect speculative gossip and attention away from their own migratory experiences. Shame is highly gendered, intimately linked to and produced by socioeconomic insecurity and opportunity. In a context of normalized transnational labor migration, the circulation of shame in discussions of migration in Central Javanese villages, however, is largely directed at influencing women's mobilities and motilities. Nevertheless, this chapter has also highlighted the less common cases where feelings of humiliation and shame provoke violence or depression in some men, or prompt their decisions to delay their return to their villages of origin.[17] Malu or shame is thus a fundamental moral condition that organizes and mediates Central Javanese villagers' gendered mobility and motility.

While internal migration is not new to these Central Javanese villages, the pressures to migrate overseas are relatively recent. These pressures are directed at and experienced more strongly by women, due to the ways that migration infrastructure, at least in Java, unevenly offers more opportunities and credit for women to migrate than men. Women in Central Java are better positioned than ever before to financially support their parents and spouses, afford siblings' or children's education, buy prestige goods, and build concrete houses to boost their family's social status. In focusing on shame and migrant failures in this chapter, I do not mean to suggest that most Central Javanese are against the migration of women and supportive of the migration of men, as is the case in countries where male migration is the norm (Bylander 2015; Rao 2014). On the contrary, women make up the majority of migrants from my field sites, and parents, husbands, and even some children, encourage women to migrate.

Villagers' talk about migration appears inconsistent because their expressed views and responses to migratory outcomes or practices are highly contextual. Rather than simply being "for" or "against" the migration of women and men, circulations and cultivations of shame respectively urge and constitute certain precautionary measures or behaviors which aim to avoid failing at migratory projects or return as failures. Looking at the production, mobilization, and negotiation of shame thus provides alternative viewpoints to how return migrants and others perceive, evaluate, and respond to migration-associated risks.

Attention to the various ways migrants, neighbors, and relatives negotiate shame and its risk sheds light on seemingly irrational or ignorant migrant decisions and practices, such as moving from documented to undocumented work or visa status, agreeing to disproportionately large amounts of debt, cutting off contact with family in Indonesia, or committing extreme acts of violence. These seemingly irrational acts make sense when considering migrants' temporal and often hopeful orientation to the future, in relation to the precariousness of the present. Tracing the mobilization and cultivation of shame in migrant-origin villages illuminates villagers' everyday practices of "getting by" and "moving on," amidst these "pulls" of transnationalized futures, or in response to lost futures and plans. In these ways, villagers' mobilizations and cultivations of shame play a key role in shaping how, where, and when individuals produce, circulate, and value their labor and money.

Notes

1. The video was shared on Buruh Migran's Facebook Page on August 5, 2014. Accessed March 9, 2016. https://www.facebook.com/photo.php?v=751811514864793.

2. While most people typically use malu to describe all of the various forms of shame from feeling shy and embarrassed, to feeling ashamed in relation to causing dishonor to the family name, many Javanese-Indonesian speakers make the distinction between two

kinds of shame: malu and *aib* (or *isin* and *wirang*, their equivalents in the Javanese language; cf. Fessler 2004). Isin refers to more common forms of shame, such as being caught stealing, or being poor. A female former migrant said that wirang or aib was rarely used, and only in severe cases. She cited an example of aib: if a woman returns pregnant from abroad, but she is already married in Indonesia. Someone caught having an affair (*selingkuh*) should feel aib which in turn causes the family to experience aib. Aib refers to a more public form of disgrace, dishonor, and humiliation, in relation to violating social taboos.

3. Several Central Javanese women I knew and interviewed were active members of *Pembinaan Kesejahteraan Keluarga* (Family Welfare Guidance).

4. For comparison, see Elmhirst 2007 on unemployed men in a context of female rural-urban migration; and on male unemployment, alcoholism, and gambling in a context of feminized transnational migration in Sri Lanka, see Gamburd 2000 and 2008.

5. In Java, migration is a feminized trend since more women migrate. To my knowledge, men who stay behind are very rarely, if at all, shamed for being "feminine" in their nonmigration, unlike in other contexts where most men migrate, and where most migrants are men (Bylander 2015; Hernández-Carretero and Carling 2012).

6. It is not uncommon for couples to move into a wife's family's house after marriage, if they have yet to build their own house, as Javanese parents tend to prefer living with daughters over sons. This arrangement is sometimes further encouraged when the couple has children and when maternal grandparents can help with childcare.

7. A wife's duties to fulfill her husband's sexual needs are explicitly part of the Indonesian Presidential Instruction 1/1991, on the Compilation of Islamic Laws specifically referring to the Marriage Law 1/1974, Part 6, Article 84.

8. Internet memes, broadly defined, are ideas, activities, and phrases, often in the form of visual media such as photographs or videos, that spread among individuals via the Internet. As the term suggests, memes typically involve forms of mimicry and creative reinterpretation of what it mimics or references. For a discussion of how Internet memes can provide social commentary or responses to journalistic reportage on critical issues of the day, see Rintel (2013).

9. The meme cannot be reproduced here, but the full caption reads: "*Asik/ PT buka lagi/ mau ke Jeddah/ mau kabur ke kamar supir*" (Great/ Recruitment agencies are open again/ I want to go to Jeddah/ to run away to the driver's room). I encountered this meme first on the public Facebook group, *Buruh Migran Indonesia Saudi Arabia* (BMI-SA). It was circulated via Facebook in 2014 in response to news that the Indonesian state would end the moratorium against migration to the Middle East.

10. KEMLU 2014. "Muhammad Hartati: Kisah Anak TKI yang ditinggalkan Ibunya di Saudi," Kementerian Luar Negiri Indonesia. September 24. Accessed October 25, 2014. http://www.kemlu.go.id/riyadh/Pages/Embassies.aspx?IDP=250&l=id. (This link is no longer available, but the incident and report are also mentioned in Patnistik 2014.)

11. In Hans Ladegaard's (2013a) analysis of Indonesian and Filipina foreign domestic workers' narratives of trauma with their employers and jobs in Hong Kong, he argues that the women's laughter in addition to their tears were crucial to understanding how they cope with traumatic experiences. By introducing laughter or creating situations where laughter is present in their narratives, Ladegaard argues that these women "use laughter to create and reify their own superiority in relation to their adversities. Thus, laughter becomes a survival mechanism; like crying, it becomes a very human response to dehumanizing experiences" (2013a, 405).

12. Such attitudes contrast with ethnographies of Filipina labor migrants, who tended to represent their lives abroad to families in terms of entertainment and pleasure (McKay 2012).

13. Of course, as many scholars have shown, and I have discussed in chapters 1 and 2, Indonesian women's mobilities are neither "free" nor "unchecked." A complex migration infrastructure constrains and regulates their transnational movements (Xiang and Lindquist 2014).

14. 2,320 migrants were officially reported as having lost communication with their families (*putus hubungan komunikasi*). See BNP2TKI 2013.

15. For similar observations of the phenomenon, see DedeMit Jarank Onlen 2011.

16. On how aspiring Senegalese "boat" migrants frame risky endeavors in terms of the necessity to maintain personhood and masculine dignity, see Hernández-Carretero and Carling 2012.

17. This gendered bias in the data is also likely due to the fact that in my field sites, women's migration was much more common than that of men. This meant that I also interviewed fewer men overall. Nevertheless, the stories and narratives that circulated among villagers about migration largely involved women's mobilities and motilities.

5 Faith

When I asked a former migrant woman in Cilacap why people still migrate despite horror stories in the news, she said,

> They migrate ... for economic reasons. But mostly it is *nasib*. Your nasib can change, but it is something personal. It depends on people themselves.... If you get a bad employer, you can find out how to change your situation. If not, for those who are lazy or ignorant, they will get stuck in their situation. But nasib to some extent is determined by God, of course. Or how do we explain why some people land in much worse situations than others? It is a bit like luck.... Good people can have bad nasib and the reverse is also true. It depends on how you handle your given life situation.

Nasib, or "fate," was a central element of how return migrants or nonmigrant residents explained migrant tragedy or success. Typical responses included that migrant success or failure depends on fate, or that everyone has their own fate (*nasib-nasiban*). Fate was not necessarily always used in a fatalistic sense. Instead, the meaning of nasib in relation to human agency and uncertainty shifted in context, along a spectrum that emphasized both "human effort" (*usaha*) and God's "will" or "destiny" (*takdir*). Nasib discourse was also salient among migrant activists, mainstream journalists writing in Indonesian and in English (who use the term "fate"), as well as state authorities.

Through discourses of fate and destiny, migrants and their families can sometimes temporarily or contextually be absolved of blame and responsibility for their "shameful" actions. Furthermore, human responsibility can also be displaced and reconfigured by acknowledging the role of divine agency in human strivings (Liebelt 2008; Pingol 2008). In a conversation with Nurul and Bu Musliah, two former migrant women, I asked, "What does nasib depend on [*tergantung apa*]?" The following discussion ensued.

Bu Musliah: [Fate depends on] God, but also our own selves [*kita sendiri*].

C: Can we change our nasib?

Nurul: Yes, if we make an effort [*berusaha*], we can change what God has given to us. For example, God gives us our destiny [takdir]. This is the first level. But we can, with effort, get to higher levels ... have better lives than what we are given.

C: But what is the difference between takdir and nasib?

N: Actually, sometimes they can be the same ...

C: Bu Musliah, do you think we can change our nasib?

Bu M: Nasib depends on God too, and what he wants for us. But if we are in a bad situation ... of course we can work hard to change it. If we are lazy, then we won't be able to change our fate.

Various former migrants and residents—like Nurul and Bu Musliah—often emphasized that human effort was central to changing and shaping one's fate. I argue that villagers' nasib discourses enable a view of faith as a form of labor central to their decisions to migrate, stay, or return. For the Central Javanese I met, practicing one's faith was intimately tied to caring for kin and community in gender-specific ways. This chapter elaborates on how the development, mobilization, and practice of faith is an important way for former migrants, prospective migrants, and their families to negotiate uncertainties, risks, and shame associated with migration, return, and staying behind.

Nasib is not only an abstract or theoretical concept used to refer to or evaluate others' efforts or circumstances. It is also invoked to reflect and act on the present, based on an understanding of how one's past actions and hopes show promise or not. For example, a young mother from Cilacap framed her own failure to migrate in terms of nasib. She said, "People here believe in nasib.... If your nasib is good, and you make an effort, it will be ok, but you must make an effort." She compared it to destiny, saying, "It is similar ... but [unlike destiny] you can change your fate, and make your fate, if you try." She was taking care of some plantations and agriculture (*tanaman*) at the time. Her circumstances may be modest now, she said, gesturing to her small and cramped house with bare cement floors. "But hopefully I can change my nasib slowly. Maybe my nasib wasn't to be a TKW [migrant worker] ... but hopefully with the tanaman, it will get better. I can only make an effort." By reframing past experiences, nasib discourses were also self-evaluations of one's present circumstances. They served to reorient persons' hopes and actions toward different futures. In other words, not all who had failed to migrate saw themselves as "bad" people who deserved their bad fates, but simply that being a migrant was not their fate at a particular point of time, and the solution was to work harder or differently at achieving better futures.

My approach to nasib is informed by Hirokazu Mizayaki's criticism of scholars who view faith as "beyond ... analytic scope" (2000, 44). Indeed, scholars of Islam in Indonesia have framed their focus on material or ritual practices, symbols, or discourse, in relation to how "true" piety is difficult to prove and ascertain empirically (Blackburn 2004; Jones 2010). Following Miyazaki, I take the "character of faith" as "ethnographically accessible," through a focus on how individuals generate, through discourse and practices, "the capacity to place one's agency in abeyance" (Miyazaki 2000, 44). This chapter examines how and when Cilacap and Yogyakarta residents suspend, displace, or reconfigure their agency in relation to nonhuman actors. This offers a complementary but different perspective to migrant research that typically focuses on structural processes and regulation, human agency, and social networks.

Mainstream media, village leaders, and government officials often cast villagers' narratives of fate and destiny in terms of their ignorance and resignation to broader structural and supernatural forces (Prusinski 2016a). Instead, I argue that narratives of fate and destiny are grounded in villagers' awareness of the complicities and dispersed responsibilities of employers, recruitment agents, and state institutions when things go wrong for migrants. Responsibility, human intentions, and decisions are always intersubjective and fundamentally socially constituted (Duranti 2015; Keane 2014). Narratives of fate and faith serve to shape transnational migration flows by continually reconfiguring villagers' agency in relation to what they are willing to risk (e.g., debt, sickness, loneliness, adultery, death), and what they are not willing to forsake (e.g., social interdependency, patron relations to local government officials, and hope for long-term success). In this chapter, I argue that villagers' talk about fate, destiny, and spirit possession are partial yet ultimately ineffective responses to the state's inability to guarantee villagers' transnational security or livelihoods. This chapter thus traces the ways villagers have come to depend on the ambiguities and ambivalences present in unevenly implemented state regulations of migration, even as these very ambivalences have contributed to the risks of their endeavors.

Fate and faith discourse and practices in these field sites are partially influenced by Islamic ideas and discourse. While anthropological and theological approaches to Islam have been the subject of much debate among anthropologists (Asad 2003; Varisco 2005), I align with ethnographers who focus on how and to what extent Indonesians negotiate their beliefs and practices with reference to ideas about Islam (Bowen 1993; Varisco 2005; Woodward 1989; Kim 2007). Interpretations of the Qur'an and Islam in people's lives are diverse and often conflicting, as evident in enduring public debates over the nature of "Indonesian Islam" and the presence of "radical" Islamic groups (Munjid 2012). Nevertheless, Islamic discourses or associated notions—such as fate and destiny—are salient and important to Central Javanese residents' discussions, evaluations, and reflections of their own actions and those of others. Everyday talk about or debates over morality and the role of human agency—based on a shared orientation to God, other supernatural agents, and the afterlife—illuminate how Islamic subjectivities and ideas are explicitly and intimately negotiated in the context of transnational labor migration.

Faith as Labor

Perceptions and use of the term nasib among villagers as well as activists were not always consistent or compatible, in terms of how human agency and effort was emphasized in relation to God's will. I first became aware of this during an informal discussion about trafficking and undocumented migration (often referred to as "illegal" migration) facilitated by a women's NGO in Yogyakarta. Participants were mostly former migrant women, who were sharing their negative experiences abroad, such as forced confinement and food deprivation. A few described how Singapore-based recruitment companies marketed and treated them like commodities to be "bought and sold" (*jual-beli*). In response, the oldest woman in the group, who had migrated in the 1980s and returned in late 1990s, dismissed these bad experiences as due to individual nasib. She challenged the NGO and the forum's framing of these experiences as related to "trafficking," and said that she doubted that stories about trafficking were that common. To support her claim, she said she had personally never had bad experiences. Maintaining that she had always had good nasib, partly due to having treated others well, she described her generous employers and agents, and how she could rely on the kindness of strangers in foreign countries.

The NGO staff facilitating the discussion disagreed with what they saw as a circular argument and fatalistic view. Addressing all participants present, a young Javanese female NGO staff member said,

> Nasib can be changed, especially with effort. Don't mix up fate with destiny. How can we change our fate? With learning about employment contracts, being skilled and informed, so that you won't become a victim of trafficking. Bargain and negotiate [*nilai tawar*], learn ... about laws, and the processes of making a passport, and so on. Allah doesn't just give you bad fate. That alone doesn't explain why your fate is bad. Your fate is not bad because you are supposed to have bad fate. That is wrong.

Despite these disagreements on the extent to which people can change their life circumstances, both approaches towards nasib, whether as primarily influenced by God or by human effort, recognize the *limits* of human agency in ensuring success, safety, and health, as constrained by a migration infrastructure involving power hierarchies across national, socioeconomic, and gender lines. The elderly migrant was also arguably aware of these structural limits, in highlighting that the (unguaranteed) "kindness" of others had been key to her safety and relative success as a migrant woman navigating a foreign land and culture. As the vocal NGO staff member's remarks reveal, participants should learn to change their nasib in relation to very specific risks, including a range of potentially misleading practices by employers and migration intermediaries. Ellen Prusinski's research attests that NGO staff and migration activists often "reinforce the idea that migration is safest when women follow proper channels," and thus tend to emphasize distinctions between regular and irregular migration processes (2016a, 507).

Many women subtly criticized the workshop facilitators for "misunderstanding" trafficking during informal conversations after the workshop. A young mother who recently returned from Taiwan said that she disagreed with the elder villager's deterministic view of nasib, but she also disagreed with the facilitators' view that many return migrants' experiences were similar to "trafficking." This was likely due to the fact that the term "trafficking" was popularly associated with victimhood, abduction, and sex work (Brennan 2014; Choo 2013; Ford and Lyons 2012). During the workshop, it was clear that women emphasized their everyday and "hidden" strategies to mitigate the risks of going abroad. Common examples included hiding food or important phone numbers of NGOs and the Indonesian Consulate inside of ballpoint pens or their bras. Despite taking such subtle precautionary measures, the women "allowed" employers to keep their passports and "allowed" recruitment agents to falsify their documents. Women's awareness of and justifications for these strategies contrasted with NGO workers' views that women were either "forced" to do things, or passively "accepted" these exploitative and illegal practices. Furthermore, unfair practices by recruitment agents and employers were taken for granted by prospective migrants and return migrants as part of "regular" or "formal" channels of migration, and could not be avoided as simply as suggested by the NGO staff.

Gendered moral assumptions, as well as a mainly theoretical-legal understanding of migration processes, prevented the workshop's facilitators from grasping the women's apparent resignation to and complicity in trafficking-like practices. This was evident in a young staff member's moralizing tone when she admonished the women for "not thinking" before choosing to go abroad and leaving their "poor children" behind.[1] She pleaded with them to think of the social and not only economic consequences of their movements, thus limiting her ability to perceive how social and economic obligations were intimately linked for many prospective and current migrants (Constable 2014; Gamburd 2000; Parreñas 2005; Pratt 2012). Even the "trafficking expert" and invited speaker, who had apparently written several books on the issue, repeatedly asked very basic questions about the situations women found themselves in. Former migrant women patiently explained the many ways in which they could not simply demand their passports from recruiters or employers: that might mean being fired and then being sent back to Indonesia with a lot of debt. Most women were able to point to specific laws in destination countries such as Singapore where these common practices by employers and recruiters were technically illegal. Yet, they were also well aware of the limitations, biases, and failures of foreign states to actively enforce laws and monitor the behavior and practices of citizen-employers.

The situated knowledges and experiences of return migrants thus contextualize and explain why most Yogyakarta and Cilacap villagers' understandings of nasib, and associated notions of human choice and risk, departed significantly from those of some NGO workers, government officials, and trafficking experts. Central to return migrants' expressions of how people can change their fate was that God was the final judge of the consequences of human strivings and efforts (see Qur'an, 95.6). For example, in a discussion with Rina in Cilacap about whether or not local shamanistic healers [*dhukun*] had real power [*sakti*], she reframed my question to imply that the source of shamanistic power is ultimately God. She said, "Yes, this power is from God. For us, we just make an effort. When we are sick, we look for who and where can heal us. Maybe it will be a dhukun or someone else. If it's suitable, yes of course you can [recover]. We only make an effort. God is the one who decides."

This emphasis on the role and limit of human effort in influencing nasib opens the possibility for thinking about residents' labor in terms of faith, and faith as a form of labor. Villagers' labors of faith and faithful labor critically contribute to morally sustaining and shaping the transnational circulation of human bodies, labor, and finance. Attending to the culturally specific notion of human effort and agency in relation to nonhuman agency can clarify particular tensions in migration research on migrants' individual and relational subjectivities. Broadly, scholars have emphasized how migrants sustain emotional and transnational connections through remittances and other communicative practices (Huang and Yeoh 2000; Kwon 2015; Madianou 2012; McKay 2007). Yet, scholars have also highlighted the sense of adventure and dreams of self-actualization that form the "hidden motivations" of many migrants (Madianou 2012; Parennas 2001). Ming-Yan Lai, for example, observed how migrant domestic workers in Hong Kong may temporarily "forget" homelands and their families. She writes, "while some ... may willingly perform the gendered sacrifices expected of female migrant workers, others may have mixed feelings and even resentment towards the demands on them from home even though they maintain the diasporic connections for various reasons" (Lai 2011, 571).

Attention to faith and religious-ethical practice elucidates further layers of migrants' and residents' subjectivities, particularly in how they may use Islamic discourses or identities to justify or reconcile competing desires and responsibilities at stake in migrating or staying. Iwan Prawiranta has highlighted the relationship between Islamic faith, effort, and intention in his research on Central Javanese and Sundanese Muslim entrepreneurship, writing that "as Muslims, they believe that what they do is dependent on intention [*niat*]. It is a faith that niat needs effort and after a strong effort they said 'we'll get what we are intended to get'" (Prawiranta 2013, 134). In similar ways, Cilacap and Yogyakarta residents emphasized niat or intention as important to directing one's effort in daily and religious strivings in order to realize their hopes and plans in general and migration success in particular. As mentioned in the previous chapter, gossip or speculations about the intentions guiding human action, decisions, and responses feature centrally in discussions of nasib or piety.

In the context of processes of industrialization, state decentralization, and globalization, Islam offers a vocabulary and identity for rural Indonesians to allow them to negotiate social, economic, and moral anxieties that people face with regards to shifting and contradictory gendered expectations. The intersection of Islam and gender is thus a key site of performance and debate over "authentic subjectivity" or "self-actualization" through the negotiation and cultivation of piety (Boellstorff 2005; Brenner 1996; Hefner 1987; Wichelen 2010). In contemporary as well as preexisting observations of social life in Central Java, a mix of Javanese and Islamic ideas about appropriate behavior and obligations towards others importantly shape subjectivity and behavior (see Brenner 1996; Keeler 1983). It is this practical and embodied orientation—how to perform and fulfill one's proper obligations to others within a social hierarchy—that arguably underlies Nurul's and Bu Musliah's references to the ways that "effort" can change one's given life circumstances. The elder former migrant woman at the trafficking workshop also justified her good fate, with reference to how she had treated others according to what they were "properly and rightfully due" (Chittick 2000, 583).

These subtle meanings of effort, intention, and nasib point to some ways that experiences of shame and agency are morally intersubjective. Shame and agency are related to material practices and ideas about appropriate behavior, and are influenced by historical and contemporary Islamic-based teachings and discourses in Java. Cilacap and Yogyakarta villagers' faith practices and "human efforts" can be understood as a form of self-governance linked to negotiated notions of gendered social obligations. Moving on from these meanings of nasib, the next section discusses some examples of how nasib discourses are metadiscursively commented on by migrant-origin villagers to explain migrants' and residents' subjective and structural situations within migration processes, as well as to illustrate how nasib grounds the kinds of "human effort" employed to forge worthwhile futures whether abroad or in Central Java.

Making Fates Abroad

Villagers' faith in nasib was sometimes reflexively viewed as part of the problem behind migrant failures, by migrant-origin villagers, activists, and authorities. A community organizer in Yogyakarta noted that "belief in nasib" was a reason why women made seemingly irrational and risky decisions to migrate, according to an informal report and conference presentation she had written for Koalisi Perempuan, the largest women's organization in Indonesia. During a discussion about promises by state officials to solve the "problem" of migration, chiefly by preventing women from migrating as domestic workers, I asked Hazam (a "former migrant" who failed to leave Indonesia due to fraud, see chapter 3) if he saw migration as a problem. He replied,

> I don't think migrating is a big problem, only the process is problematic. Many people, myself included, believe in nasib. People here are simple minded, narrow minded. Regardless of the news reports they read about Saudi, or what their neighbors have experienced over there, they believe they might have better luck because everyone has their own destiny.

He elaborated that this belief in fate meant that people did not try very hard to understand the proper migratory procedures, or the working and living conditions abroad, prior to leaving their villages. As he had experienced for himself, this meant that when some become victims of fraud by recruitment agents, sympathetic fellow villagers may simply see this as "bad luck," while others may blame a migrant for not being cautious, or trusting the wrong agent.

The options for prospective migrants to take such systematic precautions are often limited by resources and the kinds of information available. Prospective migrants' relationships to migration-related information can be complicated in terms of how the information can be dismissed or disregarded as irrelevant or unreliable (see also Hernández-Carretero and Carling 2012). Since it is relatively expensive and time-consuming for many rural residents to travel to the nearest town where there is a formal government agency for migration or migrant workers, prospective migrants often turn to local and informal recruitment agents or former migrants for advice. Informal recommendations and information by brokers, friends, or family can be inaccurate, too specific (to their unique broker, center, job, employer, or destination country) or simply not that useful. Indah, a prospective migrant in Cilacap who failed to migrate, told me that there were few options in the village regarding which recruitment agents to trust. She eventually chose an agent whom she did not trust completely, but whom she perceived as the "lesser evil" (*kurang jahat*). Whatever fears or limited alternatives migrants or prospective migrants may have regarding the uncertainties of migration are mitigated by the belief that they may have good fates abroad.

In several interviews with those who went abroad with falsified passports or documents, former migrants sometimes said that they were not sure if they would come back dead or alive. This statement always shocked me, and I would ask, "Weren't you afraid? If you knew there was a possibility you might not return alive, why would you leave in the first place?" Some said that life and death were matters of destiny and thus in the hands of God. Other common responses included that they believed that they would have good fates, an acknowledgment that they were reckless (*nekad*), or that there was no room for fear, especially in circumstances where women were divorced and had to find a way to support their children and/or ageing parents. As Nicole Constable (2014) argues in her ethnography of Indonesian and Filipina migrant mothers in Hong Kong, women may migrate to "atone" or financially compensate for the ways they are judged to have failed as mothers, daughters, and wives. Such migrations or decisions to migrate can be seen as acts of faith, in women's hopes that migration will lead to their moral redemption and social acceptance.

Thus, despite past negative migration experiences or failures, Cilacap and Yogyakarta residents may strive to change their present circumstances or fates by migrating, or migrating again. These individual acts of faith draw on a broader collective faith in migration to negotiate better futures and fates for themselves and/or their families. Nevertheless, these acts of faith should not be misinterpreted as due to romantic illusions of a good life overseas. While people fantasized aloud about experiencing life overseas, nobody ever described or recounted—without disclaimers—dreaming of working abroad as TKI or TKW. Instead, as I have argued and will further elaborate below, some migrations out of faith are strategies based on a recognition of the limited opportunities in Indonesia for such women and men to radically change their "fates" in the country.

A migrant's chances of success or failure abroad are importantly perceived to largely rely on personality—a combination of confidence, capability, wit—that is linked to religious piety and individual morality, so that God will provide the migrant with good agents, employers, fortune, and solutions for their problems. In short, nasib discourse is linked to broader Islamic-inflected discourses on responsibility, morality, and God's will.[2] One of the few "model migrants" in Yogyakarta told of how prayer and faith in God helped her navigate difficult circumstances at the training center, when a fellow prospective migrant colluded with a recruitment agent to delay her departure. Her account of this incident, which included cultivating patience and the belief that God will help her find a way out of an unfair situation, was later described again to me in very similar ways by her parents, who thanked God for their daughter's safe and successful return. Nasib and faith feature importantly in narratives of migration, in guiding persons' aspirations, patience, endurance, or gratitude prior to, during, and after migratory journeys. Nasib tends to individualize the circumstances of every migrant failure or success, and promotes the view that most pious and skillful individuals will likely succeed (Chittick 2011, 8–10). The focus on moral human agency and effort partially contributes to mobilizing either faith in or fear of migration, according to villagers' sense of their self-discipline, or capacity for self-discipline.

Making Fates at Home

Not everyone believed that migrating would lead to good fates for them. I asked Hazam (above) in the same conversation, "If so many people believe in fate, why do other people stay, and not migrate?" He cited three reasons that many NGO workers also often gave me. The first was that some people decided to stay because they might feel they had enough (*cukup*) to live on, and were not greedy for more. The second was fear—people did not migrate because they were afraid of what would happen overseas, and thus lacked the self-confidence and courage to leave. The third was that some had tried to migrate, but did not pass health requirements, or medical or language tests, and thus could not leave. These three reasons for "not migrating" contribute to understanding how shame conditions decisions to migrate or stay in temporal ways, in comparing possible futures and their present lives.

First, the perception that some choose to stay because they are content and "not greedy" implies judgment on a category of migrants who are perceived to leave out of selfish desires and greed. Second, others who stay out of fear are often contrasted with capable, skillful, adventurous, and self-sacrificial migrants. Yet, this fear also reflects how they have "shame" and self-knowledge that migration is not their nasib, or that they are not suited for migration. Third, as I have elaborated (chapter 3), others who tried and failed to migrate, due to apparent inadequacies or health and physical "deficiencies," contribute to the subtle ways that bodies are valued in these villages, in relation to a person's potential capacity and eligibility to migrate. Such implicit value judgments and categories fuel desires for some to achieve success and social respectability through migration, or to pursue other efforts to earn a living in Indonesia in modest but respectable ways.

These three broad categories, perpetuated by state and media discourses, are also internalized and self-identified by migrants, return migrants, and villagers themselves. Several residents explained that their children or siblings did not migrate because they were stupid, ignorant, or lazy. Nonmigrants who told me they stayed due to fear spoke of themselves as "not mentally strong enough" (*kurang kuat mental*), and susceptible to temptations (*takut digoda*) or to becoming "addicted" to life overseas (*takut kecanduan*). The list also included fears of sickness, going missing, or never returning (a euphemism for returning dead). These fears share in common a fear of the lack of self-discipline, and anxiety about unknown, powerful, negative forces that would cause migrants to become sick, disappear, or return as corpses. Thus the faith of some in migration—and the associated emphasis on self-discipline—conversely mobilizes in others a fear of migration.

In these fears there is little room for the recognition that migrants do not labor alone in these foreign lands, and that they often will have a broader community of migrant workers, Indonesians, or labor organizations to turn to for help. Notably, prospective migrants and their kin seldom viewed local recruitment agents or the Indonesian Consulate abroad as potential sources of help should anything go wrong during a migrant's stay in other countries. Cilacap residents, in particular, seldom knew that families were entitled to insurance in the event of a migrant who returned from overseas sick, depressed, or dead. Even for those who were aware that migrants were typically insured by recruitment companies, they rarely knew how to go about seeking compensation, and nobody I knew of had access to insurance documents. In contrast, Yogyakarta villagers' many links to NGO groups and direct ties to BP3TKI substantially contributed to their awareness of medical insurance for migrants' families, alongside infrastructural help (via NGO staff and some recruitment agents) to formally file claims.

In a context where uncertainty and risk characterized the lives of many villagers in Cilacap and Yogyakarta, residents strived to change or determine their uncertain fates in diverse ways. Apart from the risky journeys that migrants embarked on, others who stayed might also participate in risky business ventures. Interdependence among kin and neighbors meant that there would always be something to eat, especially since many households had their own rice fields, or grew cassava and other edible plants and fruit on their land. Nevertheless, while many villagers usually said they had enough to eat and live on from day to day, their main sense of insecurity was in terms of the future, in anxieties about funding children's education, medical expenses, or affording important social events such as births, circumcisions, weddings, and funerals.

When I conducted the majority of my fieldwork in 2014, shrimp farms, selling distilled water, and selling coconut cakes were burgeoning and apparently profitable businesses in Yogyakarta. In Cilacap, many return migrants were starting small restaurants, selling Taiwanese, Korean, Singaporean, Malaysian, and Middle Eastern cuisine. Remittances or savings were seldom enough to establish these businesses, and many return migrants additionally relied on kin, neighbors, moneylenders, banks, or local microcredit systems for funding. These businesses were uncommon and virtually nonexistent in 2012. However, by early 2015, even as more agricultural land was being cleared to establish more shrimp farms in both Yogyakarta and Cilacap, villagers began to realize that shrimp farms were susceptible to epidemics. Farmers lost a lot of shrimp, time, and money while waiting to purify the waters from disease. In Cilacap, even as new food businesses were starting up, villagers told me that such shops were not so profitable, since locals seldom had the spending power to eat out, and were not used to foreign cuisine. Despite efforts by BNP2TKI to encourage entrepreneurship as a solution to unemployment and an increasing rate of migration in such rural areas like Cilacap and Yogyakarta, villagers said that starting businesses was risky and largely unprofitable. Yet, in the same sentence or conversation, they expressed hopes that one day they would be able to open their own shops.

The question of why villagers participate in risky migration journeys and seemingly unprofitable business ventures was the focus of Fioratta's (2015) research in the highlands of New Guinea. She argues that striving for success itself was more important than whether or not these efforts and ventures paid off. By looking at locals' criticisms of "uselessness" or "useless" persons, Fioratta argues that the highlanders' seemingly irrational decisions and economic activities make sense in the context of achieving a respectable social personhood that emerges precisely in the striving itself. These observations are partially applicable to these migrant-origin villages of Yogyakarta and Cilacap. In contrast to current migrants, or those who have small businesses or factory jobs, unemployed individuals or return migrants who do not appear to work are criticized as simply "sitting at home" (*duduk di rumah*), being lazy, or not contributing to the family's needs.[3] Conversely, striving or making an effort in these Central Javanese contexts indexes one's responsibility and sense of shame in the *attempt* to achieve a sense of social worth.

To illustrate the role of faith and morality in villagers' business or economic endeavors, profit or money that one earned was tellingly referred to as *untung* (the same word as luck), and *rejeki* (fortune). Minah, as a respected nonmigrant community leader in Yogyakarta, often gave pep talks to return migrants about business practices and attitudes. She explained to me that money was "good fortune" from God (a common refrain), but she also emphasized how, in order to be wealthy, one should not look for money, but instead look for God, and have good relations with neighbors and community members. People who "look for money" (*cari uang*) directly and purposefully end up worshipping money.[4] Minah's explanations echo Prawiranta's (2013) discussion of how Islamic-inflected niat or intention in business was expressed by Central Javanese and Sundanese entrepreneurs as being central to influencing the outcome of their endeavors.

Others strived to maintain faith in migration and make better fates through everyday acts of waiting and patience (Kwon 2015). Another element of how human effort can change one's fate includes the idea that one should endure, be patient (*sabar*), and not act impulsively (chapter 4). If one is patient, God could provide an opportunity or a sign. Cultivating patience allows for a recognition that circumstances and social relationships can change. A Yogyakarta woman who returned from Taiwan told me that her patience and faith in God as well as faith in her husband's capacity to change, enabled their marriage to survive his adultery. Despite her anger at the time, she knew that he had sinned only because his faith was not yet strong enough (*belum yakin*). But her belief in the possibility that he would eventually be loyal to her enabled them to mutually work on renewing their trust and marriage. Faith thus mediates patience and villagers' labor of waiting, in allowing for an openness towards a future that can be different from the limiting present. One example of such faith in the possibility of change is when stigmatized individuals cope with gossip and public shaming by acknowledging that "This will pass … soon people will forget," or "Soon someone else will be the target of gossip."

Depoliticizing Migrant Death and Destiny

I was first drawn to the most basic distinction villagers made between fate and destiny (takdir) when I encountered Bu Isti. Bu Isti, a former migrant woman from Yogyakarta, told me that her niece had died mysteriously in Saudi Arabia. Her niece was working as a domestic worker. The employer had hidden her body and the death, and had forbidden other employees to tell anyone about it. Her family only found out a year later when an employee, the chauffeur—who was also Indonesian—reported the death to the Indonesian Consulate after feeling haunted. When I suggested to Bu Isti that this could be a case of abuse and violence, she disagreed. She said, "If it is abuse or torture, this is usually done by the employer.… But with death, that is God's doing. This is destiny."

Hundreds of Indonesian migrants die abroad every year, ostensibly due to "accidents at work" and illness (Mahmudah 2013). Evaluations of death in general and migration-related death in particular are commonly linked, within Indonesia, to Islamic discourses about one's destiny (chapters 2 and 3).[5] I have previously highlighted how not all migrant deaths are equal: some deaths (and abuses against migrants) are seen as deserved or destined, while a minority of deaths are viewed as unjustified (chapter 2). That migrants' deaths are unequally valued is evident in public discussions of migrant women who were sentenced to death in Saudi Arabia. While some villagers may perceive this as due to destiny and divine punishment for adulterous women, others may view such death sentences as unfair, and linked to corrupt, discriminatory, and overly strict legal interpretation of Islam in Saudi Arabia. In contrast to nasib discourses, stories about deaths of migrants, migrant kin, recruitment agents, and employers can thus more strongly provoke a sense of divine justice or human injustice. As I will elaborate, evaluations of deaths were thus related to ideas about destiny or the unjust *thwarting* of one's due destiny.

Statistical data on deaths and problems faced by Indonesian migrants are often unclear and debated among government agencies as well as nongovernmental organizations (see chapter 2, note 4). Additionally, before 2015, there were no official national statistics collected on the rate of suicide in Indonesia (Jong 2014). However, in 2015, the Central Bureau of Statistics reported that the largest proportion of suicides in the country occurred in Central Java (331 out of a national estimate of 812) (Databoks 2016). The actual rate of suicide is likely much higher due to unreported incidents (ibid.). These inconsistent and unreliable data on migrant deaths and local suicides, combined with local emphasis on deaths as destined, influence how Cilacap and Yogyakarta villagers cope with local deaths by suicide or accidents, or migrants who return as dead bodies. Indonesian sociologists, anthropologists, and Health Ministry officials have criticized cultural explanations of suicide in Java, which generally represent death as inevitable and unpreventable (Darmaningtyas 2002; Puspito 2014; *Tribunnews* 2011). These scholars argue that such representations normalize preventable deaths, such as suicides, accidents, and murder.

Seeing death in terms of destiny appears to evoke a sense of resignation and acceptance. As a Yogyakarta villager whose kin died overseas said, "It's Javanese *adat*. When death happens, we should just resign ourselves. Don't ask too many questions. Talking about insurance, or autopsy.... It will only bring more pain to the [deceased's] family." Such apparent resignation is often expressed in the rhetorical question many villagers gave in brief references to migrants who died or fell sick overseas, or upon return: "Who knows?" (*Siapa tahu?*) Although I repeatedly heard such a refrain, no villagers I knew demanded autopsies of dead relatives, or official explanations for why some bodies took so long to be repatriated (in one case, three months; in another, over a year). Although scholars have emphasized that Indonesian recruitment agents often depend on their social and moral reputations for business (Lindquist 2010; Rudnyckyj 2004; Spaan 1994), I found that operating recruiters in Cilacap and Yogyakarta typically had terrible moral reputations—as liars and thieves—based on their track records with fellow villagers who migrated. Despite bad track records, including providing little information about the circumstances of migrant relatives' disappearances or deaths abroad, residents still approached these recruitment agents for help to migrate.

What accounts for the apparent collective political inaction of villagers, in the context of evident mortal, social, and economic costs of migration on families and villagers? This situation is in stark opposition to widespread labor activism particularly in Java, in the 1980s and 1990s, when workers generally organized along the lines of occupation and gender (Silvey 2003a; Tjandraningsih 2000). I disagree with the view that villagers' beliefs in destiny simply point to their passive resignation to existing socioeconomic and political disorders. Instead, as I have argued in previous chapters, villagers' discourses of destiny and fate should be contextualized in terms of how and when responsibility for migration has been institutionally and discursively dispersed and refracted. In this scenario, a partial explanation for collective inaction is that unlike factory uprisings, there is no longer a single or "external" actor to blame (Dang et al. 2013) for migrant fatalities, sickness, or debts—particularly from the viewpoint of migrant-origin villages. Even in the example of migrants sentenced to death in Saudi Arabia, or cases that might formally qualify as "trafficking," villagers, migrant activists, and state representatives are aware that the Indonesian state, local recruitment agents, and extended family relations are implicated, to varying degrees, in women's migratory journeys (Ford and Lyons 2012; Palmer 2012).

Villagers' acknowledgement of a complex migration infrastructure is evident in stories of death that are recounted simply to remind others that even the best laid plans fail. Such tragic stories of sickness and death partly serve to remind migrant-origin villagers and migrants that they have limited control over the outcomes of their efforts, and ultimately God is in control of a migrant worker's destiny to succeed or fail, live or die. One such story with no clear moral takeaway was the following, told to me by a Yogyakarta nonmigrant, about her migrant neighbor.

A migrant domestic worker in Saudi Arabia regularly sent money home for her only child, a son, to get a good education. Her son graduated from high school with above average grades. Pleased, his migrant mother sent even more money for him to buy a motorbike when he turned eighteen. Unfortunately, a few days before she returned for Idul Fitri holidays, her son got into a road accident and died instantly. To this resident, the migrant had failed in her migratory project because she had lost her son—the reason for which she migrated in the first place.[6] The story was made more tragic by the fact that this migrant had bought the motorbike for her son with her remittances, which ultimately led him to his death.

It may be that most villagers accept deaths because they believe that no action can bring the dead back to life. Yet, attributing death to destiny may also be a way that villagers negotiate the uncertainties of migration, through emphasizing individual strategies of self-discipline, and highlighting the limits of human agency to cope with and avoid certain risks. Of course, some residents do acknowledge the responsibility of and place blame on the Indonesian and foreign states for perpetuating these precarious labor migrations, particularly former migrants, failed migrants, and individuals involved previously or currently with the political and social activism of NGOs. Nonetheless, as noted in chapter 3, former migrants who have had sustained interactions and experiences with NGOs are also often those who qualify as "failed" migrants who encountered NGOs due to circumstances in which they needed assistance regarding their (un)documented status or working conditions. As such, such persons may withdraw from explicitly defending other "failed" migrants in political terms—such as attributing blame to states or recruitment or labor laws—so as not to draw attention to or publicly recall their own less than ideal migratory experiences. Nevertheless, as I elaborate below, villagers' vague acknowledgment of state complicity and inefficacy regarding migration's problems ground their discourses of fate and destiny. Talk of fate and destiny are also productive of faith in alternative and hope-filled futures. Through refrains of nasib and takdir, residents learn to live with and negotiate the social and physical costs of migration, while maintaining hope in its promises in a socioeconomic context where alternative pathways are limited and political action is experienced as ineffective.

Locating Responsibility, Agency, and Hope

Migrants' deaths and failures are often linked to sickness (*sakit*)—either their own or a member of their family. Explanations of sickness—sickness etiologies—often involve moral rationales in many social contexts, and in Java, sickness is also often associated with supernatural or spiritual issues (Nitibaskara 1993). This section focuses on sickness etiologies in Cilacap and Yogyakarta to examine some ways in which residents employ narratives of sickness and injury to variously locate responsibility, agency, and hope in relation to migration. Sickness etiologies often imply that migrants and their families can insure against physical, financial, and moral risks of migration by performing gendered moral expectations and practicing religious faith.

Narratives of migration-related sickness do not only serve to blame, shame, or cast judgment on migrants and their kin. Some stories may not target individuals, but criticize circumstances where migration is perceived to disrupt normative familial structures or deprive individuals of social support from or companionship of their migrant kin. A local "cautionary tale" in Yogyakarta involved a neighbor whose wife and daughter were both working in Taiwan. He was a bit "stressed" (*stres*, an Indonesian term borrowed from the English language, usually used as a euphemism for someone who is mentally unstable) due to loneliness and being left behind (see Good and Brodwin 1994; Klein 1988). Whenever his wife returned, however, he appeared well again and the house was often peaceful and quiet, with no domestic arguments. While such tales also contain or imply cautions against adultery, divorce, negligent parents, or unfilial, ungrateful children, they mainly highlight ways migration can disrupt social and familial harmony and order. The moral aspect of these sickness diagnoses is evident in how the suggested "cures" (*obat*) involve exhortations for people to be religiously pious (*taqwa*), to fulfill familial obligations, or formally ask others for forgiveness for any wrongdoings (*minta maaf*). This tale in particular criticizes the necessity of the wife and daughter to migrate for work, though the tale leaves ambiguous whether structural conditions or individual agency is to blame for their migrations. Regardless, the tale expresses the "evidence" as well as the hope that when migration objectives are accomplished, and the man's wife and daughter finally return home for good, he, and individuals like him, will be healthy and whole again.

Sickness etiologies are thus also narratives of and responses to uncertainty and risk in a context where migration and recruitment processes are experienced as uneven and unstandardized. Villagers' focus on individual and divine agency in times of sickness reflects their awareness of and responses to the multiple and powerful political, economic, and social constraints that produce their structural vulnerability. Perceptions and evaluations of migration-related sickness must be understood and contextualized in relation to medical tests that migrants are subjected to prior to migration. When migrants return to Indonesia physically or psychologically unwell, neighbors and kin reasonably attribute the sickness directly to conditions abroad or the processes of migration, due to the common acknowledgment that only physically and psychologically "fit" and healthy individuals were allowed to leave the country to work in the first place.

According to the Presidential Regulation of the Placement and Protection of Migrant Workers 2004, migrant candidates should undergo certified physical and psychological medical checkups in order to be formally placed with an employer overseas (Articles 31, 50, and 51). In practice, the medical examinations are not formally regulated or standardized. Medical certificates can be and often are falsified by doctors and clinics, since recruitment agencies can select which medical practitioners to affiliate with. Due to the lack of formal standardization or elaboration on what such medical tests entail, some of these checkups are simply "cursory visual health inspection[s]" (Rudnyckyj 2004, 416), or based on recruiters' subjective observations that female migrant candidates have the "mental capacity" to be domestic workers (ibid.). Indeed, a female former migrant worker from Wonosobo who often accompanied her neighbors on such clinic visits told me that some of these medical checkups were as rudimentary as "Open your eyes, open your mouth, and you pass."

Since some prospective migrants do not undergo thorough medical examinations or even go for the examinations at all (in the event of false or "bought" certificates), women in their early days of pregnancy may be allowed to migrate despite national regulations forbidding pregnant women to do so (Article 35, U/U 39/2004). In these cases, women may realize that they are pregnant only months after arriving in the country of destination, and husbands and kin in Indonesia may doubt that the child is fathered by her husband. Such a situation can happen in migrants' destination countries where medical examinations are also not standardized. In Singapore, however, prospective migrants are also subjected to medical examinations before they can work. These tests are mainly to detect cases of pregnancy or sexual and other contagious diseases. A migrant from Wonosobo had passed the lax medical tests in Indonesia, but her early pregnancy was detected by medical practitioners in Singapore. As a result, she was deported immediately to Indonesia, without a day's work or pay, and deeply indebted to her recruitment agents.

The lack of standardization in medical examinations in Indonesia was perceived by prospective migrants as both a bane and boon. For those who had known medical conditions such as asthma, the inability to pass a more stringent medical test in Yogyakarta only meant that they could try their luck in other cities or recruitment agencies known for their lax or corrupt medical examination processes. The loosely regulated practices of clinics thus offered them hope and opportunity that despite their health problems, there might be alternative ways to migrate with all the required documents. Yet, other prospective migrants might find the latter medical examinations unfair, since medical practitioners might label all candidates "unfit" to migrate unless they are bribed to provide a fraudulent medical certificate.

The unevenness with which medical certificates are issued contributes to an Indonesian migration landscape where prospective migrants navigate a great deal of ambivalence and uncertainty. Even upon receiving news from clinics that they are physically or psychologically "unfit," migrant applicants often do not have the means to determine (and thus file complaints about) whether or not the report is reliable or simply based on routine and corrupt procedures aimed at extorting more money from them. Importantly, the medical certificate is only one of many documents that prospective migrants require in order to "legally" migrate via state-recognized recruitment agencies.

Although return migrants, kin, neighbors, and migrant activists might explain mental or physical illnesses due to individual biology, vices, or moral weaknesses, sickness narratives also often explicitly comment on the broader structural landscape of migration and illness. These include references to financial anxieties due to familial conflict, the lack of stable employment opportunities locally, and an awareness that the types of work migrants do are largely confined to "undesirable" labor that is dirty, difficult, and dangerous, and thus, work that risks migrants' health and lives. It is important to understand migration-related suffering and illness as intimate and shared, in the sense that migrants and their kin can experience a heightened sense of loneliness in their physical and mental ailments, and shared moral and financial pressures (Duncan 2015). The conditions of suffering are also intersubjective, due to the importance of social circumstances and obligations influencing whether or not persons experience hardship as exploitation or self-sacrifice, and whether or not they experience and interpret hallucinations as due to mental illness or as a result of spirit possession and black magic. Most Central Javanese villagers I spoke to were aware of the risks of "stress" resulting from the specific kinds of work migrants do abroad. Nevertheless, villagers tended to emphasize and circulate rumors about supernatural, divine, or individual moral causes behind such sickness.

In several forums organized by former migrants' associations to exchange information about migration practices and entrepreneurial opportunities, former migrants highlighted that migration requires great patience and mental strength in the face of temptations and harsh working conditions (see also Prusinski 2016b). Prospective migrants acknowledged that the spiritual and emotional support of neighbors and kin, as well as divine or supernatural protection are essential to safe migratory journeys and their path towards seeking good employment and wages abroad. Thus a farewell ritual for most Central Javanese is to go from door to door in the village to informally ask for "permission" and blessings for their journey (*pamit*). Sometimes, especially if it is an individual's first time, his or her family might organize ritual feasting (*slametan*) to ensure a safe migration journey, to bring the migrant fortune, as well as to prevent spirit possession. Some migrants might also bring charms with them as a form of protection against bad spirits.

Under conditions of relative poverty, risk, and uncertainty, prospective migrants, return migrants, and their kin tend to focus on what they perceive is within their control—cultivating individual mental strength and moral discipline, as well as faith in divine agency and divine justice. Expressions of faith in supernatural and divine agency can be viewed as suspensions, displacements, and reconfigurations of human agency in shaping and renewing hope for their futures, whether overseas or in Indonesia. Below, I describe three broad kinds of local interpretations of and responses to migration-related sicknesses: 1) as divine justice or intervention, 2) in terms of spirit possession or madness due to the patient's or victim's lack of or weak self-discipline, and 3) as mainly the work of God and spirits, where individual, collective, and state responsibilities are temporarily downplayed and dismissed.

Divine Interventions

Many villagers gave me examples of "mysterious" or spiritual healings that supported their perceptions that religious piety and practice can and often do ensure physical health. One story involved a former migrant woman from Cilacap who worked in Singapore and was diagnosed with HIV. The former migrant woman who told me the story defended her friend's honor, and said that the virus was not due to the woman's fault—her boyfriend had secretly had multiple sexual partners and she had caught the virus from him. Since her diagnosis, she escaped to Batam, where she worked in a hotel. Though she kept her illness a secret from her family, some close friends knew about it. Fellow Indonesian migrants visited her in Batam and claimed that she looked "too well" and healthy for someone diagnosed with HIV.[7] She seemed happy, and the salary she earned was enough for her to support her family and her disabled brother. The mystery or miracle of how this "sick" girl could appear so healthy was explained to me in terms of her favor with God, and that she must have received God's blessing.

Conversely, there were numerous stories of ill-intentioned or deceptive recruitment agents and employers who mysteriously fell ill. Their illness was often framed in terms of divine moral retribution for their sins and wrongdoings against others. Rendra from Yogyakarta, who was in his early thirties, had tried to migrate to Korea twice and to Japan once. All of these attempts failed. The second time that he tried to go to Korea he lost 38 million rupiah (approx. USD 3,800) that he had paid the recruitment agent. Upon realizing that he had been conned and was not likely to go to Korea, he went to the agent's house to demand compensation. However, the agent was not home, and her family informed Rendra that she was hospitalized. At first, Rendra thought the family was simply lying to avoid a confrontation, so he went to the hospital to verify their claim. To his surprise, it was true: he saw the agent herself lying in a hospital ward in Yogyakarta city. She had just had a heart transplant. Her husband, who worked with her in the same recruitment business, was also very ill around the same time. He had suffered a sudden stroke, and was also hospitalized. Rendra left the hospital surprised by how God had punished the scheming couple who stole his hard-earned savings.

These narratives of sickness and healing commonly point to the idea that divine or social justice prevailed, despite irreversible circumstances. The woman with HIV cannot be cured, but she found a way to continue fulfilling her familial duties without causing them great shame. While Rendra's narrative of the deceptive agent's sickness was one of divine punishment, he simultaneously expressed resignation, as it would now be unlikely that he would recover his financial losses. These narratives suggest villagers' recognition of the limits of addressing the gendered and structural circumstances of their shame or failures. Yet, they also provide discursive and embodied ways for individuals to negotiate some measure of agency and justice.

Self-Discipline, Madness, and Spirit Possession

Stories about spirit possession and mental illness were common and closely interrelated in Cilacap and Yogyakarta. These stories often invoked fear and exacerbated or confirmed sources of anxiety and ambiguity about particular social phenomena. Spirit possession and mental illness are sometimes referred to as *ngamuk* in research on Indonesia, which Kevin Browne argues "sometimes work[s] to marginalize those suffering from mental/emotional affliction by designating them as mentally ill" but also "provides a culturally meaningful dialogue on the politics of emotion currently at play" (2001, 158). For example, residents told me that spirit possession was common in Islamic boarding schools (*pesantren*), due to the ways that the schools were "isolating" for the students, particularly girls, since they had to be away from their family for such long periods of time. When such spirit possession occurred in boys' pesantren, they were linked to some Cilacap villagers' suspicions that religious leaders in specific cities were using the pesantren to radicalize boys into committing violent jihad, which was unacceptable and wrong for many of their parents. Thus, talk about spirit possession, its causes, and consequences often reveal people's ambivalent feelings, which, in this case, centered on the question of whether or not families should send their children to pesantren, despite the associated prestige, and the well-known benefits of producing pious and disciplined Muslims.

Villagers' ambivalence towards migration was also evident from stories about spirit possession and mental illness involving prospective, current, and former migrants. I met May when she wandered into Nurul's home one day in her dressing gown. May was a woman in her early forties from Cilacap, and she had worked in Taiwan for eight years. Speaking in an incoherent mix of Mandarin and Indonesian, she told Nurul and me that she loved us very much. She said that her daughter was getting married, and that she herself was going to be a grandmother soon. As May grabbed a pillow and mimed breastfeeding a baby, Nurul told me that this was all part of May's active imagination—none of her story was true. Nurul gave her some fruit to take home, explaining to me that May's husband seemed to deprive her of sustenance, in addition to locking her up at home. Nevertheless, May sometimes managed to wander outdoors to ask her neighbors for food. It was public knowledge that when May returned from Taiwan, she was largely "normal," but went "crazy" (*gila*) only after she found out that her husband had spent all her remittances and left her no savings. Villagers spoke of how May's husband had engaged a local dhukun (healer) to cast black magic on her, making her blind and mad. May's neighbors also reportedly witnessed her husband physically hitting her and throwing plates at her. Although her relatives had sent her to a traditional healer, the healer only managed to partially salvage her eyesight, but not her mental faculties.[8]

"Why didn't her family help? Why does May still live with her husband? What about her parents or siblings?" I asked. Nurul replied, "Her family blames her for her own downfall, since she was foolish enough to trust her husband. You see, May sent him all her money from Taiwan, while her family did not get a single cent. They were angry and jealous. For them, her madness is a kind of punishment or retribution." The rejection and moral condemnation of May by her own family was harsh, but not so uncommon among those who experience mental health issues. Her circumstances exemplify the abuse and isolation that mentally unstable migrants may face upon return.

May's situation within the village points to how migrants' sickness can be attributed to multiple causes, whether by traditional medical practitioners, villagers in Yogyakarta and Cilacap, or the state. Discussions of sickness in Indonesia often provoke informal evaluations about the sick person's daily habits and regular activities, sometimes including relationships at home, at work, with other neighbors, with spirits, God, or Satan (Lee 2001). Mental illness provokes and highlights multiple and sometimes competing understandings of the causes of illness, and methods of healing. Looking at perceptions of mental illness in Central Java throws into relief what the stakes are for villagers who choose or prioritize one explanation over another, especially when possible explanations for sickness seem incompatible (Hunt and Mattingly 1998). For example, a person's hysteria may be caused by severe guilt due to sin, genetic predisposition, or overwork and abuse abroad. In contrast, other forms of predictable and preventable physical sickness such as diabetes and high blood pressure may be attributed both to bad diet, as well as to individuals' moral character such as laziness or overdependence and exploitation of a migrant kin. These reasons are in fact complementary, regardless of whether villagers emphasize one or another, or disagree about which factors "came first."

Discussions of other kinds of sickness share much in common with those of mental illness in the ways that sickness is commonly attributed to familial shame and the structural circumstances of an individual's life, such as poverty, debt, and forms of overwork in menial or domestic labor industries where low wages and long hours are the norm. Apparently incurable (physical) diseases and untimely or unexpected sickness or death, may also invite explanations regarding spirit or magical attacks, or divine justice and punishment. While there is more social stigma attached to mental illness, the perceived causes of all illness have implications for effective methods of healing and treatment. Perceived causes affect people's strategies in dealing with not only the sickness, but also sick individuals. Sickness etiologies in Indonesia must be contextualized in relation to its biomedical and traditional medical industries, social stigma associated with mental illness and suicide, and how state representatives deal with and respond to sickness and death. Relevant to this chapter's discussion is that attributions of spirit and magical attacks in migrant-related cases were not only speculative, diagnostic, or discursive. They were also productive of fear and faith, in deterring ambivalent villagers from deciding to leave, while mobilizing faith in others who are determined or pressured to migrate.

The predominant understanding of mental illness in Central Java, and arguably throughout the Indonesian archipelago, is that these cases are caused by spirit attacks or black magic. Such explanations—as described above in May's situation—are often accompanied by the recognition that these individuals are likely already susceptible to such attacks, in either having offended someone through their own attitudes, words, or actions, or in being mentally and spiritually vulnerable to attacks by feeling stressed, dreamy, or confused (*bingung*) (Lee 2001, 118; Browne 2001). Villagers distinguish between temporary spirit attacks, in which spirits may enter and leave a human body within minutes or within an hour, and spirit possession, in which spirits tend to stay for a much longer time. It is the latter phenomenon that Cilacap and Yogyakarta villagers associate with a more damaging problem for the individual and community—that of mental illness (*mental tidak sehat*, or simply, *punya mental*) or "brain damage" (*otaknya rusak*). The majority of villagers and urban migrant activists I spoke to were skeptical that mentally ill persons can ever fully recover from their conditions, though they acknowledged that biomedicine or traditional healers may reduce the symptoms or temporarily cure the patient (see also Good et al. 2010, 66–67).

Fears of spirit possession associated with mental illness and suicide are likely driven by the social stigma of mental illness. "Soul sickness" (*sakit jiwa*) or "crazy" people (*orang gila*) are associated with violent outbursts, hysteria, talking to themselves, talking to others about improbable past, present, or future events, and general incoherence. Across the archipelago, persons with serious mental disorders typically also experience domestic violence, such as physical or verbal abuse by their kin. In a press interview, Irmansyah, a scholar and the Health Ministry mental health chief in 2012, explained that "Some families restrain their ill family members to prevent harm to others and the sufferer.... This is done because the patient is usually an embarrassment to the family" (Faizal 2012a; *Jakarta Post* 2010a). While most mentally unstable and depressed individuals in the Cilacap and Yogyakarta villages were nonviolent, I observed that they were largely avoided and were associated with fearful supernatural phenomena such as "talking to themselves" or "hearing spirits' whispers." Although the state, national media, and international health and development organizations have recently increased efforts to educate citizens on biomedical models of mental illness, many sufferers, such as May, still have very limited or no access to medical treatment.

Not all spirit attacks are considered mental illness. In nearly all stories that take place in domestic workers' predeparture training centers (*penampungan*), women either witnessed or personally experienced spirit attacks. In these episodes, the attacked person may suddenly faint, scream, cry hysterically, or tremble visibly, before "acting like a completely different person." Women who were tired, stressed, hungry, dreamy, or worried were the target of these spirit attacks, since they were perceived as vulnerable and weak. These women usually served as a medium for spirits' communication to the other prospective migrants at the center, conveying messages such as tidying up the place, or obeying certain instructions in order to prevent the spirits from harassing them again (cf. Ong 2010). I suggested to former migrants in Cilacap and Yogyakarta who shared their personal experiences with spirits in the centers that maybe some women were experiencing psychological problems, and might already be susceptible to hallucinations prior to entering the training centers. One former migrant categorically rejected my suggestion, explaining, "It cannot be due to sakit jiwa. Everyone who is in there passed their medical tests, right? They are all fit." Except for a Yogyakarta-based recruitment agent, all persons I spoke to on this subject said that spirit attacks in women's training centers could not be attributed to psychological issues.

The effects and consequences of spirit attacks in women's predeparture training centers followed a standard pattern, according to the stories told to me by dozens of former migrant women. Spirits were often chased away by reciting Islamic prayers either by an individual or by the women as a group. As a result of the spirit attacks, victims and other women became more explicitly mutually accountable and responsible for one another. After the attacks, women emphasized that a way of coping and finding mutual support was for everyone to focus on their tasks, not think too much about their families or financial worries, to be mentally resilient, to follow the rules of the center, and to maintain order in their rooms and the center in general. In these stories, spirits were always women, and the majority of these spirits were women rumored to have died in the compound as a result of either overwork or suicide. Former migrant women typically mentioned an "eerie" and "unclean" atmosphere about the training centers, including details about illicit graveyards in the garden where the staff and owners of these recruitment and training agencies presumably hid the deaths of prospective migrants from their families.[9]

These stories provide some context for understanding that even though these spirit attacks were nearly always temporary, the perceived presence of spirits in training centers meant that women lived in fear of actual and more damaging and permanent spirit possession, which could lead to untimely death or suicide. This fear of being permanently possessed or influenced by spirits shaped women's attitudes and actions in the training center in many ways. It not only helped them build solidarity against these attacks, it also often resulted in practical strategies to cope with homesickness, and to endure the long hours and poor living conditions of the training centers, sometimes by being more attentive and meticulous workers and trainees. While there were sometimes cases of women who ran away with or without the help of fellow candidates or their family members, the most commonly cited response to spirit attacks—and to the conditions in general—in these centers was collective prayers, and collectively produced discipline through mutual care (cf. Ong 2010).

I argue that such strategies of self-discipline to ward off spirits and avoid possession reflect women's awareness of broader structural disorders within the Indonesian migration industry and state. This includes awareness about their limited options to change their minds about migrating, to change recruitment agents, or to inform relevant authorities and neighbors about things their narratives often involved: mistreatment, lack of food and access to communications, unhygienic living conditions, and "illegal" graveyards. Police reports were viewed as ineffective since police often worked to "protect" illegal or blacklisted recruitment agencies (Gunawan 2015). There were few consistent or thorough efforts by relevant state agencies to monitor or standardize training processes or living conditions in such centers. Running away from the centers risked great financial debt and social stigma as failed migrants (see chapters 3 and 4).

Return migrants perceived as having severe mental health issues are sometimes identified by immigration officers at ports or airports upon return. They are then referred to BNP2TKI officials, or prominent migrant-centered NGOs.

These organizations may direct the return migrant to the nearest mental health hospital, usually RPTC in Jakarta (Rumah Perlindungan Trauma Center). According to the chief of the Ministry of Social Protection and Social Security (*Perlindungan dan Jaminan Sosial Kemensos*), all irregular migrants, upon return, must undergo a medical checkup in RPTC before returning to their hometowns. Return migrants typically stay at the center for two weeks at most, and longer stays are accommodated to suit patients' specific "physical and mental conditions" (*Detik News* 2014). However, resources and training for health-care staff at RPTC seem woefully inadequate to address the long-term effects and the possibility of reintegration into families and society for return migrants upon leaving the center. Such necessary reintegration processes, which includes informing and educating migrants' kin on mental health issues, or working conditions abroad, were sometimes voluntarily facilitated by staff from women's or migrant-centered NGOs.

The figure of the dangerous and "crazy" return migrant and the ever-present threat of spirit attacks on migrants in training centers, overseas workplaces, and also upon return home produce ways to manage migration-related fears for some Yogyakarta and Cilacap residents. Explanations of why and how spirit attacks or mental illness occur serve to fuel as well as domesticate fears associated with psychological and spiritual costs of migration. May, for example, served as a local moral precautionary tale that married migrants—especially women—are still obliged to partially provide for their parents and siblings who need or request financial help. Women's transnational migration has clearly changed Javanese women's financial obligations towards their parents and siblings. Previously, women's monetary household contributions had never been so important to their social status and familial relations, though scholars have noted greater familial dependence on women's autonomous income as rural women's factory work grew more common in the 1990s (compare Wolf 1992 in Java; Elmhirst 2002 in South Sumatra). May's social abandonment reminded neighbors that although marriage and motherhood are important social identity markers for women, the long-term emotional and social support of parents and siblings are also fundamental to ensuring one's social recognition in the community, particularly in a context where migration is seen as a risk to marital stability. Similarly, stories of spirit attacks and possessions always imply other practical and pious strategies to avoid becoming a target of such attacks.

Downplaying Individual, Collective, and State Responsibility

Amidst such harsh judgements and treatment of those with mental health problems, narratives of suicide offer insights into more sympathetic attitudes towards mental or emotional instability and spirit possession. In all of the stories

I encountered, suicide was partially attributed to spirit possession or satanic influence. When Nurul's relative hung himself from a tree in the back garden, his suicide was generally understood by residents to be related to his financial debt and marital conflict. However, Nurul and her neighbor also suggested that his death was not entirely of his volition, since he was said to be "not like himself" or "not normal" immediately prior to the incident.

When the deceased's family pieced together the events leading to his suicide, they noted that he had seemed confused, restless, and unaware of his own surroundings. A relative heard him talking to himself or to an unseen presence, and he had seemed unsure of how he got to his relative's house in the first place. He spent the days prior to his death sleeping, unmoved, on a couch. Some villagers also noticed that when his body was hanging from the tree, his eyes were wide open, which they took as a sign of a spirit attack. Nurul suggested that he was able to hang himself without being noticed by others only because of supernatural influence. Sometimes spirits could make bodies invisible, or alter others' perceptions of them, in such a way that explained why neighbors only noticed the dead body an hour after it happened. Such collective participation in reconstructing the man's suicide suggested efforts to partially exonerate him for the act of suicide, which constitutes a grave sin to most Muslims. This explanation of his suicide which focuses more on spirit possession than on human agency importantly shifts blame away from individual shame and cowardice. Instead, Nurul's relative emerged as a sympathetic character who was concerned about his family's financial future, but was momentarily confused and vulnerable to a malicious spirit attack.

Ultimately, Nurul was convinced that her brother-in-law had died because he had been possessed. For months after the incident, she and some neighbors lived in fear of nearby spirits and ghosts. For a while they prayed more fervently to keep the spirits away, and asked for God's protection. Thus, stories of illness or death caused by spirit or magical attacks can mobilize concerned others to perform acts of faith. This pertains not only to faith in God (and the preventive or healing properties of individual and communal prayer), but also to a lesser degree to faith in spirit ancestors and the power of local traditional healers or sorcerers.[10]

Collective interpretation and reconstructions of suicide can also undermine the potential of such desperate acts to serve for communities and families as a critical commentary on the effects of shame and stigma in relation to debt, failed masculine roles, and marital conflict. Stories attributing suicide to spirit possession obviate the potential benefits of social support for those deemed vulnerable to mental illness, "confusion," and the influence of spirits. Although emphases on supernatural agency behind acts of suicide can help to reduce the shame potentially confronting the deceased and his or her kin, such narratives can also serve to normalize suicide as an act that "makes sense" in the context of the man's worries and the nature of certain spirits (Darmaningtyas 2002; *Republika* 2011). Narratives and discussions of spirit attack and possession thus often appear contradictory, with paradoxical effects on how villagers seek preventative or healing measures.

The state was seldom cited as a factor in explaining more serious forms of sickness confronting migrants and nonmigrants, although as mentioned earlier, residents may include financial debt, family conflict, conditions of training centers, and hard work (at home or abroad) as likely causes alongside supernatural factors. Except for cases where the mass media or NGOs intervened, state institutions were seldom explicitly considered part of the problem or the solution to migration-related processes (such as training center conditions) and illness. The absence of the state in these sickness narratives and healing strategies suggests a lack of faith in the state's ability to address the everyday medical, financial, spiritual, or social concerns of villagers of Yogyakarta and Cilacap. In place of the state's unreliability, social networks provide a critical safety net when dealing with uncertain futures (Dang et al. 2013, 65). In his study of rural poverty, Geof Wood argues that "risk management in the present involves loyalty to institutions and organizations that presently work and deliver livelihoods, whatever the long term cost" (cited in Dang et al. 2013, 665). Like other rural poor, Cilacap and Yogyakarta villagers enter into a "Faustian bargain" with commercial recruitment agencies and informal migrant brokers, who may be a kin, friend, or neighbor. Faith discourses and practices enable villagers to negotiate and live with the financial, physical, social, and moral costs and risks of migration, while remaining acquiescent to and less explicitly critical of social and migratory institutions that offer access to livelihoods and promises of socioeconomic mobility.

Developing Faith in Migration

Scholars have observed how religion plays a central role in framing the migratory experiences, trajectories, and subjectivities of migrants in destination countries (Aguilar 1999; Johnson 2010; Liebelt 2008; Pingol 2010). Migrants draw on faith narratives or the support of religious communities in destination countries to endure and sometimes justify harsh working and living environments abroad. In contrast, I have shown how in migrants' villages of origin in Central Java, residents also develop, mobilize, and practice faith as a strategy to negotiate risks and shame associated with migration, return, and staying behind. NGOs, state officials, and some scholars tend to explain migrants' risky migratory decisions in terms of their ignorance, lack of relevant information, extreme poverty, greed, or "gamblers'" agency (Aguilar 1999; Cohen and Sirecki 2011; Suzuki 2003; Stoll 2013; Massey et al. 2005). Instead of simply reflecting obliviousness or superstition, I argue that villagers' fate and faith narratives enable them to act in pragmatic and strategic ways.

In Central Java, nasib or fate often implies human effort in relation to divine agency, while takdir or destiny emphasizes the ultimate authority of God in human life and strivings. The multiple and context-specific uses of these faith narratives can serve to overemphasize, suspend, or displace the role of individual's agency in their present life circumstances, with reference to nonhuman actors. On the one hand, acknowledging supernatural and divine agency encourages a sense of resignation and fatality, particularly when individuals have already been possessed or are very ill. On the other hand, such recognition of the limits of human agency mobilizes faith in the preventive or redemptive power of Islamic (and to a lesser degree, Javanese) prayers, chants, and rituals. Local discussions of suicide and mental illness illustrate how resignation and faith-driven human efforts, blame and empathy, are not contradictory but constitutive of one another.

Despite the lack of explicit criticism of the state and labor regimes, villagers' discussions of fate and destiny are grounded in an awareness and acknowledgment of the complicity and partial responsibility of employers, recruitment agents, and state institutions when things go wrong for migrants. Instead of fully articulated critiques of exploitation in class or feminist terms, villagers' talk about fate, destiny, and spirit possession are partial yet ultimately ineffective responses to the state's failure to guarantee villagers' transnational security or livelihoods (cf. Ong 2010). In the absence of alternative access to livelihoods, fate and faith discourses are tactics to assert and defend one's moral status when migrants confront an exploitative, risky, yet potentially rewarding migration landscape (ibid.). The example of spirit possession, however, is a clear example of how discourses of religiously inflected moral discipline and faith can produce collective action and solidarity through communal prayer and mutual care and attentiveness. Besides commenting on broader social and political disorders, in such scenarios spirit possession and responses to the phenomenon focus on the limits of individual responsibility vis-à-vis unpredictable human and nonhuman actors. These situations highlight the ways that neighbors, kin, and peers share precarious lives and specific circumstances, and suggest that mutual care and solidarity could be an effective way to confront vulnerability.

Villagers' labors of faith and faithful labor morally sustain and shape the transnational circulation of human bodies, labor, and finance. Instead of focusing on how migrants and kin make individual or household-based decisions and arrangements (Hoang et al. 2013; Massey et al. 2005; Paul 2015), I have highlighted the importance of villagers' collective discursive processes of "making move and letting stop" (Salter 2013), as well as how these processes allow certain forms of life and death to continue. Narratives of fate, destiny, and faith are villagers' attempts to collectively explain and reduce migration's "collateral damage," in deterring some to go while managing fears and producing discipline in others. Simultaneously, they also serve to maintain faith in the "Faustian bargain" with migration-related agents and institutions, for the promises of migration's eventual rewards.

Notes

1. Despite their differences in age (the NGO staff member was in her early thirties while workshop participants were women largely between the ages of thirty and fifty), the NGO staff member was able to adopt a relatively authoritative position vis-à-vis the participants due to her educated and urban background, as well as her role in the workshop to "educate" the mainly rural women participants who had received little or no formal education.

2. Since nasib is an Indonesian word, it is also used by non-Muslim Indonesians, such as Christians and Catholics. Nonetheless, how nasib draws on takdir, is contrasted to takdir, and influences discussions of morality in Central Java is linked to Islamic discourses propagated by regionally influential Muslim leaders. Muslim sermons in Java as elsewhere often emphasize that the doing of deeds in conjunction with faith is important to gaining favor with God (see Chittick 2001). How villagers' "efforts" are performed and viewed in terms of such "deeds" are thus heavily influenced by Muslim gendered discourses as discussed in other chapters.

3. A similar example is found in Julie Chu's (2010) fieldwork in a migrant-origin Fuzhounese village in China. Chu argues that young men in their twenties and thirties who stay behind are viewed as incapable, hardly even perceived as men, partially due to the fact that they seem to have "nothing to do" (242–256). In her account, villagers go so far as to deny that there are any men in the village who wish to stay or do not wish to migrate. Thus nearly all men are deemed as desiring to migrate, but those who fail to do so in their productive years pass on their migratory aspirations to children before they can deflect a sense of shame, or in the Chinese cultural context, a lack of "face" in being a nonmigrant man (ibid.).

4. Iwan Prawiranta, in his dissertation on microfinance among rural villagers, argues that an Islamic moral framework is central to the business ethics of rural Central Javanese and Sundanese residents. He found that many Muslim respondents spoke about faith, intention, and effort in approaching their business practices. Thus work or business in contemporary Indonesia's entrepreneurial economy is reconfigured as an act of devotion (*ibadah*), where faith, through practicing the right intention and effort, will hopefully result in God's blessings and a profit (2013, 137; see also Rudnyckyj 2010).

5. Interestingly, in other Islamic contexts of migration, migrants also frame death in terms of destiny, and thus completely beyond one's control (Hernández-Carretero and Carling 2012).

6. The narrator had begun this story by saying that her neighbour too was a "failed migrant."

7. It is likely she was taking antiretroviral drugs, but I was unable to confirm this. Current medical research acknowledges that not all persons diagnosed with HIV exhibit symptoms (Johns Hopkins Medical Institutions 2008).

8. Dukhuns have generally been defined as healers, but a more accurate translation is: "practioners who are recognized as specialists and are labeled according to whether they treat certain specific conditions or perform according to the sources of their specialist power: possession by spirits, ownership of magical items, innate skill, and so on" (Nitibaskara 1993, 125). Dhukuns who deal with supernatural forces are also typically categorized in terms of black (dark) magic (*sihir*) or white magic (*putih*). Others may be experts in more practical matters such as childbirth, making land fertile, preventing bad luck, or preparation of traditional medicine.

9. These stories were supported by news reports about police recovering corpses and human remains in some predeparture training camps. See for example, Probo 2014; *Republika* 2014.

10. As mentioned in chapter 1, in Cilacap, *kejawen* was in the extreme minority, and only some elders practised Javanist animism. Despite increasing outward rejection of Javanism as being incompatible with Islam, I observed that some Cilacap villagers still subscribed to many Javanism-linked beliefs about spirits, and sometimes turned to local men known to be knowledgeable about such affairs to advise them on matters of "luck" and healing. Despite the endurance of some such obviously syncretic Javanese-Muslim practices, it was much more common for residents to posit a dichotomy between Muslims and Javanists.

6 Contesting the Terms of Belonging: Views of/from Elsewhere

"I worked hard for this family, for the children.... I've never asked for anything else. All I want is a divorce."

> —Overheard, Anisa, a migrant woman in her late 30s who recently returned from Taiwan, shouting at her husband, Cilacap.

"Before I left [Taiwan], we [my employers and I] cried and cried. They understood I had to leave because I have family too in Indonesia.... Why did it have to be like this? It was like we were fated to be, you know, *yuan fen*, and it was so sad that we had to part....[1] I was really at home there. They took me as part of the family."

> —Titin, a migrant woman in her late 30s who recently returned from Taiwan, Yogyakarta.

"I just want to see the world.... I think I'm just really bored here, there's nothing to do."

> —Indah, a prospective migrant woman in her mid 20s who tried and failed to migrate, Cilacap.

MIGRATION MAY CREATE new differences and exacerbate existing ones, not only in terms of material wealth, but also diverging gendered behavior and related moral-religious perspectives. In the preceding chapters, I have suggested ways that migrant-origin villagers were aware—to varying degrees—of the working and living conditions of migrants abroad. This chapter explores the villagers' views of foreign places and the threats they pose. Cilacap and Yogyakarta residents do not only attribute blame or responsibility for migrants' successes or failures to divine agency, recruitment agencies, or migrants themselves. They also locate such blame or responsibility in foreign employers and foreign countries, which is evident through their representations and discussions of "foreign" gender and sexual practices. Such talk often encodes knowledge about different immigration and labor regulations abroad, which villagers may attribute to foreign "cultural" norms. Discussions among former migrants and nonmigrants about foreign gender and sexual norms may challenge, reaffirm, or destabilize ideas about what kinds of gendered relations are locally acceptable, such as divorce and premarital cohabitation.

Through such work of imagining the self in relation to others, migration presents wider alternative venues and possibilities—liberating, dangerous, or ambivalent—of how villagers experience and understand gender identity and relations, the world, and their place in it. Feminist and queer migration scholarship has looked at the ways in which migration has enabled women and gender-queers to achieve, contest, or escape heteronormative expectations in their places of origin (Luibhéid 2004; Mahler and Pessar 2006; Manalasan 2003). Ethnographers have looked at the ambivalence migrants feel prior to returning to their home countries and families (Cheng 2010; Constable 1999; Lai 2011; Margold 1995), and diasporic processes of "making home" elsewhere (Fortier et al. 2003; Schiller et al. 1995). While some migrants may return with a sense of relative pride and prestige (Thai 2014), others may feel a sense of cultural alienation upon return, where, by contrast, their hometowns may seem shamefully underdeveloped (McKay 2005). Indeed, the migration of some Cilacap and Yogyakarta villagers has not only shaped the subjectivities of migrants in relation to home and family, but their mobilities have also influenced the subjectivities and anxieties of their kin and neighbors who have never left the country.

Through villagers' idioms of restlessness (*bosan, tidak betah*), desires for elsewhere (*ingin pergi, merantau*), feeling "at home" (*betah, kerasan*) or not, this chapter points to how migration to other Islamic and non-Islamic countries presents subtle but significant challenges to local gendered expectations, moralities, and kinship. Narratives of "home" and "belonging" in terms of identity—Javanese, Indonesian, Muslim—are often attempts to either challenge or domesticate the boundaries of ethnicity, citizenship, kinship, gender, sexuality, and moral communities. What constitutes households and families is never a given, nor are they necessarily harmonious. Being "part of the family"— whether at "home" or "away"—is typically fraught with power hierarchies and tensions (Bapat 2014; Ehrenreich and Hoschschild 2004; Lai 2010; 2011; Paul 2015; Wolf 1992). In addressing cases of migrants who struggle between competing desires to stay abroad or to return home, to escape or to conform to gendered expectations, Sealing Cheng asks, "What happens to the excess affects that refuse to be domesticated?" (2010, 169). With this provocative question in mind, I now turn to experiences of "restlessness" and feeling "at home" (or not) in Cilacap and Yogyakarta. These illuminate residents' dynamic processes of domesticating, resisting, or exceeding the gendered and moral boundaries of "home" and "elsewhere."

Restless in Central Java

Indah's situation exemplifies the restlessness and ambivalence that I refer to. Despite her repeated resolutions not to migrate, Indah's desire for transnational mobility sat in tension with her attempts to contain these desires. When

I first met her in Cilacap in 2012, she told me that she had never considered migrating abroad like other young women in her village, mainly because she was afraid. Although some migrant women could send money home to build concrete houses and wear fashionable clothes, several others returned sick, in debt, or worse. By 2014, however, Indah had applied to work in a factory in Taiwan. As per Indonesian state regulations at the time, she was living in a privately owned predeparture training center in the nearest city, where she began learning Mandarin. Within ten days, she began to feel uncomfortable (*tidak enak*) and sick (*sakit*). No medicine (*obat*) was available for her or the other women at the center. After much pleading with a recruitment agent in charge of her journey, she was allowed to return home for a few days. Indah cried when she saw her two young sons. When narrating this experience to me, she said, "How could I have ever thought of leaving them? At that moment I regretted my decision so much." Her husband eventually convinced Indah to stay. For months, the recruitment agents (who lived nearby) harassed Indah, urging her to return to the training center. By then she owed them one million rupiah, ostensibly for the food, lodging, and lessons during her temporary stay at the center.

Yet, four months after this upsetting experience, Indah began telling me and close friends that she was very bored. She applied to work abroad again, despite her husband's and sons' reluctance, and the disapproval of her family, in-laws, and neighbors. She admired the modern fashion of return migrants, and followed her migrant friends' seemingly glamorous lives abroad via Facebook. "I just want to see the world," she told me,

> I think I'm just really bored here, there's nothing to do.... But where would I go? What would I do? Of course ... there are the children. But I also know what people think of me here. That I'm lazy, the worst mother, the worst daughter-in-law, and my house is in such a mess. They don't lead my life. I've learned not to care what they say. It's okay.

It was true that Indah was not well regarded by her husband's family and neighbors. They saw her as too lenient with her misbehaving children, and lazy and undedicated to household chores. Since Indah's husband was later unemployed during the time of my fieldwork, Indah started working as a door-to-door salesperson, and considered working overseas. In addition to her curiosity about living abroad, Indah also suggested that migration would enable her to be away from the judgemental neighbors. By sending money home, she could potentially recuperate her reputation as a good mother. Theoretically, migration sounded like a win-win situation from Indah's point of view (though she was reluctant to leave her children). Yet her family and neighbors were against her migration, partly because there was no other female kin to care for the children (e.g., a grandmother or aunt who was available or willing), and partly because of their general assessment that, due to her personality, Indah would not be able to navigate the risks and trials of migration well. The common view of Indah's unsuitability for migration was ostensibly confirmed after her first failed attempt to migrate. This generated further judgemental remarks by those around her, sometimes in front of Indah herself, that she was not "mentally strong" enough or that she did not really try hard enough to persevere through the conditions of the training center, unlike other candidates who managed to migrate.

A few weeks after her application to migrate for the second time, Indah changed her mind. However, whenever we met ostensibly successful migrant women who returned from working overseas, Indah still asked them, "Do you have a job for me? Take me with you!" On one such occasion, out of confusion, I asked Indah if she really intended to go abroad, or if she was still resolute about staying. She replied that she was only joking about leaving. During one such conversation, a nonmigrant neighbor joked, "Yes, Indah, even when you're near you don't feel at home (betah), what more if you go somewhere far away." Indah then asked herself aloud, "Why, Indah? Before you went to the [recruitment] agency, why didn't you think of that?"

This sense of ambivalence and restlessness "at home" and the suggestion that some persons might be "at home" elsewhere powerfully illustrate how feminized labor migration from Central Java has troubled and unsettled gender and kinship in embodied ways, even for those who do not leave Indonesia. Indah's restlessness highlights how gendered migration from Central Javanese villages has also shaped the subjectivities of residents who have not (yet) moved.[2] Attention to residents' varying potential and desire to migrate shifts analyses of migration away from indicators of "accessibility" to material and financial resources to embark on journeys (Reeves 2011; Stoll 2013). Instead, residents' potential to migrate encompasses and shapes gender-specific anxieties and desires, where questions of social belonging and displacement are intimately linked to transnational movement (Fortier et al. 2003; Manalasan 2012). This goes beyond an analysis of mobility versus immobility, migrant versus nonmigrant, to examine also those "who are stopped before they start" (Salter 2013, 10; Kellerman 2012), including those ambivalent about migrating, or in the process of making decisions about moving or staying.

Focusing on the "loose ends" of residents' attitudes towards home and away balances the previous chapters' emphasis on how villagers contain the effects or threats of shame, stigma, and migratory risks. Another example of such undomesticated, "loose" affects is Titin's quote in the beginning of this chapter about her reluctance to leave her employer-as-kin in Taiwan. Such kinship is based on mutual care and affinity that transcends and comments on biological, ethnic, or national boundaries of kinship. Significantly, Titin's longing for her fictive kin in Taiwan is intimately linked to her obligations to stay in Central Java as a wife and mother. It is important to recognize that factors contributing to migrants' feeling "at home" elsewhere are enmeshed in broader socioeconomic inequalities (Constable 1999), such as when imaginations of the ideal "home" and "family" are built on experiences with wealthier households overseas. Yet, feeling "at home" in other cultures and places can also offer critiques of local gender and moral norms, and suggest that alternative moralities and gendered subjectivities are possible, not just elsewhere. Before discussing forms of gendered transgression and negotiations of gender norms in Cilacap and Yogyakarta, the section below first explores some responses by villagers to perceived threats to the terms of belonging as Muslim-Javanese Indonesian men and women, such as residents' desires for elsewhere and/or different ways to be "here."

Reaffirming "Local" Gendered Morality

Reproducing Javanese Islamic Morality or Adat

I first met Adi when he returned from working in Taiwan. He had dropped by Indah's aunt-in-law's house to visit her son, who was a close friend. This aunt, with whom I had spent many afternoons and evenings chatting, urged us to speak to each other in Mandarin, and told me that "Adi's fiancée [*calon istri*] is from Taiwan." Adi had left at a young age (after high school) to work in a Taiwanese automobile factory, against his parents' wishes. There, he met a Taiwanese girl who worked in a nearby restaurant. After his three-year work contract was up, Adi returned to Cilacap. According to him, his Taiwanese girlfriend insisted on "following" (*ikut*) him back to Cilacap, because she wanted to see where he was from, and meet his family. When I met Adi, his "fiancée" had already returned to Taiwan. I asked if he intended to return to Taiwan and settle there, or if he preferred to stay in Cilacap with his future wife. He said that he would "of course" prefer to live in Cilacap, to be close to his parents. The work that he did in Taiwan—smelting metal—was exhausting and dangerous. He added that he was not sure if his "girlfriend" (*pacar*) could ever adapt to village life, such as learning the Javanese or Indonesian language, and eating Javanese-Indonesian food.

Adi and his Taiwanese partner became the topic of conversation later that day when I was at Indah's house, and in the company of her husband, sister-in-law, teenage niece, and young sons—who all knew Adi. I told them about my meeting with Adi, and that he had surprised me with how fluent his Mandarin was. Indah asked, "Did you meet Adi's wife?" I replied that she had returned to Taiwan, and that I had the impression the couple were not yet married. Indah's husband corrected me, and said that they were already married (*sudah nikah*). The group collectively confirmed that Adi had undergone religious marriage rites (*nikah siri*) the same day his Taiwanese girlfriend arrived. Indah explained that it was *adat,* or local customary law based on Islam. The couple had to marry, or else they would be considered guilty of *zina* (an Islamic term referring to forbidden, usually nonmarital, sexual relations). Adi's parents had invited a *kyai* (local Islamic religious leader) to perform the ceremony, and insisted that the couple go through the rites.

When I met Adi again, he confirmed this, saying that they had had to get married, since the girl was "afraid of sleeping alone" (*takut tidur sendirian*). Being "married" would allow them to share the same bed and sleep in the same room. Despite this "marriage," Adi referred to his Taiwanese partner as his girlfriend, while his friend's mother clearly referred to her as his "fiancée." This example illustrates the ways that adat and associated rituals maintain and preserve the appearance of social gender norms in order to domesticate gossip about sin or morally transgressive behavior. In Adi's case, adat and the religious marriage rite prevented potential accusations that the couple were engaged in nonmarital sexual relations, despite the fact that to some villagers, they were only engaged and not yet married.

The conditions of adat often emerged in discussions of gender and sexual relations in Cilacap and Yogyakarta. Adat was typically used to justify particular judgments or community actions in terms of "traditional" or "normal" gendered and sexual practices. In these sites, where transnational migration was pervasive, adat was sometimes idealized and often implicitly contrasted with perceived foreign heterosexual norms. The example of Adi's relationship with his Taiwanese partner shows that adat cannot merely be understood as a description or an informal code of actual "normal" or "traditional" gendered practices. Instead, it often served to reaffirm particular heteronormative ideologies of proper "Javanese" and "Islamic" gender relations, even as it enabled potentially subversive practices.

On several occasions, I witnessed district officials giving advice or speeches addressed specifically to prospective and former migrant women, to morally and sexually discipline themselves (*jaga diri*) and not return pregnant (chapter 2). In nonmigration-related settings more generally, such as at a village-level Islamic gathering (*pengajian*) in Yogyakarta, the district's chief police officer explicitly addressed the rise of rape cases in the area, saying that "Sometimes when rape occurs, not only the rapist is to blame." He then warned parents to monitor their daughters' movements, and asked women not to dress provocatively. Such speeches and formal advice by state representatives built on and reinforced local gender attitudes that women are responsible for disciplining their own as well as men's sexual desires (see chapters 3 and 4; Brenner 1998; Bennett 2005a, 152).

That local narratives of migration tended to overwhelmingly focus on women's transgressive sexual behavior as opposed to men's suggests a perception and unease, especially among local male leaders, that women's migration threatened heteronormative Islamic gender roles. Importantly, although female labor migration is often targeted in Cilacap and Yogyakarta as a main concern because of its ubiquity and popularity, the fears of some local leaders and residents about the "breakdown" of the Javanese family structure or gender norms are also related to ongoing anxieties about "Westernization," and the effects of United States-produced popular and consumer culture shaping Javanese and Indonesian moralities (chapter 1). Against these broader and influential national debates and discourses, repeated references to adat in Cilacap and Yogyakarta, or exhortations to preserve "local" gendered moral practices, can be seen as attempts by some villagers to bridge the gap between perceived ideal gender norms and the diversity of actual desires and practices.

While many residents openly frowned upon adultery and divorce, for example, I encountered many such cases among migrants and nonmigrants. Homosexuality was viewed as deviant and nearly nonexistent locally, yet not unheard of among older residents in both Cilacap and Yogyakarta. It was also an open secret that adolescents dated, although not always with the approval of their parents. One Cilacap woman in her early twenties who had dated once before getting engaged to her second partner, told me that "actually, Islam forbids dating" (*tidak boleh pacaran*). Her statement, clearly drawn from elders and local religious sermons, struck me as particularly conservative in an area known for being "less circumscribed by patriarchy or Islam than counterparts in West Java" (Wolf 1992, 256), thus suggesting an increase in the local adoption of more literalist readings of Islam. In the context of transnational migration from Cilacap and Yogyakarta, local discussions of appropriate gendered behavior and sexual relations were contextually targeted at instilling moral self-discipline in migrant women and at domesticating the desires of young women who do not move.

Constructing Immoral Foreign Cultures

Two broad categorizations of "foreign cultures" emerged in Central Javanese representations of migrant-destination countries: non-Islamic countries of East and Southeast Asia (Hong Kong, Taiwan, Korea, Singapore), and Islamic countries (Malaysia, Saudi Arabia, Kuwait, Dubai). Locally circulated stories and stereotypes about these foreign cultures and peoples often provoked local discussions about race, religion, and "freedoms" regarding gender, sexual, and family relations. These included restrictive or progressive labor laws overseas, different moral and religious beliefs, and cultural norms. These informal evaluations about non-Indonesian Asians and Muslims also produced and reaffirmed what constituted "Javanese" or "Indonesian" cultural-religious norms.

Despite the fact that all residents I spoke to in Cilacap and Yogyakarta were Muslim, for whom the pilgrimage to the Islamic holy land of Mecca in Saudi Arabia was religiously important and socially prestigious, local perceptions of

Saudi Arabia (and its Muslim neighboring countries) were largely negative. One former migrant I spoke to, Sumi, could speak four languages and had worked over twenty years in Singapore, Hong Kong, and Macau. When her friend misremembered that Sumi had also worked in Saudi, Sumi recoiled and cried, "No! Never Saudi." "Why not Saudi?" I asked. She echoed several other former migrant women's responses and said that she was scared (*takut*) of being forbidden to leave the employer's house (*gak bisa keluar*), and the uncertainty of even returning to Indonesia alive.

Representations of Saudi Arabia generally focused on its strict interpretation of the Qur'an, the "extreme Islam" that people seem to practice there, and the high rate of executions and death sentences for adultery, witchcraft, and murder. Stories emphasized the restrictive labor laws based on the *kafala* system of employer-sponsored work visas (Mahdavi 2016), and how women are not allowed to leave their houses without veiling their entire bodies, or without male companions. Due to these regulations on women's mobility, villagers perceived Saudi Arabia as a dangerous place for women to work. Anecdotal evidence in these villages suggested that the majority of cases of women who died overseas, or returned home pregnant, had worked in Saudi. A former migrant man who had worked in Korea linked Saudi Arabia's strict laws to the perceived high levels of sexual violence against women there: "Whether or not people are married, Koreans have affairs. There is always a phone number for a sex worker around. That's why there is no rape or violence there. Unlike in Saudi, [where] men resort to desperate actions because there is no other outlet."

Women and men made negative observations that polygyny in Saudi Arabia was still the norm, with one return migrant reporting that his employer had up to fourteen wives. Even though Saudi employers and families were represented as being incredibly rich, with big houses in which extended families lived, they were largely depicted as being outwardly religious yet immoral in their treatment of women and workers. Islam as practiced in Saudi Arabia was often presented by villagers as being "very different" from the "moderate" Islam that they associated with Indonesia. Villagers commonly explained this difference in terms of the "culture" that also shaped laws and law enforcement in Saudi Arabia. Significantly, these discourses focusing on "cultural" differences and variations of Islam echo dominant public, media, and state discourses on Indonesian Islam, and the often reported abuses and death sentences facing Indonesian migrant workers in Saudi Arabia.[3]

In contrast to the lack of freedoms in Saudi Arabia, some former migrants and nonmigrant villagers represented other migrant-destination countries in Southeast Asia and East Asia as having "too much freedom" and "no religion." On the one hand, villagers tended to stereotype return migrant women who worked in Hong Kong and Taiwan as having "forgotten" Javanese-Indonesian cultural norms, when they return wearing "inappropriate" (*tidak cocok*) attire such as miniskirts, high heels, tight clothing, and lipstick. Gossip about such women included stories of them smoking and drinking in bars and cafes abroad, and doing sex work in addition to domestic or factory work. Many women and men initially expressed surprise at how in Hong Kong, Singapore, and Taiwan, couples could apparently live together prior to marriage without social stigma or judgement. Former migrant women reported how their employers' families accepted such living arrangements. One female former migrant who worked in Taiwan said, "People in Taiwan don't think about tomorrow, there is only today for them. They have relationships outside of marriage, and don't think of the consequences of their sins.... I mean there is too much freedom [*maksudnya kebebasan*]."

Former migrants were also critical of how religious worship and rituals in Hong Kong, Singapore, and Korea, appeared to be explicitly directed towards material pursuits. As a former migrant who worked in Korea put it, "I was shocked [*heran*].... People pray everywhere to gods, for cars, business, money.... Their prayers are for themselves [*mereka sendiri*], and to idols. They pray to anyone or anything that will give them success and the things they want. Unlike Islam." Hong Kong was also singled out in terms of seeming to promote a "culture" (*budaya*) or "tradition" (*tradisi*) of lesbianism (Adrian 2015; *Republika* 2015). Some Indonesian women were said to be influenced by lesbianism, and stories were told of how a few local women turned "sick" (*sakit*) or encountered "problems" (*khasus*) when they were transformed into "men" there, despite being engaged or married prior to migration.

In comparison to Saudi employers or ethnic-Malay employers in Singapore and Malaysia, ethnic Chinese women as employers in general were considered extremely fussy, strict, paranoid, vain, and jealous. Stories about these female Chinese employers in Singapore and Hong Kong tended to focus on how they were beautiful, fair, and had expensive clothes, but also on how much they controlled domestic workers' movements and salaries. Such female employers in Saudi Arabia were not as homogenous or prevalent. Many former migrant women with Chinese employers recounted that they were forbidden to talk to anyone outside the household or to step outside the house on their own. Indonesian migrant women—who were assumed to be practicing Muslims—were typically not allowed by ethnic Chinese employers to pray or wear a veil in their employers' homes, and many were required to cook pork.

Negative stereotypes of other Asian or Islamic countries and people implicitly and explicitly create and reaffirm ideas about Javanese or Indonesians as being morally righteous and religiously pious. Implicit in these narratives is the claim of moral superiority over Chinese and Koreans by rejecting "free sex," showing respect for marriage and family institutions, and by treating others with greater human dignity. These tales also imply the moral superiority of Indonesians over their Muslim counterparts in Saudi Arabia and the Middle East, through citing Indonesia's "moderation" in regulating women's mobility and sexuality. For example, Muslim women in Indonesia can walk or drive alone outside the home, but they must informally seek permission from their husbands. Proper Muslim women have to wear the hijab (veil), but not only in black, and burqas (full-body veils) are not compulsory. Significantly, these affirmations of Javanese-Indonesian identity also reinforce intranational stereotypes of "bad" Islam in terms of "bad" Indonesian-Muslims, such as in Aceh, who are perceived to be influenced by "radical" Islam from the Middle-East. Stereotypes of ethnic Chinese abroad also build on and reinforce intranational perceptions that Chinese-Indonesians are wealthy, arrogant, and vain (see also Brenner 1995, 25). Furthermore, narratives of immoral migrant behavior tend to focus on female adultery, and what are seen as "loose" sexual or "sick" homosexual identities and behavior associated with wealthier Asian cultures. Together, these produce their implied opposite: an ideal Islamic and normative Javanese femininity in relation to normative Javanese masculinity.[4]

Reasserting the Husband's Authority

When the absence of migrant wives and mothers proved challenging or threatening for some men who stayed in Cilacap and Yogyakarta, women were requested or told by husbands to return. In several cases, men demanded that their wives return to Indonesia, despite the women's reluctance. Such former migrants often framed their return to Indonesia specifically in terms of "being asked to return" (*disuruh pulang*), as opposed to simply "return," "asking to return" (*minta pulang*), or "wanting to return" (*mau pulang*). Despite this, most women I spoke to framed their acquiescence to husbands' requests in terms of the proper obligations of a Javanese-Muslim wife.

Titin's story stands out for her direct honesty about her reluctance to leave Taiwan, where she worked for five years. In the presence of her husband, she told me that she was "forced to leave [Taiwan]" (*maksa pergi*) before her contract ended. Her husband had asked her to return, because he could not handle their three teenage children anymore. She returned specifically to take over the household chores and childcare. When her husband first asked her to return, she was reluctant, because she already felt "at home" with her employer's family in Taiwan. The elderly man she was caring for was a "soul-mate," and the family also felt that she was the perfect "match." Notably, Titin's narrative suggested that she had little choice regarding whether or not to return to Indonesia. Instead, she emphasized her reluctance, her husband's decision and pressure, and that when she returned, she simply "took heart" in the fact that she needed to fulfill her duties as a wife and mother.

Many women in similar circumstances as Titin deferred to their husbands' decisions, even if they expressed a reluctance to comply. Some women also told me that they wanted to migrate, or wished to migrate for a second time, but did not, because their husbands, fiancés, or boyfriends did not permit it. They suggested that their partners did not approve of their desires to migrate largely due to fears that the women would be unfaithful, or that other migrants or foreign employers would sexually abuse them. Titin's framing of her return in terms of her gendered familial duties echoes Anju Paul's (2015) observations that some Filipina migrant women tended to reinforce normative gendered expectations through their narratives of migration, rather than transforming gender roles through independent labor migration. That some Central Javanese women frame their mobility practices by reproducing kodrat-inflected discourses suggests that older Javanese-Islamic ideas about men as rightful heads of households can no longer merely be seen as "lip service" (Brenner 1995; see discussion in chapter 1), since such patriarchal discourses are in these cases used to exert and justify some men's control over women's lives.

Transgressing Gender Norms

While some migrant women reluctantly returned to their husbands and child-caring duties, there were also others who responded to these local heterosexist attitudes by explicitly rejecting or transgressing adat. However, explicitly transgressive acts, such as cohabitation out of wedlock, or migrating without a male kin's formal permission, could provoke or result in harassment, discrimination, or even expulsion from communities by local leaders, family members, and fellow villagers.[5]

When Geno was working in Singapore, she brought her Singaporean Muslim boyfriend back to her village for Idul Fitri to meet her family. The couple was formally engaged, and Geno explained to her family and neighbors that she could not marry him in Indonesia, since she had heard that it might hurt the chances for their marriage to be legalized in Singapore (see Constable, forthcoming). Legal marriage documents from Singapore would help her and her children obtain future citizenship. Although villagers received Geno's boyfriend warmly at first, the couple began to feel pressured to undergo religious marriage rites. Neighbors and even distant relatives began to mutter offensive names behind their backs, and spread word that they were living in sin, or "*kumpul kebo*," literally "getting together like animals." A local village leader called Geno a "dirty woman," and the couple received anonymous threats to their physical safety and the house, if the couple did not marry soon, or if Geno's boyfriend did not leave the village immediately. Fearing for their safety and the welfare of her children, Geno and her boyfriend packed their bags and left the next day. The couple stayed away until Geno felt it was safe to return to the village alone.

In cases of explicit moral transgression, as Linda Bennett observed in Eastern Indonesia, it is not "enough to ignore or tacitly disapprove of cohabitation but [some villagers must] publicly condemn, stigmatize, and harass" (2005b, 108). Similar responses to Geno and her partner by fellow villagers point to the ways that patriarchal norms are reinforced and upheld through fear and shame, despite women's attempts to disrupt them. Very few neighbors were sympathetic to Geno's position and plight. The explicit and damaging name-calling and threats cautioned other women of the ugly consequences of trying to introduce—reasonably or not—perceived "foreign" heterosexual practices locally.

Not all residents feared stigma and gossip, particularly when the desire for other worlds and experiences proved greater than desires to belong or return to Central Java. Anisa had worked in Taiwan for three years, and in that time she had sent back enough money to build a modern concrete house in Cilacap for her husband and three children. Despite (or perhaps because of) her evident financial success, gossip circulated about Anisa's infidelity and sexual promiscuity. There was talk that she boasted about how foreign men in Taiwan propositioned her, and in Cilacap, she openly flirted with men on her mobile phone, which villagers said was "obvious" from her tone of voice and body language during those calls.

I met Anisa upon her return from Taiwan, while she was waiting to migrate again. The first time we met, she was dressed in a sleeveless top that defied what was considered appropriate dress for women in rural Cilacap. That evening, she sat outside her new house with an electronic tablet device. Addressing a group of female neighbors—including myself—who had gathered at her home, Anisa spoke about the cool winters in Taiwan, and showed us a flirtatious Facebook conversation she was having with a Bangladeshi man. Although this was in English, and, among those present, only Anisa and I could make sense of the words, it is generally unacceptable for married women to boast of or even openly discuss private friendships with other men. Definitions of *selingkuh*—having an affair—can sometimes be based merely on a sighting of a married woman chatting in the market in a too friendly manner to an unfamiliar man (i.e., someone who is not a known fellow villager or kin). Anisa had asked me what a certain word meant, and I told her that her online friend had told her she was "pretty."

Appearing to anticipate gossip, she reasoned aloud to me and the other women present, "[Through Facebook] I just want to learn about the world, and make new friends." I empathized with Anisa's desire for travel, knowledge, and new experiences. At the same time, I sympathized with her children, the youngest of whom clung to her the entire time, and another who was very quiet and withdrawn. I also sympathized with her husband, whom I saw every day, without fail, climbing trees to collect material to produce coconut palm sugar for sale.

Through my own shifting sympathies and judgements, I realized that villagers' perceptions of such situations were also complex and situational, linked to their own temporal restlessness and varying attachments to the village. Indeed, while the few young women who lived nearby sometimes seemed to admire Anisa's possessions (e.g., her tablet) and stories, at other times they shook their heads at her open flirtations and signs of rebellion.[6] Still at other moments, they expressed genuine concern about Anisa's well being abroad. Wondering aloud about why she had lost so much weight and alluding to Anisa's sporadic complaints about stomach pains, some neighbors speculated that her employer might have been mistreating her through inadequate food provision, and suggested to her various remedies for her apparent malnourishment.

Many neighbors witnessed Anisa's public fight with her husband that same evening. Sitting with Indah and her sons after dinner, we heard Anisa shouting angrily, "What have I ever done to deserve this? I worked hard for this family, for the children.... I've never asked for anything else. All I want is a divorce." She called her husband a "bastard," much to our shock and mirth. The next day, villagers close to Anisa's husband told me that the fight was over two things. One was that her husband had had enough of her flirtatious phone calls to other men; she had showed absolutely no respect for him as her husband. Second, he pleaded with her not to go to Taiwan again, since he assured her that he could earn enough from making coconut palm sugar so that she could stay and take care of the children.

A few days later, Anisa left for a premigration training center, despite the fact that her husband had not signed the required documents granting her the permission to migrate. Neighbors blamed the recruitment agent who was notorious for "playing" such games with migrants and their families. Anisa's unauthorized departure shocked no one; she already had a reputation for her independence. Months later, she called her husband to ask for a divorce, and informed him that she was religiously married to another Indonesian man in Taiwan.

Unlike Geno, who carefully tried to reason with villagers about her delay in marrying her foreign boyfriend, Anisa defied several implicit and explicit social rules in Cilacap, and resisted attempts to govern her movement and behavior as a woman, wife, and mother. Unlike Geno who was threatened with explicit violence, I sensed that Anisa was discussed and gossiped about by families and neighbors in terms of an emerging "normal." This meant that her experiences—her migration without her husband's permission, her apparent infidelity abroad, her inappropriate dress, and her demand for a divorce—arguably all conformed to villagers' stereotypes and perceptions of the "collateral damage" that migration inflicted on families and the broader community. Few spoke about Anisa with anger or bitterness, but mostly with ambiguity and pity for her husband and children. I heard very little talk that explicitly blamed or shamed Anisa.

This could be because her financial contributions were physically evident and thus undeniable. Her remittances had funded a house built on her husband's land, and according to existing marriage and property laws, it would be difficult to divide the property, since the land would still solely belong to her husband after divorce, and the house built with her remittances was on his property.[7] In contrast, Geno lived sparsely and modestly after decades of working abroad. Neighbors also gossiped that Geno was stingy and unfilial, that she did not send enough money to feed her elderly mother. As both of these cases suggest, women's autonomy is tied at least in part to their economic contributions to the family (Wolf 1992).

Contrasting Anisa's and Geno's situations shows how some acts of gendered transgression are increasingly anticipated and met with ambivalence by villagers. Shortly after Anisa left the village, her eldest son dropped out of middle school, to his father's distress. I recalled how Anisa had spoken of her hopes that she would send her son to college with the Taiwanese dollars she earned. Even accounting for Anisa's financial contributions to the family, residents' relative lack of moral blame targeted at Anisa is notable, due to her apparent disregard for her reputation as a "good" woman, wife, or mother. Her departure produced instead many new and unanswered questions about the future of her children and husband, and other families in similar circumstances.

Deep ambivalence characterized the prevalent attitudes of villagers toward those who opt to "exit" and reject local gender norms linked to familial obligations. As an openly unfaithful wife and a reliable remittance-sending mother, Anisa's position seemed to challenge existing moral judgments of women (see chapters 3 and 4). Unlike other women who might wish to dispel or avoid gossip that their remittances were based on "non-halal" sources, Anisa displayed fearless indifference to being perceived as an unfaithful wife, alongside a self-confidence in her sacrificial contributions to the family ("I worked hard for this family, for the children."). This arguably destabilized villagers' ideas of moral subjectivities or diffused feelings of moral righteousness. Such ambivalence, in the form of open and unanswerable questions about the strength of kinship and broader community norms in fostering ties of belonging and obligation, importantly shaped the mobility and restlessness of other onlookers and observers.

Towards Alternative Gendered Moralities

In contrast to Geno and Anisa's explicit social transgressions, other men and women might choose more careful or subtle ways to question local gender norms. Former migrants might contest local norms by talking about their observations and experiences of gender and sexual identities and behavior that seemed acceptable in countries where they had worked and lived. This included questioning local expectations of unmarried female chastity, stigma against divorce, and the illegitimacy of sex work. A few former migrants carefully offered explanations and justifications for same-sex intimate relationships such as lesbianism associated with migrant women in Hong Kong, or gay (U.S.-born) employers. However, homosexual identities were almost always considered deviant or a "sickness," even as these discussions of gender and sexuality expanded and shifted the boundaries of appropriate heterosexual identity and relations.[8]

Instead of focusing on negative stereotypes of "too much freedom" in Hong Kong, Singapore, Taiwan, and Malaysia, some return migrants spoke appreciatively about the relative freedoms in these countries, in terms of having days off (for those who did) and for having employers who trusted them to be independent workers. A few migrant women spoke positively about how people can dress and talk "however they want," without fear of stigma or judgement by others, in contrast to the small rural villages they came from. As noted earlier, a former migrant man suggested that the availability of commercial sex workers reduced the rate of sexual abuse and violence in Korea relative to Saudi Arabia. These positive representations of sexual freedom, and freedom of dress and movement abroad, however, were usually expressed only in the company of close friends, or in private conversations with me.

Former migrants who worked in Hong Kong, Taiwan, and Korea sometimes said that the apparently more "liberal" sexual norms abroad could be understood as also being rational in the context of another culture, and not objectively immoral. I see these views—expressed both by men and women—as contributing to publically cultivating a sense of cultural and moral relativism, as opposed to moral judgement. For example, some women stated that it is "okay," "not wrong," and "not a sin" in Hong Kong for unmarried couples to cohabit, in order to decide whether or not they want to marry. As a middle-aged female former migrant to Taiwan said, "it may not be acceptable here due to adat, but there are no laws against it in Singapore." Another former migrant woman rationalized premarital cohabitation as such: "If [the couple] does not like living together, they can break up. If not they can marry. In Indonesia, you find out only after marriage ... and then if you don't like each other, you have to divorce!"

In making such statements, women were also aware that divorce in foreign contexts follows different laws from divorce for Muslims in Indonesia. Several women said that "In Islam, women are not allowed to divorce men" or that "Islam does not permit divorce, and people who divorce are just less pious Muslims." These local perceptions of divorce and marriage regulations in Indonesia are only partially true—women can request divorce, but only after three months of proven financial neglect, six months of physical neglect, or in cases where the husband has clearly physically abused the wife. In contrast, men need not fulfill these conditions (Katz and Katz 1975; Grace 2004). Nevertheless, discussions of divorce and marital practices or norms overseas can be read as implicit criticisms of how Indonesia's marriage regulations unfairly disadvantage women.

Additionally, many return migrants pointed out how adultery, divorce, or premarital sexual relations are also common among Indonesians abroad and at home. This challenged the sometimes implicit idea that Javanese or Indonesians are morally "better" than their foreign Asian counterparts, due to perceived differences in essentialized cultural attitudes towards sexuality. As I describe below, the generosity of nonreligious Chinese employers, compared to stereotypes of abuse in Islamic Saudi Arabia, also disrupts any easy associations of religious identity and practice with ethical behavior.

Rethinking Transnational Kinship

Despite having visited the Cilacap site at least thrice over three years, particularly during the religious holidays, I had never met Bu Henny, a friend's mother who had been a domestic worker in Saudi Arabia for nearly ten years. Every year, I was told that Bu Henny would retire and return to Cilacap soon. Her daughter, who was in her mid-twenties, eagerly awaited and regularly requested her return, so that she herself could embark on her own journey and leave her children in her mother's care. Yet, Bu Henny continued to extend her contract abroad, and as of 2015, she had not returned to Cilacap for five years. As her sister-in-law explained, "I think she's already at home there. [Her employers are] probably like family. What is there for her here? She's widowed; her children have their own families. But she's still sending money home regularly."

Unlike migrant women in their twenties to forties who might be accused of promiscuity or infidelity if they stayed abroad too long, older migrants (over 50) who were divorced or widowed experienced less stigma if they did not return or send money home. This is likely since, being past childbearing age, the women would typically be associated with the desexualized identity-positions of "grandmothers" (*nenek*) (Winarnita 2016). Older women's local absence and sustained presence abroad was thus often explained in terms of their "kinship" ties to foreign employers. Unlike patterns of emigration, in which migrants typically settle and form families in the destination countries (Schiller et al. 1995), migrants and their kin from Central Java often assume that transnational journeys will be temporary (see chapter 1). An exception is the case of migrants who left for Malaysia in the 1980s or early 1990s, where some migrant men and women married ethnic Malay citizens or fellow Indonesians who obtained residency there (see also Spaan 1994, 100–101). A small but increasing number of migrant women are also reported to formally or religiously marry and live abroad with men from Taiwan (Lu 2005; Tsay 2004), Hong Kong (Constable 2014), Singapore (Jones and Shen 2008), Australia, Britain, Germany, and the United States. Thus, a main reason villagers understand migrants' overly prolonged stay and work abroad is that they must feel "at home" there, and having or making "kin" there is an important part of feeling "at home." Simultaneously, villagers recognize that these "foreign" kinship ties—whether to employers or spouses—tend to also financially benefit migrants' biological kin and neighbors at home. The possibility of migrants having fictive kin abroad largely applies to women, partially due to the fact that women work within their employers' households, and sharing and cooking food together has been central to conceptions of kin and household in Java and other Southeast Asian contexts (Carsten 1991; Errington 1987; Retsikas 2014).

Consequently, there were also stories of kinship and affection across borders, based on mutual care and concern. These bonds were not necessarily based on religious values, ethnicity, or nationality. However common or compelling these stories of positive affinity were, they were still often perceived as exceptions rather than the norm. Cilacap and Yogyakarta perceptions of migrants and their "foreign kin" nevertheless existed alongside the pervasive idea that transnational labor migration was threatening Javanese marriage and parent-child relations, whether or not migrants were cast in the role of parents or children, or both. Stories about fictive kinship and fears of social disruption point to the multiple ways that transnational migration is gradually reconfiguring and extending the geographic, ethnic, national, and religious boundaries of kinship and relatedness in Central Java.

Titin's story as told above was representative of some women's narratives of uncertainty about leaving their "foreign kin" abroad to return to their biological families in Indonesia. Such affective narratives of employers as family contrast with studies of how employers of domestic workers extract and justify workers' extra-domestic work or delayed wages in terms of workers being "part of the family" (Bapat 2014; Romero 2002). As Titin's case illustrates, the pressure to return "home" to Indonesia can exist in tension with the bonds forged with their "soul mates" and "other family" overseas. Several narratives included teary farewells and emotional pleas by migrants' employers to stay. Stories of Taiwanese employers in particular focused on positive affinity and good working conditions: women spoke about how their Chinese-Taiwanese employers treated them like daughters and sisters, taking them out for family holidays and meals, and buying them gifts such as clothes, shoes, and other material luxuries. Narratives focusing on mutual care and concern between employers and domestic workers were more common in cases where women lived alone with and took care of the sick and elderly in rural parts of Taiwan. Chinese employers in Singapore and Taiwan, as well as some Saudi employers, were also known to give large sums of money to workers in order to acquire new skills in computing, hairdressing, or language, or to start businesses in their hometowns. These employers also went beyond their formal or legal obligations of care for domestic workers, by paying for medical bills and school fees for migrants' own families in Central Java.

Such ties were maintained over years in a few cases, even after the contractual labor relationship had formally ended. Foreign employers from Singapore, Malaysia, Saudi Arabia, Taiwan, and Hong Kong sometimes paid for migrants to reunite with them overseas. A Singaporean Malay family made annual trips to visit and stay with their former domestic worker in the Yogyakarta village. They also helped to fund her wedding, which was not only a very generous gesture, but a contribution that strongly symbolized and intensified kinship-like relations in the context of Central Java, since close kin participated actively in the organization of such an important life ritual. The former migrant's parents saw her former employers as fictive kin who took extremely good care of their daughter.

These affective bonds and generosity sometimes contrasted vividly with women's experiences of financial and emotional pressure from their families in Indonesia to send more money or to return home to perform domestic duties. Thus women's narratives of foreign kin sometimes served to implicitly criticize the social pressures they felt to fulfill narrowly defined and doubly burdened family roles as caregiving and breadwinning mothers, wives, and daughters. However, the generosity of foreign employers also highlights the unequal capacities of "family" members to perform or meet financial obligations, much less exceed these expectations.

Negotiated Selves and Families

The boundaries of gendered selves, morality, and kinship are intimately linked to local terms of belonging—meanings attached to being Javanese, Indonesian, Muslim, man, or woman. Migrants' destination countries and their associated cultural moralities are thus commonly framed in ethnic, national, religious, or gendered terms. Former migrants' and villagers' narratives of aversion to foreign gender norms, and affective ties of foreign kinship, contrast with international and national migration policies that tend to prioritize migrants' economic motivations and experiences. Instead, migrants may view other-Asian or other-Islamic people and practices as culturally familiar, yet foreign; appealing, yet dangerous, or repulsive. "Freedom," as associated with migration and other countries, often embodies contradictory tensions. People weigh greater risks, freedoms, or restrictions, and various gendered and moral "trade-offs" between staying behind and migrating to specific countries.

While some former migrant women and men contest or transgress local customary gender norms through divorce, marital infidelity, or premarital cohabitation, others are deterred by the threat of expulsion, shame, or violence against such transgressions. This chapter has discussed the subtle ways that migration experiences have enabled women and men to criticize perceived strict regulations or laws targeting sexuality or women. Nevertheless, these narratives and practices are still ultimately subordinate to and do not question the heteronormativity associated with Javanese-Indonesian Muslim selves and families.

The emerging gender dynamics described in this chapter—greater attempts by Islamic religious leaders and some husbands to regulate women's mobilities, and villagers' harsh or ambivalent responses to women's moral and gendered transgressions—are not entirely new, but depart in several ways from previous ethnographies of gender in Central Java. Before industrialization, Javanese women and men shared equal agricultural workloads and women were not particularly restricted in terms of mobility (Brenner 1995; Wolf 1992; for a comparison to Sulawesi, see Elmhirst 2002). The gradual development of social and village networks around some rural women's internal migrations in the 1980s for factory work arguably curtailed moral panic about young women's mobilities. In contrast, current migrations of women to labor in intimate household spaces so culturally and geographically distant from "home," as well as the uncertainty linked to the vastly uneven outcomes of such journeys, have fueled stronger patriarchal discourses locally, alongside the greater influence of Islamic leaders and groups in other areas of political and social life in Java and Indonesia. This chapter has outlined some of the desires of and actions by women's families, and local and national authorities in Cilacap and Yogyakarta, to exert control over women's mobility, sexuality, and behavior, often effectively. Yet, in exceptional cases, transnational migration has also radically offered unprecedented economic, social, and geographical opportunities for some women to make new identities, "homes," and kin elsewhere.

Whether the benefits of migration have outweighed its costs for migrant-origin villagers, or whether transnational migration has led to more gendered freedoms or constraints, these remain open-ended questions. The answers depend on who is speaking, for whom, and what moralities, identities, or sense of security or "homeness," are at stake. For many women—like Indah who has never left the country, and Titin, a former migrant—the ubiquity of transnational gendered migration and the option to move away, as long as they are willing, have resulted in their sense of restlessness in and ambivalence toward their (migrant-origin) villages. These feelings are accompanied by a questioning of their attachments to "home" and "family," in terms of their expected duties as mothers, wives, and primarily female members of the village. Although she has not migrated, Indah's ambivalence about staying or going may point to larger shifts within local gender norms over time. Such growing restlessness and discontent may well inspire residents to make the village a kind of place where, barring extreme economic needs, people decide to stay, not one that they desire to escape.

Notes

1. *Yuan fen* is the Mandarin term for fate and has subtle differences from the Indonesian term nasib. Rather than emphasizing the tension between human and divine agency as nasib does, yuan fen refers to a predestined coincidence that governs how people meet and part (Yang and Ho 1988).

2. A recent study conducted in a migrant-origin village in East Java describes similar accounts of women wishing to migrate to escape domesticity temporarily, or simply due to desires to explore the world beyond familiar places (Khoo et al. 2015, 17).

3. On characterizations of Indonesian Islam as moderate, see Halim 2015, Hefner 2000, and Woodward 1996.

4. There were very few stories or generalizations about Malaysia in terms of a "culture," perhaps due to the fact that Malaysia is very similar to Indonesia in terms of some of the countries' ethnic and religious politics. Domestic workers also often worked for Chinese employers in Malaysia, and those who did work for Malay employers in Malaysia or Singapore would comment more generally on how they were strict. These complaints were thus less about characterizing the Malays as a cultural group than simply noting that these employers were fussy and particular. While there were certainly women who worked for Caucasian employers in these countries (Singapore, Malaysia, Taiwan, Hong Kong, UAE) who come from the North America, Europe, or Australia, these were in the minority. I noticed that although two women had unpleasant experiences and relationships with their Caucasian female employers, they nevertheless did not broadly stereotype "Westerners" negatively, but rather, continued to reproduce the common idea among migrant domestic workers that working and living conditions would be good and better with Caucasian employers as compared to employers of other ethno-cultural backgrounds.

5. The responses of individuals to migrants' transgressions importantly depend on the relationships between residents of particular villages. Rural villages such as the field sites in Cilacap and Yogyakarta seldom have residents who can be considered nonkin in a broader sense of the term, and hence tend to have a stronger sense of ingroup identity and boundaries (Carsten 1991; Errington 1987; Retsikas 2014).

6. Single mothers or divorced women were typically able to gain relative social acceptance if they conformed to other gender norms such as performing religious or filial piety, remaining frugal, maintaining a modest appearance (nothing glamorous, luxurious, "sexy," or "modern"), and conforming to other expectations of a good mother or daughter. Remittances and financial contributions were a factor in these moral evaluations, but not the only one, as discussed in chapter 4.

7. Generally, however, the wealth a couple acquired after marriage was viewed as common and shared, as opposed to wealth or property that each partner already possessed prior to marriage.

8. This observation coincides with the official "medical" view of Indonesian psychiatrists on homosexuality. With reference to Law No.18/2014 on Mental Health, the Indonesian Psychiatrists Association (PDSKJI) "categorizes homosexuals and bisexuals as 'people with psychiatric problems,' while transgender people have 'mental disorders.' According to this classification, a psychiatric problem is condition in which a person is at risk of developing a mental disorder" (Yosephine 2016). Against prominent LGBT groups and LGBT activism in Indonesia, in early 2016 the influential MUI officially declared homosexuality-related activities "haram" or forbidden (*Jakarta Post* 2016).

Conclusion: Gendered Moral Economies of Migration

Residents in migrant-origin villages of Cilacap and Yogyakarta appear to remain both hopeful and fatalistic about the future. "*Kalau orang baik, nasib baik*" was a common refrain in response to my persistent questions about what residents in migrant-origin villages thought about migrants' money and sickness, successes and failures. "If a person is good, (his/her) fate will be good." One woman claimed that nearly all migrants were "successful." Yet simultaneously and paradoxically, she participated alongside fellow villagers in the circulation of individualized stories of migrant injuries, debt, and failures, concluding that nobody could really be considered successful *yet*.

This book has shown how stories of failed migration journeys and projects tend to mobilize fear and gendered shame in migrant-origin villages. While the threat of shame strongly encourages some against migrating or frames decisions to stay in positive terms of "having shame," shame also discourages some migrants from returning to the villages or Indonesia before having achieved (or appearing to achieve) "success." Simultaneously, through employing discourses of fate and destiny to explain and individualize migration failures, residents of migrant-origin villages actively develop and sustain faith in the promised "successes" of migration. Villagers thus mutually shape and cultivate relative mobilities and motilities in relation to risk, by mobilizing and dispersing gendered responsibility and blame for migration's losses and gains.

By circulating and developing faith and shame, villagers draw on gendered and religiously inflected discourses of fate and morality to frame and explain the past, to act strategically on the present, in order to construct "better" futures. Villagers' moral narratives, including those about (deserved, desirable, or inevitable) fate and destiny, must be contextualized in terms of the way in which moral responsibility for migration has been institutionally and discursively refracted by invested institutions and individuals—through discussions over who ought to intervene, and in what ways, in processes and consequences of migration. State agencies, national newsmakers, migrant labor NGOs, recruitment agents, and residents of migrant-origin villages interact in dynamic ways to account for migrant successes and failures. This book has shown how these various discourses of migration in terms of development, exploitation, faith, or destiny collectively shape attitudes in the village and nation towards what kinds of bodies and subjects should (or should not) circulate transnationally.

How a society values people gives them their sense of "social worth," and the negotiations of the value of persons, their time, and labor is "a central aspect of what the economy is about" (Narotzy and Besnier 2014, S10). *Gendered moral economies of migration* refers to these ways in which transnational migrations from and returns to Central Java are actively shaped and sustained by multiscalar gendered and moral discourses about bodies, labor, and finance. I have argued that the lack of or pursuit of money is not what keeps people in motion, but rather how people value (and contest other ways of valuing) money and mobility in gendered and moral ways. Appreciating how residents of migrant-origin villages—whether as "stayers," "nonmigrants," "failed" or "successful" migrants—experience and shape these places and social relations within them critically demonstrates how "economic" reasons for migration are deeply enmeshed in local and cultural regimes of value such as morality.

Stories of "immoral" migrants and gender practices that destabilize the figure of the ideal parent, spouse, or child, however, may illuminate alternative paths to current forms of migration and work, to achieve different kinds of hopeful futures. By weaving together the views and narratives of migrant-origin villagers—including return migrants, prospective migrants, current migrants who are back for short visits, and those who have never migrated—this book has complicated common categories or analyses associated with mobility/immobility and migrant/nonmigrant. Instead, in migrant-origin villages, migrant categories are much messier. For example, those who have never left Indonesia are considered former transnational migrants in their failed attempts to cross national borders. These cases of nondeparture demonstrate the expansive social and spatial effects of migration infrastructure beyond the facilitation of transnational movement. Instead, the same infrastructure enabling some people to leave the country substantially shapes relative immobilities, intranational movements, and associated subjectivities within migrants' countries of origin.

Narratives about Islamic-inflected fate and destiny in the Cilacap and Yogyakarta villages show that "nonmigrants" are not passively "left behind," but that they actively negotiate the terms of migration, mobility, and motility. "Failed migrants" and those who have not migrated draw on fate and destiny narratives to justify reasons for staying, in staking their faith in alternatives to migration such as local agriculture, opening small shops, selling homemade snacks, or working in urban Indonesian cities. While the banner of Islam appeals to various demographics for diverse reasons (chapter 1), scholars of Indonesia generally agree that Islamic discourses and identities enable citizens to negotiate moral anxieties in the context of a sense of greater individual responsibility and liability that comes with more opportunities, mobility, and choice (Brenner 1996; 1998).[1]

Assumptions about the agency, intentions, or knowledge of prospective migrants and their fellow villagers significantly impact how policymakers, development workers, migrant activists, recruitment agents, and state representatives approach migration as a problem or solution to issues of rural unemployment, education, poverty, health, and gender equality. Scholarship and discussions about migration that examine or assume moral or economic rationality behind human behavior do not provide holistic accounts of the ways that ideas about the "moral" is gendered, organized, and mediated through situated forms of communication and exchange (see Mattingly 2014). Indeed, how migrant money is perceived to be earned and used produces its value and meaning partially through village talk. In addition to the role of national and international media, this book has shown how gendered moral economies of migration are constituted and sustained through seemingly mundane everyday village talk about migrant success and failure: their money, houses, sickness, and deaths.

Although longer term research is required to elucidate the fine and fragile social dynamics and bonds of villagers of Cilacap and Yogyakarta, migrant-origin villagers' (variously positioned) moral judgments of migrants and migration can also be read as ethical and practical responses to the moral and existential anxieties regarding the inherent risks and arbitrary nature of the migration process. Villagers' circulation of stories of failure and shame can serve as cautionary tales to prospective and current migrants, by explaining migration's many known risks. As partial criticisms of the debts and moral and mortal risks of migration, stories of migrant failure and shame are used by some villagers to justify and validate their desires and decisions to stay amidst social pressures to migrate. At the same time, discourses of shame exert immense pressures on those who leave to put in the "proper effort" and faith to return with "good fates."

Surprisingly, even though the Indonesian state strongly promotes and facilitates migration, partially through regulating and licensing commercial recruitment and insurance agencies, migrant-origin villagers seldom held the state accountable or responsible for migrants' risky journeys. With the exception of cases where mass media and NGOs intervened, state institutions were seldom considered by the Cilacap and Yogyakarta villagers as viable options for migration-related problem resolution or compensation. Apart from a few outstanding examples that I am aware of in Wonosobo and East Java, there is a notable paucity of village-level political action or grassroots organization in migrant-origin villages around migration-related issues.[2]

This does not point to a general political indifference in Cilacap and Yogyakata: there were organized protests against foreign corporations and their foreign workers in Cilacap city during my main fieldwork period. In the same year, farmers and villagers near the Yogyakarta field site held widely publicized protests against state plans to build an international airport nearby (*Jakarta Post* 2015a). A partial explanation for villagers' collective inaction in the case of migration is thus that, unlike factory uprisings or protests over land rights, the complexity and interrelated institutions involved in transnational migration infrastructure mean that there is no longer a single or "external" actor to blame for migrant fatalities, sickness, or debts. Even in cases officially identified as "human trafficking," villagers, migrant activists, and state representatives are aware that the Indonesian state, local recruitment agents, and extended family relations are implicated, to varying degrees, in women's migratory journeys (Palmer 2012). Existing overlapping and contrasting discourses about migration's overall costs and benefits, the blame and responsibility for migrants' wealth and injuries, obscure how actors and institutions are actively maintaining the highly uneven transnational distribution of capital and risk.

The absence of the state in villagers' discourses, alongside the presence of fate narratives, demonstrates the inadequacy and neglect of state institutions in addressing the many ways migration has negatively affected the lives and economies of migrant-origin villages. Some glaring examples are: the high recruitment and migration fees paid by migrants, how victims of fraud seldom get compensation while errant recruitment agencies continue to operate, the lack of a second autopsy in Indonesia for migrants who died abroad, the lack of thorough medical or police reports regarding the circumstances of these deaths, inadequate or inappropriate medical attention or social support provision to migrants who return in states of trauma or mental illness, and bureaucratic and logistical obstacles for migrants and their families to claim insurance and financial compensation in the event of migrant death, injury, or fraud.

The lack of political criticism in matters regarding migration constitutes villagers' partial acquiescence to and indifference towards the ability of relevant state and migration institutions to address the absence of competitive alternative access to livelihoods. The superficially apolitical narratives of migration also illuminate some villagers' gendered desires for other kinds of lives elsewhere, and show how many have come to even *depend* on the very uncertainties and arbitrary outcomes in the migration processes that are ostensibly the state's responsibility to address. This was evident in Indah's (chapter 5) multiple attempts to find a financially sustainable job as a high school dropout, and her response that choosing the "less evil" local recruitment agent was a better option than going through nonlocal agents. Her ambivalence and indecision about migrating, alongside her relatives' strong disapproval of her migration, provides the context to understand that her relatively risky decision to apply with the ill-reputed recruiter was nonetheless an informed one, and partially shaped by competing gendered desires and obligations, not simply out of ignorance or desperation.

This book could be criticized for focusing too much on the "collateral damage" of migration, while overlooking the ways that remittances have contributed to building concrete houses, increasing children's education, increasing consumption capacity, and paying medical expenses for migrants' families and neighbors. I do not wish to deny or underemphasize how remittances have enabled migrant-origin villagers to better afford these opportunities and resources. However, this book has argued for the need to challenge the impetus to justify these "gains" of migration, at the expense of arguments by migrants and migrant activists that these "gains" entail unnecessary and preventable risks and costs to migrants and their families. Indeed, the Indonesian state and migrants' destination countries often emphasize the "positive" developmental potential of migration in order to shift discussions away from structural or legal changes that favor improving migrants' labor rights and migration safety. As Nicole Constable has observed, a form of humanitarian reason "clearly underpins attitudes toward the employment of migrant workers from regions of the world that are considered poor . . . by wealthier labor-importing regions" (2014, 18). In this view, the low wages and lack of legal protection for labor migrants are justified through a discourse of employment as assistance or charity (ibid.), in which workers are treated as unappreciative "recipients of 'gifts' that create an obligation in the form of obedience and gratitude to the benefactor, as opposed to the expectations of labor rights, fair wages for their work, and the right of abode" (ibid.).

Currently, the Indonesian state's main solutions to migration's "problems" are to encourage migrant entrepreneurship and banking, to "stop" all domestic work migration by 2017, to open more international markets for Indonesian labor in "skilled" industries (mainly manufacturing and nursing), and to increase the regulation of prospective migrants, such as imposing stricter "psychological checks" (*Detik News* 2015; *Indosuara* 2014).[3] To address specific forms of migration deemed undesirable by state authorities, destination countries' governments, or the Indonesian public, the Indonesian state has banned female migration to the Middle East following diplomatic disputes over death sentences of Indonesians in certain countries, and forcefully repatriated undocumented migrants from Malaysia. In short, the Indonesian's state's solutions to the problems of migration have been to encourage *more* migration—for "formal" and nondomestic work—and to regulate and improve the "quality" of migrant workers.[4] These discursive promotions of certain migration projects are accompanied by intergovernmental agreements to increase Indonesia's expansion into more foreign labor markets, and redirecting or renaming migration flows.

I join other scholars and activists who argue that current "solutions" by the Indonesian state may have the opposite effect of placing greater risks and burdens on migrants (see Susilo 2017). Banning migration will very likely only expand the market for clandestine movement, while "psychological checks" for prospective migrants increase the costs of migration and symbolically target migrants' own mental conditions as a root "problem" of migration. These programs and discourses importantly diffuse what Aihwa Ong (2010) calls "idioms of resistance" (such as spirit possession, chapter 5), by reinforcing popular perceptions that migrant success and failure mainly are a matter of individual responsibility or luck, while at the same time, paradoxically overregulating migration.

Due to a complex set of historical and contemporary factors, Cilacap and Yogyakarta villagers, like the vast majority of Indonesian citizens, perceive and experience increasing pressures to identify with Islam, or find Islamic practices more relevant to their life worlds than before (Bennett 2005a; Boellstorff 2005; Bowen 1993; Brenner 1996; 1998; Hefner 1987; 2000; Smith-Hefner 2007). This book has shown some of the ways that these emerging Islamic subjectivities limit and/or enable the critique of exploitative or unfair labor and migration laws, and local norms of gendered morality, through a focus on individual fate, divine punishment, and divine justice, as opposed to (worldly) social justice. While some migrants and activists draw on and reinforce gendered moral expectations to draw sympathy for their causes (often successfully), such as in representations of the ideal feminine victim or migrant worker, there are also many that challenge or sidestep these assumptions.[5]

Some Indonesian activists employ ethical and moral rhetoric based on Islam and citizenship to advocate for and participate in programs involving migrant welfare and rights, while suspending judgement on individual actors. Several activists affiliated with migrant-centered or women's NGOs have politicized nasib (fate) discourses, in expressing that migrants' nasib depends on employers (*majikan*), the law (*hukum*), and education (*pendikikan*). This effectively reworks dominant nasib discourses pointing to luck, destiny, and migrants' moral character or efforts in explaining migrants' problems and failures. I met many activists, whether based in cities like Yogyakarta or Jakarta, or local community leaders, who perceived their roles in migrant-origin villages as changing people's apolitical attitudes towards migration in terms of nasib. Many, such as those attending the workshop I described in chapter 5, sought to change the discursive context of nasib from one that emphasizes individual human effort and faith to one that supports public sharing and collective action to change aspects of the migration infrastructure or status quo. These efforts include consulting former migrants for their input on reforming official migration procedures and regulations, documenting and highlighting to local governments and state agencies the nature and extent of institutional and procedural inconsistencies, and facilitating discussion forums for return and prospective migrants to more openly and publicly share negative or traumatic experiences of work and life abroad. Activists have also developed online platforms as working models for geographically diverse prospective migrants and current migrants to share experience-based information on specific recruitment agencies and insurance companies.[6] Those who see nasib as grounded in national and foreign laws, such as SBMI, have also focused on paralegal training for village leaders and local volunteers, so that they may address the needs of fellow villagers who seek compensation or satisfactory answers from recruitment companies and local governmental representatives in the event of fraud, disappearance, sickness, or death of a migrant kin or peer.

Some of these NGO and activist efforts have resulted in important infrastructural changes in some migrant-origin villages, such as the building of BP3TKI or its subsidiary P4TKI closer to migrant-origin areas. I agree that an effective way to reduce irregular migration and costs is to make it simpler for prospective migrants to independently navigate migration procedures (Patunru and Uddarojat 2015), and one way to do so is through providing the necessary and accessible infrastructure to populations more likely to migrate. Reducing unnecessary bureaucratic procedures is also a potentially effective strategy, as opposed to the current impetus to increase bureaucracy and checks ostensibly to "protect" migrants from exploitation and high fees; these efforts have instead been found to increase migrants' dependence on brokers, and the associated vulnerabilities and costs (ibid; Killias 2010). In the case of the Yogyakarta site, the presence of NGO actors helps the facilitation of insurance claims and access to skill-training programs for return migrants who may have experienced legal, financial, or medical issues abroad. The lack of access to these in Cilacap arguably contributes to more precarious forms of migration from Cilacap as compared to Yogyakarta, as well as higher levels of migration and more failed attempts to migrate. Nevertheless, both structural and discursive interventions can be effective in addressing migrant-origin villagers' concerns and anxieties only if they are sensitive to their situated knowledges and gendered experiences of risk.

Many Indonesia-based migrant-centered activist groups have also been advocating for changes to current migration regulations in order to place more legal responsibility for the welfare of migrant workers on Indonesian and foreign state agencies, rather than mainly limit the state's role to ensuring and regulating the recruitment and placement of Indonesian migrant workers abroad. In the 2015 discussions over how to redraft the National Regulation of Placement and Protection for Migrant Workers (which, at the time of writing, is still under revision), SBMI recommended that although recruitment agencies can be commercial entities, they should not be solely responsible for setting up and running predeparture training facilities as well as medical insurance (Buruh Migran 2015). The current regulations make recruitment agents solely responsible for these processes, which activists argue increases the vulnerability of migrants and prospective migrants to these brokers. The flipside is also that recruitment agencies may be bearing too much responsibility in running training processes and facilitating migration paperwork, and are sometimes easily and unfairly targeted as criminals in discussions about precarious migration. Instead, Indonesian-based migrant organizations like SBMI suggest that the presently highly commercialized training facilities could be run as public (or semiprivate) educational institutions. Migrants' associations in destination countries are also drawing attention to the negligence of some Indonesian Consulates and Embassies abroad that are inadequately staffed or unprepared to deal with cases of migrant abuse and labor disagreements (see also Palmer 2016).

These actions and proposals that focus on changing or improving infrastructural and legal provisions for migrant workers and migrant-origin villagers often require the discursive reframing of moral, legal, and financial responsibility within migration processes and the migration industry.[7] Seeing migration in terms of gendered moral economies reminds us that the stories we tell about migrants and where they come from relative to where they are going to—in terms of their work, pay, sexuality, and family lives—all contribute to dismissing or legitimizing certain perspectives and actions or inactions regarding people's abilities, capacities, and desires to move or stay in their place or country of birth. In future extensions of this project, it would be productive to focus in more detail on comparing the gendered experiences and perceptions of contemporary intranational migration and associated livelihoods in relation to transnational migration. The migration of men has also become increasingly vulnerable in recent years (see Palmer 2017). More migrant seafarers are involved in illegal fishing industries, and the migrants involved were often misled into thinking that they are going to work in cruise ships or in construction work abroad. Irregular forms of migration and brokerage—mainly of men—to Korea and Japan have also grown. Ironically, these migration corridors have been increasingly popular due to general perceptions of better wages and stricter labor protection laws, perceptions which are reinforced by the Indonesian state's determination to promote all state-facilitated and predominantly male migration to Korea and Japan as "formal" (hence, not precarious) work. In this context, the Indonesian government has declared it an achievement that the numbers of documented female domestic labor migrants seem to be decreasing, which they link to their effective ban against migration to the Middle East. Such statistics disguise the fact that risks are not reduced for all migrants, but may be simply justified, hidden, or transferred to other gendered industries. Future enquiry should attend to how migrant-origin villagers themselves, alongside other invested actors including researchers, participate in sustaining or containing faith in these new and continuing forms of precarious mobilities.

Notes

1. These meanings associated with Islam and capitalism are uniquely different from other Muslim-majority countries, such as those in the Middle East, which typically do not share Indonesia's history of secularism, democracy, and explicit state focus on women's rights and education.

2. Certain grassroots migrant welfare organizations have been effective both in facilitating legal and economic redress for return migrants who have experienced abuse or fraud, as well as in highlighting migrant labor issues at the national level. I argue, however, that these are exceptional cases in which individual former migrants "brought home" advocacy skills typically learned in Jakarta or from migrant-centered NGOs in destination countries. The vast majority of migrant-origin villages, however, lack such access to local grassroots organizations and NGOs and their discourses of migrant and labor rights.

3. The Indonesian government did not fulfill its plan to ban the migration of all domestic workers by 2017. "A senior official at the Manpower Ministry told the Thomson Reuters Foundation that Jakarta would not go ahead with the ban but it has been in talks with countries to ensure Indonesian maids are treated in a 'humane' way" (Beh 2017).

4. For example, in 2015, the Ministry of Foreign Labor helped to publish a book distributed to migrant-origin villagers titled "99 Tips to Become a Successful TKI." See *Solopos* 2015.

5. As discussed in chapter 2, activists and advocates for migrants' and labor rights often have to creatively employ various strategies that they perceive can best foster solidarity among different individuals and groups, bolster public support for, and draw forms of institutional attention to their causes. Thus, the discourses and actions of individual activists and groups can sometimes be inconsistent, in terms of attending to representations of gender and morality, such as when focusing on labor rights abroad, or educating prospective or current migrants on laws or rights (see also chapter 5 and Lai 2010; 2011).

6. An example is Pantau PJTKI: http://pantaupjtki.buruhmigran.or.id/. Accessed September 9, 2017.

7. For an example of such a reframing of moral responsibility in advocating for migrant and labor rights, see Koh et al. 2017. The authors show how civil society actors in Singapore, in their successful campaign to give migrant domestic workers a weekly day off, carefully avoided explicit references to rights discourses and instead strategically reframed their campaign in terms of a moral appeal within the cultural and discursive norms of Singaporean society. Simultaneously, the activists also employed other forms of reasoning (in terms of cost-benefit analysis and market mechanisms) to respond to anticipated fears by employers of workers' moral transgressions.

Bibliography

Abu-Lughod, Lila. 2008. *Writing Women's Worlds: Bedouin Stories*. 2nd ed. Berkeley: University of California Press.

Adrian, N.H. 2015. "WNI Terjebak Penyimpangan Seksual di Hong Kong." *Kompasiana*, June 26. Accessed March 9, 2016. http://www.kompasiana.com/m.abdul.gani /wni-terjebak-penyimpangan-seksual-di-hong-kong_54ff9c41a33311ec4f5104c6.

Agence France Presse. 2004. "Indonesian Maid Avoids Death Penalty after Killing Abusive Boss." *Singapore Window*, September 24. Accessed March 9, 2016. http://www .singapore-window.org/sw04/040924a2.htm.

Aguilar, Filomeno V. 1996. "The Dialectics of Transnational Shame and National Identity." *Philippines Sociological Review* 44: 106–36.

———. 1999. "Ritual Passage and the Reconstruction of Selfhood in International Labour Migration." *Sojourn: Journal of Social Issues in Southeast Asia* 14, no. 1 (April): 98–139.

Ahmed, Sara. 2012. *The Cultural Politics of Emotion*. New York and London: Routledge. (Orig. pub. 2004.)

Åkesson, Lisa. 2010. "Cape Verdean Notions of Migrant Remittances." *Cadernos de Estudos Africanos* 20: 139–59.

Al-Alawi, Irfan. 2011. "Indonesian Bans Labor to Saudi Arabia after Beheading of Grandmother." Gatestone Institute, August 15. Accessed July 2, 2014. http://www .gatestoneinstitute.org/2347/saudi-beheading-grandmother.

Anjalah, Veeramalla. 2015. "RI's Migrant Workers Remit Record $8.55 Billion in 2014: WB." *Jakarta Post*, April 20. Accessed March 9, 2011. http://www.thejakartapost.com /news/2015/04/20/ri-s-migrant-workers-remit-record-855-billion-2014-wb.html.

Antara News. 2012a. "Kiriman Uang TKI Asal NTB Rp 27.4 Milyar." July 23. Accessed July 1, 2014. http://www.antaranews.com/berita/323066/kiriman-uang-tki-asal-ntb -rp274-miliar-juni-2012.

———. 2012b. "Remittances from Migrants Soften Global Economic Crisis Blow." August 9. Accessed March 8, 2016. http://www.antaranews.com/en/news/83864/remittances -from-migrants-soften-global-economic-crisis-blow.

Anwar, Ratih P., and Carol Chan. 2016. "Contrasting Return Migrant Entrepreneurship Experiences in Javanese Villages." *International Migration* 54, no. 4: 150–63.

Aradou, Claudia. 2013. "Human Trafficking Between Data and Knowledge." Keynote lecture for the conference "Data Protection and Right to Privacy for Marginalized Groups: a New Challenge in Anti-Trafficking Policies," Berlin, September 25–27.

Ardyan, Mohamad. 2014. "Merasa Rugi Malaysia Lega Ribuan TKI Ilegal Enyah." *Merdeka*, December 24. Accessed April 18, 2016. http://www.merdeka.com/dunia/merasa-rugi -malaysia-lega-ribuan-tki-ilegal-enyah.html.

Arijaya, R. 2011. "Why Divorce in Indonesia is Increasing." *Jakarta Post*, September 12. Accessed July 2, 2014. http://www.thejakartapost.com/news/2011/09/12/why-divorce -indonesia-increasing.html.

Aritonang, Margareth. 2013. "RI Tries to Spare Wilfrida's Life." *Jakarta Post*, September 30. Accessed July 2, 2014. http://www.thejakartapost.com/news/2013/09/30/ri-tries-spare-wilfrida-s-life.html.

———. 2014. "Wilfrida Escapes Death Penalty." *Jakarta Post*, August 8. Accessed September 11, 2014. http://www.thejakartapost.com/news/2014/04/08/wilfrida-escapes-death-penalty-malaysia.html.

Arnez, Monika. 2010. "Empowering Women Through Islam: Fatayat NU Between Tradition and Change." *Journal of Islamic Studies* 21, no. 1: 59–88.

Asad, Talal. 2003. *Formations of the Secular: Christianity, Islam, Modernity*. Stanford: Stanford University Press.

Aslibumiayu.net. 2012. "Ada Apa dengan TKW di Arab … Jangan Hanya Membaca Berita Mereka Diperkosa, Tapi Baca Juga Dong Faktanya …" *Aslibumiayu.net*. June 17. Accessed September 12, 2014. http://aslibumiayu.wordpress.com/2012/06/17/ada-apa-dengan-tkw-di-arab-jangan-hanya-membaca-berita-mereka-diperkosa-tapi-baca-juga-dong-faktanya/.

Ayyubi, S. 2009. "Diduga Dianiaya Hingga Gigi Dicabut, TKW Jadi Gila." *Ecosoc Rights News Monitor* 2. Accessed July 2, 2014. http://ecosoc-monitor2.blogspot.com/2009/03/diduga-dianiaya-hingga-gigi-icabuttkw.html.

Badan Pusat Statistik Kabupaten Cilacap. 2015. "Cilacap Dalam Angka 2014." Badan Pusat Statistik Kabupaten Cilacap. Accessed August 4, 2015. https://cilacapkab.bps.go.id/index.php/publikasi/87.

Bapat, Sheila. 2014. *Part of the Family? Nannies, Housekeepers, Caregivers and the Battle for Domestic Workers' Rights*. New York: IG.

Bauman, Zgymunt. 2000. *Liquid Modernity*. Cambridge: Polity.

Bear, Laura, Karen Ho, Anna Tsing, and Sylvia Yanagisako. 2015. "Gens: A Feminist Manifesto for the Study of Capitalism." Fieldsights—Theorizing the Contemporary, *Cultural Anthropology Online*, March 30. Accessed September 9, 2017. http://www.culanth.org/fieldsights/652-gens-a-feminist-manifesto-for-the-study-of-capitalism.

Beatty, Andrew. 2002. "Changing Places: Relatives and Relativism in Java." *Journal of the Royal Anthropological Institute* 8, no. 3: 469–91.

Beh, Li Yi. 2017. "In U-turn, Indonesia Says Will Continue to Send Maids Abroad." *Thomson Reuters*, March 20. Accessed September 9, 2017. http://www.reuters.com/article/us-egypt-archaeology-discovery/egypt-archeologist-unearth-goldsmiths-tomb-near-luxor-idUSKCN1BKoFE.

Bélanger, Daniele, and Hong-Zen Wang. 2013. "Becoming a Migrant: Vietnamese Emigration to East Asia." *Pacific Affairs* 86, no. 1, Academic OneFile. Accessed October 1, 2016.

Bennett, Linda R. 2005a. *Women, Islam and Modernity: Single Women, Sexuality and Reproductive Health in Contemporary Indonesia*. New York and London: Routledge.

———. 2005b. "Patterns of Resistance and Transgression in Eastern Indonesia: Single Women's Practices of Clandestine Courtship and Cohabitation." *Culture, Health & Sexuality* 7, no. 2: 101–12.

Bennett, Linda R., Sari Andajani-Sutjahjo, and Nurul I. Idrus. 2011. "Domestic Violence in Nusa Tenggara Barat, Indonesia: Married Women's Definitions and Experiences of Violence in the Home." *The Asia Pacific Journal of Anthropology* 12, no. 2: 146–63.

Bernstein, Elizabeth. 2010. "Militarized Humanitarianism Meets Carceral Feminism: the Politics of Sex, Rights, and Freedom in Contemporary Anti-Trafficking Campaigns." *Signs* 36: 45–71.

Blackburn, Susan. 2004. *Women and the State in Modern Indonesia*. Cambridge, UK: Cambridge University Press.

BNP2TKI (Badan Nasional Penempatan Dan Perlindugan Tenaga Kerja Indonesia). 2011. "Tahun 2012 BNP2TKI Fokus Penempatan TKI Formal." Accessed June 5, 2013. http://www.bnp2tki.go.id/berita-mainmenu-231/6043-tahun-2012-bnp2tki-fokus -penempatan-tki-formal.html.

———. 2012. "Dede Khodijah TKI Asal Garut Meninggal Karena Sakit." http://www.bnp2tki .go.id/berita-mainmenu-231/6465-dede-khodijah-tki-asal-garut-meninggal-karena -sakit.html. Accessed July 2, 2014.

———. 2013. "10 Jenis Masalah Terbesar Berdasarkan Negara Penempatan Tahun 2011 s/d 2013." *Penempatan Dan Perlingundan Tenaga Kerja Indonesia Tahun 2013*. Accessed September 7, 2017. http://www.bnp2tki.go.id/uploads/data/data_22-06-2015_022721_Data _P2TKI_Tahun_2013.pdf.

———. 2014. "Kepala BNP2TKI: Kerja di Luar Negeri: Jagalah Citra Baik Bangsa." Accessed December 30, 2014. http://www.bnp2tki.go.id/berita-mainmenu-231/9757-kepala -bnp2tki-kerja-di-luar-negeri-jagalah-citra-baik-bangsa.html.

———. 2015. "Data Penempatan dan Perlindungan TKI Periode Tahun 2014." Accessed September 3, 2017. http://www.bnp2tki.go.id/stat_penempatan/indeks.

———. 2016. "Data Penempatan dan Perlindungan TKI Periode Tahun 2015." Accessed September 3, 2017. http://www.bnp2tki.go.id/stat_penempatan/indeks.

———. 2017. "Data Penempatan dan Perlindungan TKI Periode Tahun 2016." Accessed September 3, 2017. http://www.bnp2tki.go.id/stat_penempatan/indeks.

Boellstorff, Tom. 2004. "The Emergence of Political Homophobia in Indonesia: Masculinity and National Belonging." *Ethnos* 69, no. 4: 465–86.

———. 2005. *The Gay Archipelago: Sexuality and Nation in Indonesia*. Princeton: Princeton University Press.

Boellstorff, Tom, and Johan Lindquist. 2004. "Bodies of Emotion: Rethinking Culture and Emotion through Southeast Asia." *Ethnos* 69, no. 4: 437–44.

Bowen, John R. 1993. *Muslims through Discourse: Religion and Ritual in Gayo Society*. Princeton: Princeton University Press.

Brandom, Robert. 2008. *Making it Explicit: Reasoning, Representing and Discursive Commitment*. Cambridge, MA: Harvard University Press.

Brennan, Denise. 2014. *Life Interrupted: Trafficking into Forced Labor*. Durham, NC: Duke University Press.

Brenner, Suzanne. 1995. "Why Women Rule the Roost: Rethinking Javanese Ideologies of Gender and Self-Control." In *Bewitching Women, Pious Men: Gender and Body Politics in Southeast Asia*, edited by Aihwa Ong and Michael G. Peletz, 19–50. Berkeley: University of California Press.

———. 1996. "Reconstructing Self and Society: Javanese Muslim Women and the 'Veil'." *American Ethnologist* 23, no. 4: 673–97.

———. 1998. *The Domestication of Desire: Women, Wealth and Modernity in Java*. Princeton: Princeton University Press.

Brettell, Caroline, and Rita J. Simon, eds. 1986. *International Migration: The Female Experience*. Totowa: Rowman and Allanheld.

Brown, Wendy. 2005. *Edgework: Critical Essays on Knowledge and Politics*. Princeton: Princeton University Press.

Browne, Kevin. 2001. "(Ng)amuk Revisited: Emotional Expression and Mental Illness in Central Java, Indonesia." *Transcultural Psychiatry* 38, no. 2: 147–65.

Buruh Migran. 2008. "Lagi, TKW Asal Cilacap Disiksa." Buruh Migran. July 28. Accessed July 2, 2014. http://buruhmigran.or.id/en/2008/07/28/2761agi-tkw-asal-cilacap-disiksa.

———. 2014a. "Dua Orang Buruh Migran Keracunan Asap di Dubai." Buruh Migran. January 22. Accessed July 2, 2014. http://buruhmigran.or.id/2014/01/22/dua-orang -buruh-migran-keracunan-asap-di-dubai.

———. 2014b. "Miliki KTKLN, 74 ABK Masih Jadi Korban Perdagangan Orang." Buruh Migran. April 4. Accessed July 2, 2014. http://buruhmigran.or.id/2014/04/04/miliki -ktkln-74-abk-masih-jadi-korban-perdagangan-orang.

———. 2015. "UU 30 Tahun 2004 Tentang PPTKILN Tak Memiliki Naskah Akademik. Pusat Sumber Daya Buruh Migran." Buruh Migran. October 25. Accessed March 8, 2016. http://buruhmigran.or.id/2015/10/25/uu-39-tahun-2004-tentang-pptkiln-tak-memiliki -naskah-akademik.

Butler, Judith. 2006. *Precarious Life: The Powers of Mourning and Violence.* London: Verso.

Butt, Leslie, Jessica Ball, and Harriot Beazley. 2016. "False Papers and Family Fictions: Household Responses to 'Gift Children' Born to Indonesian Women during Transnational Migration." *Citizenship Studies* 20, no. 6–7: 795–810.

Bylander, Maryann. 2015. "Contested Mobilities: Gendered Migration Pressures among Cambodian Youth." *Gender, Place & Culture: A Journal of Feminist Geography* 22, no. 8: 1124–40.

Candraningrum, Dewi. 2013. *Negotiating Women's Veiling: Politics and Sexuality in Contemporary Indonesia.* Bangkok: IRASEC Research Institute on Contemporary Southeast Asia.

Carsten, Janet. 1991. "Children in Between: Fostering and the Process of Kinship on Pulau Langkawi, Malaysia." *Man* 26, no. 3: 425–43.

———. 2013. "What Kinship Does—and How." *HAU: Journal of Ethnographic Theory* 3, no. 2: 245–51.

Castles, Stephen. 2009. "Development and Migration or Migration and Development: What Comes First?" *Asian Pacific Migration Journal* 18: 441–71.

Chan, Carol. 2014. "Gendered Morality and Development Narratives: the Case of Female Labor Migration from Indonesia." *Sustainability* 6, no. 10: 6949–72.

———. 2017a. "Not Always 'Left-Behind:' Indonesian Adolescent Women Negotiating Transnational Mobility, Filial Piety, and Care." *The Asia Pacific Journal of Anthropology* 18, no. 3: 246–83.

———. 2017b. "In Between Leaving and Being Left-Behind: Mediating the Mobilities and Immobilities of Indonesian Non-Migrants." *Global Networks* 14, no. 4: 554–73.

Chen, Te-Ping. 2012. "Permanent Residency Blocked for Maids in Hong Kong." *Wall Street Journal*, March 28. Accessed May 9, 2017. https://blogs.wsj.com/chinarealtime /2012/03/28/permanent-residency-blocked-for-maids-in-hong-kong/.

Cheng, Sealing. 2010. *On the Move for Love: Migrant Entertainers and the U.S. Military in South Korea.* Philadelphia: University of Pennsylvania Press.

Chittick, William C. 2000. "Time, Space, and the Objectivity of Ethical Norms: the Teachings of Ibn al-'Arabī." *Islamic Studies* 39, no. 4: 581–96.

———. 2001. *The Heart of Islamic Philosophy: The Quest for Self-Knowledge in the Teachings of Afḍal al-Dīn Kāshānī.* Oxford: Oxford University Press.

———. 2011. "The Aesthetics of Islamic Ethics." In *Sharing Poetic Expressions*, edited by Anna-Teresa Tymieniecka, 3–14. Dordrecht: Springer Netherlands.

Choo, Hae-Yeon. 2013. "The Cost of Rights: Migrant Women, Feminist Advocacy, and Gendered Morality in South Korea." *Gender & Society* 27: 445–68.

Chu, Julie Y. 2010. *Cosmologies of Credit: Transnational Mobility and the Politics of Destination in China*. Durham, NC: Duke University Press.

Cohen, Jeffrey, and Ibrahim Sirekci. 2011. *Cultures of Migration: The Global Nature of Contemporary Mobility*. Austin: University of Texas Press.

Collins, Elizabeth F. 2007. *Indonesia Betrayed: How Development Fails*. Honolulu: University of Hawai'i Press.

Collins, Elizabeth F., and Ernaldi Bahar. 2000. "To Know Shame: Malu and Its Uses in Malay Societies." *Crossroads: An Interdisciplinary Journal of Southeast Asian Studies* 14, no. 1 (January): 35–69.

Conradson, David, and Deirdre McKay. 2007. "Translocal Subjectivities: Mobility, Connection and Emotion." *Mobilities* 2, no. 2: 167–74.

Constable, Nicole. 1999. "At Home but Not At Home: Filipina Narratives of Ambivalent Returns." *Cultural Anthropology* 14, no. 2: 203–28.

———. 2003. "Women's Agency and the Gendered Geography of Marriage." In *Romance on a Global Stage: Pen Pals, Virtual Ethnography and "Mail-Order" Marriages*, 145–74. Berkeley: University of California Press.

———. 2007. *Maid to Order in Hong Kong*. 2nd ed. Ithaca: Cornell University Press. (Orig. pub. 1997.)

———. 2009a. "The Commodification of Intimacy: Marriage, Sex, and Reproductive Labor." *Annual Review of Anthropology* 38: 49–64.

———. 2009b. "Migrant Workers and the Many States of Protest in Hong Kong." *Critical Asian Studies* 41: 143–64.

———. 2014. *Born Out of Place: Migrant Mothers and the Politics of International Labor*. Berkeley: University of California Press.

———. Forthcoming. "Assemblages and Affect: Migrant Mothers and the Varieties of Absent Children." *Global Networks*.

Contreras, Ricardo, and David Griffith. 2012. "Managing Migration, Managing Motherhood: the Moral Economy of Gendered Migration." *International Migration* 50, no. 4: 51–66.

Dagur, Ryan. 2013. "President Lambasted for Ignoring Indonesia's Migrant Workers." *UCANews.com*, December 18. Accessed September 11, 2014. http://www.ucanews.com /news/president-lambasted-for-ignoring-indonesias-migrant-workers/69937.

Dang, Trung Dinh, Sango Mahanty, and Susan Mackay. 2013. "'Living with Pollution': Juggling Environmental and Social Risk in Vietnam's Craft Villages." *Critical Asian Studies* 45, no. 4: 643–69.

Dannecker, Petra. 2009. "Migrant Visions of Development: A Gendered Approach." *Population, Space, Place*, 15: 119–13.

Darmaningtyas. 2002. *Pulung Gantung: Menyingkap Trajedi Bunuh Diri di Gunungkidul* Yogyakarta: Galangpress Group.

Das, Veena. 2007. *Life and Words: Violence and the Descent into the Ordinary*. Berkeley, CA: California University Press.

———. 2012. "Ordinary Ethics." In *A Companion to Moral Anthropology*, edited by Didier Fassin, 133–49. Malden: John Wiley & Sons.

———. 2015. "What Does Ordinary Ethics Look Like?" *Four Lectures on Ethics in Anthropology*, edited by Michael Lambek, Veena Das, Didier Fassin, and Webb Keane. Chicago: HAU Books.

Daston, Lorraine. 1995. "The Moral Economy of Science." *Osiris* 10: 2–24.

Daswani, Girish. 2010. "Ghanian Pentecostal Prophets: Transnational Travel and (Im) Mobility." In *Traveling Spirits: Migrants, Markets and Mobilities*, edited by Gurturd Huwelmeier and Kristine Krause, 67–82. New York: Routledge.

Databoks. 2016. "Di Provinsi Mana Banyak Orang Bunuh Diri?" December 22. Accessed September 9, 2017. http://databoks.katadata.co.id/datapublish/2016/12/22/jawa-tengah -provinsi-dengan-kasus-bunuh-diri-terbanyak-di-indonesia.

———. 2017. "2016, TKI Meninggal di Luar Negiri Meningkat 42%." February 28. Accessed September 9, 2017. http://databoks.katadata.co.id/datapublish/2017/02/28/2016-tki -meninggal-di-luar-negeri-meningkat-42.

Davies, Sharyn. 2014. "Surveilling Sexuality in Indonesia." In *Sex and Sexuality in Indonesia: Sexual Politics, Diversity and Representations in the Reformasi Era*, edited by Linda R. Bennett and Sharyn Davies, 30–61. London: Routledge.

DedeMit Jarank Onlen. 2011. "Cerita Pelangi Para TKI, Inilah Alasan Mereka Kabur?" *Kompasiana*, November 3. Accessed September 8, 2017. http://www.kompasiana.com /ddmit/cerita-pelangi-para-tki-inilah-alasan-mereka-kabur_550911c2813311891cb1e391.

De Haas, Hein. 2010. "Migration and Development: A Theoretical Perspective." *International Migration Review* 44: 227–64.

Detik News. 2014. "20,000 TKI Ilegal Keluar Masuk Trauma Center Bambu Apus Sepanjang 2014." December 26. Accessed March 9, 2016. http://news.detik.com /berita/2787649/20000-tki-ilegal-keluar-masuk-trauma-center-bambu-apus -sepanjang-2014.

———. 2015. "Kepala BNP2TKI Nusron Wahid: TKI Harus Jalani Psikotes." April 30. Accessed March 8, 2016. http://news.detik.com/wawancara/2903029/kepala-bnp2tki -nusron-wahid-tki-harus-jalani-psikotes.

Donato, Katharine M., Donna Gabaccia, Jennifer Holdaway, Martin Manalansan, and Patricia R. Pessar. 2006. "A Glass Half Full? Gender in Migration Studies." *International Migration Review* 40 no. 1: 3–26.

Doorn-Harder, Pieternella van. 2008. "Controlling the Body: Muslim Feminists Debating Women's Rights in Indonesia." *Religion Compass* 2, no. 6: 1021–43.

Dove, Michael R. 1988. *The Real and Imagined Role of Culture in Development*. Honolulu: University of Hawai'i Press.

Dreby, Joanna. 2009. "Gender and Transnational Gossip." *Qualitative Sociology* 32, no. 1: 33–52.

Duncan, Whitney L. 2015. "Transnational Disorders: Returned Migrants at Oaxaca's Psychiatric Hospital." *Medical Anthropology Quarterly* 29, no. 1: 24–41.

Duranti, Alessandro. 2015. *The Anthropology of Intentions*. Cambridge: Cambridge University Press.

Edisi News. 2014. "TKI Adalah Asset Bangsa Bukan Dijiadikan Komoditi." July 11. Accessed March 7, 2016. http://www.edisinews.com/berita-tki-adalah-aset-bangsa-bukan -dijadikan-komoditi.html#ixzz3EFPo1Ixu.

Ehrenreich, Barbara, and Arlie Russell Hochschild, eds. 2003. *Global Woman: Nannies, Maids, and Sex Workers in the New Economy*. London: Macmillan.

Elmhirst, Rebecca. 2002. "Daughters and Displacement: Migration Dynamics in an Indonesian Transmigration Area." *Journal of Development* Studies 38, no. 5: 143–66.

———. 2007. "Tigers and Gangsters: Masculinities and Feminised Migration in Indonesia." *Population, Space, Place* 13: 225- 38.

Elyachar, Julia. 2012. "Before (and After) Neoliberalism: Tacit Knowledge, Secrets of the Trade, and the Public Sector in Egypt." *Cultural Anthropology* 27, no. 1: 76–96.

Errington, Shelley. 1987. "Incestuous Twins and the House Societies of Insular Southeast Asia." *Cultural Anthropology* 2, no.4: 403–44.

Fadly, Tegar Arief. 2014. "Izin Operasi 16 Perusahaan Pengirim TKI Dicabut." *Bisnis*, September 7. Accessed March 8, 2016. http://bandung.bisnis.com/read /20140907/34239/516648/izin-operasi-16-perusahaan-pengirim-tki-dicabut.

———. 2015. "Mafia TKI Ilegal Dibongkar, Busron Minta Polisi Buru Para Pemasok." *Bisnis*, March 13. Accessed March 8, 2016. http://industri.bisnis.com/read/20150313/12/411585 /mafia-tki-ilegal-dibongkar-nusron-minta-polisi-buru-para-pemasok.

Faier, Lieba. 2007. "Filipina Migrants in Rural Japan and Their Professions of Love." *American Ethnologist* 34, no. 1: 148–62.

Faist, Thomas. 2008. "Migrants as Transnational Development Agents: An Inquiry into the Newest Round of the Migration-Development Nexus." *Population, Space, Place*, 14: 21–42.

Faizal, Elly Burhaini. 2012a. "Mentally Ill Often Taken to Traditional Practitioners." *Jakarta Post*, February 13. Accessed March 9, 2016. http://www.thejakartapost.com/news /2012/02/13/mentally-ill-often-taken-traditional-practitioners.html.

———. 2012b. "Returning Migrant Workers Dogged by Mental Problems." *Jakarta Post*, June 26. Accessed March 8, 2016. http://www.thejakartapost.com/news/2012/06/26/returning -migrant-workers-dogged-mental-problems.html.

Fajardo, Kale Bantigue. 2011. *Filipino Crosscurrents: Oceanographies of Seafaring, Masculinities, and Globalization*. Minneapolis: University of Minnesota Press.

Fassin, Didier. 2005. "Compassion and Repression: the Moral Economy of Immigration Policies in France." *Cultural Anthropology* 20, no. 3: 362–87.

———. 2007. "Humanitarianism as a Politics of Life." *Public Culture* 19, no. 3: 499.

———. 2012. "Introduction: Toward a Critical Moral Anthropology." In *A Companion to Moral Anthropology*, edited by Didier Fassin, 1–17. Malden: John Wiley & Sons.

Fealy, Greg. 2008. "Consuming Islam: Consuming Religion and Aspirational Pietism in Contemporary Indonesia." In *Expressing Islam: Religious Life and Politics in Indonesia*, edited by Greg Fealy and Sally White, 15–39. Singapore: ISEAS-Institute of Southeast Asian Studies.

Fealy, Greg, and Sally White, eds. 2008. *Expressing Islam: Religious Life and Politics in Indonesia*. Singapore: ISEAS-Institute of Southeast Asian Studies.

Fessler, Daniel M. 2004. "Shame in Two Cultures: Implications for Evolutionary Approaches." *Journal of Cognition and Culture* 4, no. 2: 207–62.

Fioratta, Susanna. 2015. "Beyond Remittance: Evading Uselessness and Seeking Personhood in Fouta Djallon, Guinea." *American Ethnologist* 42, no. 2: 295–308.

Firdausy, Carunia Mulya. 2006. "Indonesian Labour Migration after the 1997–1998 Asian Economic and Financial Crisis." In *Mobility, Labour Migration and Border Controls in Asia*, edited by Amarjit Kaur and Ian Metcalfe, 139–154. London: Palgrave MacMillan.

Flamm, Michael, and Vincent Kaufmann. 2006. "Operationalising the Concept of Motility: A Qualitative Study." *Mobilities* 1, no. 2: 167–89.

Ford, Michele. 2002. "Public Accounts of Indonesian Women Workers' Experiences Overseas." *Asian Journal of Women's Studies* 8: 101–10.

Ford, Michele, and Lenore Lyons. 2011. "Travelling the Aspal Route: Grey Labour Migration through an Indonesian Border Town." In *The State and Illegality in Indonesia*, edited by Edward Aspinall and Gerry van Klinken, 107–22. Leiden: KITLV.

———. 2012. "Counter-Trafficking and Migrant Labour Activism in Indonesia's Periphery." In *Labour Migration and Human Trafficking in Southeast Asia: Critical Perspectives*, edited by Michele Ford, Lenore Lyons, and Willem van Schendel, 75–94. London: Routledge.

Fortier, Anne-Marie, Sara Ahmed, Claudia Castañeda, and Mimi Sheller, eds. 2003. *Uprootings/Regroundings: Questions of Home and Migration*. London: Berg.

Frederick, William, and Robert Worden, eds. 1993. *Indonesia: a Country Study*. Washington, DC: Federal Research Division, Library of Congress.

Gamburd, Michele. 2000. *The Kitchen Spoon's Handle: Transnationalism and Sri Lanka's Migrant Households*. New York: Cornell University Press.

———. 2008. *Breaking the Ashes: The Culture of Illicit Liquor in Sri Lanka*. New York: Cornell University Press.

Gardner, Katy. 1995. *Global Migrants, Local Lives: Travel and Transformation in Rural Bangladesh*. Oxford: Clarendon.

Geertz, Clifford. 1960. *The Religion of Java*. Glencoe: Free Press.

Geertz, Hilda. 1961. *The Javanese Family*. Glencoe: Free Press.

Good, Mary-Jo DelVecchio and Paul E. Brodwin. 1994. *Pain as Human Experience: An Anthropological Perspective*. Berkeley: University of California Press.

Good, Byron, Michael M. J. Fischer, Sarah S. Willen, and Mary-Jo DelVecchio Good, eds. 2010. *A Reader in Medical Anthropology: Theoretical Trajectories, Emergent Realities*. Malden, MA: Wiley-Blackwell.

Grace, Jocelyn. 2004. "Sasak Women Negotiating Marriage, Polygyny and Divorce in Rural East Lombok." *Intersections: Gender, History and Culture in the Asian Context* 10 (August). Accessed September 9, 2017. http://intersections.anu.edu.au/issue10/grace.html.

Graham, Elspeth, and Lucy P. Jordan. 2011. "Migrant Parents and the Psychological Well-Being of Left-Behind Children in Southeast Asia." *Journal of Marriage and Family* 73, no. 4: 763–87.

Graham, Elspeth, Lucy P. Jordan, Brenda S. A. Yeoh, Theodora Lam, and Maruja Asis. 2012. "Transnational Families and the Family Nexus: Perspectives of Indonesian and Filipino Children Left Behind by Migrant Parent(s)." *Environment and Planning A* 44, no. 4: 793–815.

Grundy, Tom. 2014. "Press Release: Abuse is 'Rare'? Our Response to the Indonesian Consul." HK Helpers Campaign. January 22. Accessed September 11, 2014. http://hkhelperscampaign.com/en/response-to-indonesia-consul.

Guevarra, Anna R. 2006. "Managing 'Vulnerabilities' and 'Empowering' Migrant Filipina Workers: The Philippines' Overseas Employment Program." *Social Identities* 12, no. 5: 523–41.

———. 2010. *Marketing Dreams, Manufacturing Heroes: The Transnational Labor Brokering of Filipino Workers*. New Brunswick: Rutgers University Press.

Gunawan, Apriadi. 2015. "Maid Killer Sentenced to Five Years in Jail." *Jakarta Post*, January 6. Accessed March 9, 2016. http://www.thejakartapost.com/news/2015/01/06/maid-killer -sentenced-five-years-jail.html#sthash.59orPhUH.dpuf.

Halim, Haeril. 2015. "Congresses to Promote Moderate View of Islam." *Jakarta Post*, July 31. Accessed March 9, 2016. http://www.thejakartapost.com/news/2015/07/31/congresses-promote-moderate-view-islam.html.

Hamdy, Sherine. 2008. "When the State and Your Kidneys Fail." *American Ethnologist*, 35: 553–69.

Han, Clara. 2012. *Life in Debt. Times of Care and Violence in Neoliberal Chile*. Berkeley: University of California Press.

Hannaford, Dinah. 2015. "Technologies of the Spouse: Intimate Surveillance in Senegalese Transnational Marriages." *Global Networks* 15, no.1: 43–59.

Hannaford, Dinah, and Ellen Foley. 2015. "Negotiating Love and Marriage in Contemporary Senegal: A Good Man Is Hard to Find." *African Studies Review* 58, no. 2: 205–25.

Hannam, Kevin, Mimi Sheller, and John Urry. 2006. "Editorial: Mobilities, Immobilities and Moorings." *Mobilities* 1, no. 1: 1–22.

Hannerz, Ulf. 2003. "Being There ... and There ... and There! Reflections on Multi-Site Ethnography." *Ethnography* 4, no. 2: 201–16.

Hastrup, Kirsten. 2012. "Scales of Attention in Fieldwork: Global Connections and Local Concerns in the Arctic." *Ethnography* 14, no. 2: 145–64.

Hatley, Barbara. 1990. "Theatrical Imagery and Gender Ideology in Java." In *Power and Difference: Gender in Island Southeast Asia*, edited by Shelley Errington and Jane M. Atkinson, 177–207. Stanford: Stanford University Press.

Hefner, Robert W. 1987. "Islamizing Java? Religion and Politics in Rural East Java." *The Journal of Asian Studies* 3, no. 46: 533–54.

———. 2000. *Civil Islam: Muslims and Democratization in Indonesia*. Princeton: Princeton University Press.

———. 2008. "Islam in Indonesia, post-Suharto: the Struggle for the Sunni Center: Review Essay." *Indonesia* 86: 139–60.

———. 2011. "Where Have All the Abangan Gone? Religionization and the Decline of Non-Standard Islam in Contemporary Indonesia." In *The Politics of Religion in Indonesia: Syncretism, Orthodoxy, and Religious Contention in Java and Bali*, edited by Michele Picard and Remy Madinier, 71–91. New York: Routledge.

Hernández-Carretero, María, and Jørgen Carling. 2012. "Beyond 'Kamikaze Migrants': Risk Taking in West African Boat Migration to Europe." *Human Organization* 71, no. 4: 407–16.

Heyman, Josiah McC., and John Symons. 2012. "Borders." In *Moral Anthropology*, edited by Didier Fassin, 540–57. Malden, MA: Wiley-Blackwell.

Heywood, Paolo. 2015. "Freedom in the Code: The Anthropology of (Double) Morality." *Anthropological Theory* 15, no. 2: 200–17.

Hoang, Lan. A., and Brenda S. A. Yeoh. 2011. "Breadwinning Wives and 'Left-Behind' Husbands: Men and Masculinities in the Vietnamese Transnational Family." *Gender & Society* 25, no. 6: 717–39.

Hoang, Lan A., Brenda S. A. Yeoh, and Anna Marie Wattie. 2012. "Transnational Labour Migration and the Politics of Care in the Southeast Asian Family." *Geoforum* 43, no. 4: 733–40.

Hoang, Lan Anh, Theodora Lam, Brenda S. A. Yeoh, and Elspeth Graham. 2015. "Transnational Migration, Changing Care Arrangements and Left-Behind Children's Responses in South-East Asia." *Children's Geographies* 13, no. 3: 263–77.

Hoesterey, James. 2013. "Shaming the State: Subjectivity and Islamic Ethics in Indonesia's Pornography Debate." CURA–Luce Short Paper on Key Issues in Religion and World Affairs, Emory University.

Hondagneu-Sotelo, Pierrette. 1994. *Gendered Transitions: Mexican Experiences of Immigration.* Berkeley: University of California Press.

———. 2000. "Feminism and Migration." *Annals of the American Academy of Political and Social Science* 571: 107–20.

Hooker, Michael. 2003. *Indonesian Islam: Social Change through Contemporary Fatawa.* Honolulu: University of Hawai'i Press.

Hsia, Hsiao-Chuan. 2009. "The Making of a Transnational Grassroots Migrant Movement." *Critical Asian Studies* 41: 113–41.

Huang, Shirlena, and Brenda S. A. Yeoh. 2007. "Emotional Labour and Transnational Domestic Work: The Moving Geographies of 'Maid Abuse' in Singapore." *Mobilities* 2: 195–217.

Hugo, Graeme J. 1982. "Circular Migration in Indonesia." *Population and Development Review* 8, no. 1: 59–83.

Hugo, Graeme J., and Charles Stahl. 2004. "Labor Export Strategies in Asia." In *International Migration: Prospects and Policies in a Global Market,* edited by Douglas Massey and Edward Taylor, 174–200. Oxford: Oxford University Press.

Huijsmans, Roy. 2012. "Beyond Compartmentalization: A Relational Approach towards Agency and Vulnerability of Young Migrants." *New Directions for Child and Adolescent Development* 136: 29–45.

Hull, Terence. 2007. "Formative Years of Family Planning in Indonesia." In *The Global Revolution in Family Planning,* edited by Warren C. Robinson and John A Ross, 235–57. Washington, DC: The World Bank.

Hunt, Linda. M., and Mattingly, Cheryl. 1998. "Introduction: Diverse Rationalities and Multiple Realities in Illness and Healing." *Medical Anthropology Quarterly* 12, no. 3: 267–72.

Huwelmeier, Gertrud, and Kristine Krause. 2010. Introduction to *Traveling Spirits: Migrants, Markets and Mobilities,* edited by Gertrud Huwelmeier and Kristine Krause, 1–16. New York: Routledge.

Indosuara. 2014. "Kepala BP3TKI Semarang: 'Tes Psikologi BMI untuk Ketahui Kekuatan Mental.'" May 29. Accessed March 8, 2016. http://www.indosuara.com /headline/kepala-bp3tki-semarang-tes-psikologi-bmi-untuk-ketahui-kekuatan -mental/.

International Crisis Group. 2008. "Indonesia: Implications of the Ahmadiyah Decree." *Asia Briefing* 78 (July 7). Accessed March 8, 2016. https://www.crisisgroup.org/asia/south -east-asia/indonesia/indonesia-implications-ahmadiyah-decree.

International Organization for Migration. 2013. "IOM and the 2013 UN High Level Dialogue on International Migration and Development." International Organization for Migration. Accessed July 1, 2014. http://www.iom.int/cms/hld2013.

Irawanto, Budi. 2010. "Riding Waves of Change: Islamic Press in Postauthoritarian Indonesia." In *Politics and the Media in Twenty-First Century Indonesia: Decade of Democracy,* edited by Krishna Sen and David Hill, 67–84. London: Routledge.

Jakarta Globe. 2012. "Indonesia Plans to Stop Sending Domestic Workers Abroad by 2017." Accessed July 2, 2014. http://www.thejakartaglobe.com/archive/indonesia-plans-to -stop-sending-domestic-workers-abroad-by-2017.

Jakarta Post. 2010a. "RI to Abolish 'Pasung' Practice by 2014." October 8. Accessed March 2016. http://www.thejakartapost.com/news/2010/10/08/ri-abolish-E2%80%98pasung %E2%80%99-practice-2014.html.

———. 2010b. "Saudi Diplomat is 'Not Correct': Migrant Worker NGO." November 19. Accessed September 11, 2014. http://www.thejakartapost.com/news/2010/11/19/saudi -diplomat-%E2%80%9Cnot-correct%E2%80%9D-migrant-worker-ngo.html.

———. 2011. "Govt Fails Migrant Workers." December 20. Accessed March 7, 2016. http:// www.thejakartapost.com/news/2011/12/20/govt-fails-migrant-workers.html.

———. 2014a. "Migrant Workers Sent Home Rp 88.6 trillion in 2013." January 15. Accessed March 7, 2016. http://www.thejakartapost.com/news/2014/01/15/migrant-workers-sent -home-rp-886t-2013.html.

———. 2014b. "Thousands of Hong Kong Domestic Helpers Rally for 'Tortured' Maid." January 19. Accessed January 26, 2014. http://www.thejakartapost.com/news /2014/01/19/thousands-hong-kong-domestic-helpers-rally-tortured-maid.html.

———. 2015a. "Islands in Focus: Farmers Reject Airport Development." October 27. Accessed March 9, 2016. http://www.thejakartapost.com/news/2015/10/27/islands-focus-farmers -reject-airport-development.html.

———. 2015b. "Jokowi to Halt Sending Domestic Workers Abroad." February 14. Accessed March 8, 2016. http://www.thejakartapost.com/news/2015/02/14/jokowi-halt-sending -domestic-workers-abroad.html.

———. 2016. "Indonesian Clerics Declare LGBT Groups Haram." February 17. Accessed March 9, 2016. http://www.thejakartapost.com/news/2016/02/17/indonesian-clerics -declare-lgbt-groups-haram.html.

Jay, Robert. 1963. *Religion and Politics in Rural Central Java*. New Haven: Yale University.

Johns Hopkins Medical Institutions. 2008. "Rare Case Explains Why Some Infected with HIV Remain Symptom Free without Antiretroviral Drugs." *AIDS Vaccine Week* 2 (September 8). Accessed October 6, 2015. Academic OneFile.

Jones, Carla. 2007. "Fashion and Faith in Urban Indonesia." *Fashion Theory: The Journal of Dress, Body & Culture* 11, no. 2/3: 211–31.

Jones, Gavin, and Hsui-hua Shen. 2008. "International Marriage in East and Southeast Asia: Trends and Research Emphases." *Citizenship Studies* 12, no. 1: 9–25.

Kalleberg, Anne L. 2013. "Globalization and Precarious Work." *Contemporary Sociology* 42: 700–06.

Kankonde, Peter. 2010. "Transnational Family Ties, Remittance Motives, and Social Death among Congoloese Migrants: A Socio-Anthropological Analysis." *Journal of Comparative Family Studies* 41: 225–43.

Katigbak, Evangeline O. 2015. "Moralizing Emotional Remittances: Transnational Familyhood and Translocal Moral Economy in the Philippines' 'Little Italy'." *Global Networks* 15, no. 4: 519–35.

Katz, June S., and Ronald S. Katz. 1975. "The New Indonesian Marriage Law: a Mirror of Indonesia's Political, Cultural, and Legal Systems." *The American Journal of Comparative Law* 23, no. 4. 653–81.

Kaufmann, Vincent, Manfred Bergman, and Dominique Joye. 2004. "Motility: Mobility as Capital." *International Journal of Urban and Regional Research* 28, no. 4: 745–56.

Keane, Webb. 1996. "Money as Matter and Sign." *Etnofoor* 9, no. 1: 71–81.

———. 2007. "Materialism, Missionaries, and Modern Subjects." In *Christian Moderns: Freedom and Fetish in the Mission Encounter*. Berkeley: University of California Press.

———. 2014. "Affordances and Reflexivity in Ethical Life: An Ethnographic Stance." *Anthropological Theory* 14, no. 1: 3–26.

Kearney, Michael. 1995. "The Local and the Global: The Anthropology of Globalization and Transnationalism." *Annual Review of Anthropology* 24: 257–65.

Keeler, Ward. 1983. "Shame and Stage Fright in Java." *Ethos* 11, no. 3: 152–65.

Kellerman, Aharon. 2012. "Potential Mobilities." *Mobilities* 7, no. 1: 171–83.

Kelley, Annie, and Hazel Thompson. 2015. "The Vanished: the Filipino Domestic Workers Who Disappear Behind Closed Doors." *Guardian*, October 24. Accessed March 9, 2016. http://www.theguardian.com/global-development/2015/oct/24/the-vanished -filipino-domestic-workers-working-abroad.

KEMENPORA (Kementerian Pemuda dan Olahraga Republik Indonesia). 2017. "Pencegahan TKI Non Prosedural." Kemenpora. Accessed September 6, 2017. http://kemenpora .go.id/index/preview/pengumuman/416.

Kempadoo, Kamala. 2012. "Abolitionism, Criminal Justice, and Transnational Feminism." In *Trafficking and Prostitution Reconsidered: New Perspectives on Migration, Sex Work, and Human Rights*, 2nd ed., edited by Kamala Kempadoo, Jyoti Sanghera, and Bandana Pattanaik, vii–xxxiv. Boulder: Paradigm.

Keough, Leyla J. 2008. *"Driven" Women: Gendered Moral Economies of Women's Migrant Labor in Postsocialist Europe's Peripheries*. PhD diss., University of Massachusetts Amherst.

Kevin, Joshua. 2012. "Microsoft and US Embassy in Indonesia Launch iMULAI 4.0." Tech in Asia, March 14. Accessed September 6, 2017. https://www.techinasia.com/imulai -4-jakarta.

Khoo, Choon Yen, Maria Platt, Brenda S. A. Yeoh, Silvia Mila, Grace Baey Arlini, Theodora Lam, Julie Litchfield Sukamdi, and Endang Sugiyarto. 2014. "Gendered Migration Patterns, Processes, and Outcomes: Results from a Household Survey in Ponorogo, Indonesia." Migrating Out of Poverty, Working Paper 22, October. Brighton, U.K.

Khoo, Choon Yen, Maria Platt, Brenda S. A. Yeoh, and Theodora Lam. 2015. "Structural Conditions and Agency in Migrant Decision-Making: A Case of Domestic and Construction Workers from Java, Indonesia." Migrating Out of Poverty, Working Paper 25, February. Brighton, U.K.

Killias, Olivia. 2010. "Illegal Migration as Resistance: Legality, Morality and Coercion in Indonesian Domestic Worker Migration to Malaysia." *Asian Journal of Social Sciences* 38: 897–914.

Kim, Hyung-Jun. 2007. *Reformist Muslims in a Yogyakarta Village: the Islamic Transformation of Contemporary Socio-Religious Life*. Canberra: Australian National University Press. (Orig. pub. 1996.)

Kleinman, Arthur. 1988. *The Illness Narratives: Suffering, Healing, and the Human Condition*. New York: Basic Books.

Kloppenburg, Sanneke, and Peter Peters. 2012. "Confined Mobilities: Following Indonesian Migrant Workers on Their Way Home." *Tijdschrift voor economische en sociale geografie* 103: 530–41.

Knight, Kyle. 2013. "Looking for the Truth in the Deaths of Indonesia's Migrant Workers." *International Business Times*, January 25. Accessed July 2, 2014. http://www.ibtimes .com/looking-truth-deaths-indonesias-migrant-workers-1037974.

Koh, Chiu Yee, Kellynn Wee, Charmian Goh, and Brenda S. A. Yeoh. 2017. "Cultural Mediation through Vernacularization: Framing Rights Claims through the Day-Off

Campaign for Migrant Domestic Workers in Singapore." *International Migration* 55, no. 3: 89–104.

Kompas. 2014. "Target Kalla, Tak Ada Lagi TKW ke Luar Negeri dalam 5 Tahun Ini." November 21. Accessed March 8, 2016. http://nasional.kompas.com/read /2014/11/21/22155391/Target.Kalla.Tak.Ada.Lagi.TKW.ke.Luar.Negeri.dalam .5.Tahun.Ini.

Koo, Mee-Hyoe. 2013. "Understanding the Social Entrepreneurship Field in Indonesia." *Forbes*, September 30. Accessed March 8. http://www.forbes.com/sites/meehyoekoo /2013/09/30/understanding-the-social-entrepreneurship-field-in-indonesia /#249664775532.

Kwon, June H. 2015. "The Work of Waiting: Love and Money in Korean Chinese Transnational Migration." *Cultural Anthropology* 30, no. 3: 477–500.

Ladegaard, H. J. 2013a. "Laughing at Adversity: Laughter as Communication in Domestic Helper Narratives." *Journal of Language and Social Psychology* 32, no. 4: 390–411.

———. 2013b. "Demonising the Cultural Other: Legitimising Dehumanisation of Foreign Domestic Helpers in the Hong Kong Press." *Discourse Context Media* 2: 131–40.

Lagarde, Christine. 2015. "Poised for Take-off—Unleashing Indonesia's Economic Potential." Speech transcript, September 1, Universitas Indonesia, Accessed March 8, 2016. https:// www.imf.org/external/np/speeches/2015/090115.htm.

Lai, Ming Yan. 2010. "The Sexy Maid in Indonesian Migrant Workers' Activist Theatre: Subalternity, Performance and Witnessing." *Performing Ethos: International Journal of Ethics in Theatre & Performance* 1, no. 1: 21–34.

———. 2011. "The Present of Forgetting: Diasporic Identity and Migrant Domestic Workers in Hong Kong." *Social Identities* 17: 565–85.

Laidlaw, James. 2002. "For an Anthropology of Ethics and Freedom." *Journal of the Royal Anthropological Institute* 8, no. 2: 311–32.

Lambek, Michael. 2010. "Toward an Ethics of the Act." In *Ordinary Ethics: Anthropology, Language and Action*, edited by Michael Lambek, 39–63. New York: Fordham University Press.

Lan, Pei-Chia. 2006. *Global Cinderellas: Migrant Domestics and Newly Rich Employers in Taiwan*. Durham, NC: Duke University Press.

Lazuardi, Iqbal. 2017. "Protesters Deliver Petition, Demand FPI to be Disbanded." *Tempo*, January 19. Accessed June 17, 2017. https://en.tempo.co/read/news/2017/01/19/055837759 /Protesters-Deliver-Petition-Demand-FPI-to-be-Disbanded.

Lee, Jang Ho. 2001. *Traditional Medicine, Modern Medicine, and Christianity: a Study on the Realities of Sickness as Described by Balinese Christians in the Gereja Kemah Injil Indonesia in Bali*. PhD diss., Trinity International University.

Lensa Indonesia. 2012. "Awal Ramadhan, Remitan TKI di Kediri Mencappai Rp 454 Milyar." July 30. Accessed July 1, 2014. http://www.lensaindonesia.com/2012/07/30/awal -ramadhan-remitan-tki-di-kediri-mencapai-rp-454-milyar.html.

Levitt, Peggy. 2001. *The Transnational Villagers*. Berkeley: University of California Press.

Levitt, Peggy, and Nina Glick Schiller. 2004. "Conceptualizing Simultaneity: a Transnational Social Field Perspective on Society." *International Migration Review* 38, no. 3: 1002–39.

Ley, David, and Audrey Kobayashi. 2005. "Back to Hong Kong? Return Migration or Transnational Sojourn?" *Global Networks* 5, no. 2: 111–27.

Li, Tania. 2007. *The Will to Improve: Governmentality, Development and the Practice of Politics*. Durham, NC: Duke University Press.

Liebelt, Claudia. 2008. "On Sentimental Orientalists, Christian Zionists, and Working Class Cosmopolitans: Filipina Domestic Workers' Journeys to Israel and Beyond." *Critical Asian Studies* 40: 567–85.

Lindquist, Johan. 2004. "Veils and Ecstasy: Negotiating Shame in the Indonesian Borderlands." *Ethnos* 69, no. 4: 487–508.

———. 2010. "Labour Recruitment, Circuits of Capital and Gendered Mobility: Reconceptualizing the Indonesian Migration Industry." *Pacific Affairs* 83: 115–32.

———. 2012. "The Elementary School Teacher, the Thug and his Grandmother: Informal Brokers and Transnational Migration from Indonesia." *Pacific Affairs* 85: 69–89.

———. 2013a. "Beyond Anti-Anti-Trafficking." *Dialectical Anthropology* 37, no. 2: 319.

———. 2013b. "Rescue, Return, In Place: Deportees, Victims, and the Regulation of Indonesian Migration." In *Return: Nationalizing Transnational Mobility in Asia*, edited by Biao Xiang, Brenda S. A. Yeoh, and Mika Toyota, 122–40. Durham, NC: Duke University Press.

———. 2015. "Of Figures and Types: Brokering Knowledge and Migration in Indonesia and Beyond." *Journal of the Royal Anthropological Institute* 21, no. S1: 162–77.

Lindquist, Johan, Biao Xiang, and Brenda S. A. Yeoh. 2012. "Opening the Black Box of Migration: Brokers, the Organization of Transnational Mobility and the Changing Political Economy in Asia." *Pacific Affairs* 85, no. 1: 7–19.

Liputan6. 2014. "WNI Tersangka Pemerkosa Terancam 28 Tahun Penjara di AS." February 26. Accessed March 9, 2016. http://news.liputan6.com/read/836657/wni-tersangka -pemerkosa-terancam-28-tahun-penjara-di-as.

Lo, Clifford, and Jennifer Ngo. 2014. "Hong Kong Police to Go to Indonesia to Interview Erwiana About Abuse Claims." *South China Morning Post*, Januanry 15. Accessed March 8, 2016. http://www.scmp.com/news/hong-kong/article/1405845/hong-kong -police-go-indonesia-interview-erwiana-about-abuse-claims.

Long, Lynellyn D., and Ellen Oxfeld, eds. 2004. *Coming Home?: Refugees, Migrants, and Those Who Stayed Behind*. Philadelphia: University of Pennsylvania Press.

Lu, Melody C.W. 2005. "Commercially Arranged Marriage Migration: Case Studies of Cross-Border Marriages in Taiwan." *Indian Journal of Gender Studies* 12, no. 2–3: 275–303.

Luibhéid, Eithne. 2008. "Queer/Migration: An Unruly Body of Scholarship." *GLQ: A Journal of Lesbian and Gay Studies* 14, no. 2: 169–90.

Madianou, Mirca. 2012. "Migration and the Accentuated Ambivalence of Motherhood: the Role of ICTs in Filipino Transnational Families." *Global Networks* 12, no. 3: 277–95.

Mahdavi, Pardis. 2013. "Gender, Labour and the Law: the Nexus of Domestic Work, Human Trafficking and the Informal Economy in the United Arab Emirates." *Global Networks* 13: 425–40.

———. 2016. *Crossing the Gulf: Love and Family in Migrant Lives*. Stanford: Stanford University Press.

Mahler, Sara, and Patricia Pessar. 2006. "Gender Matters: Ethnographers Bring Gender from the Periphery toward the Core of Migration Studies." *International Migration Review* 40, no. 1: 27–63.

Mahmudah, Nurul. 2013. "Hundreds of Migrant Workers Die in Malaysia." *Tempo*, December 24. Accessed June 17, 2017. https://en.tempo.co/read/news/2013/12/24 /055539971/Hundreds-of-Migrant-Workers-Die-in-Malaysia.

Mahy, Petra, Monika Swasti Winarnita, and Nicholas Herriman. 2016. "Presumptions of Promiscuity: Reflections on Being a Widow or Divorcee from Three Indonesian Communities." *Indonesia and the Malay World* 44, no. 128: 47–67.

Malhotra, Anju. 1997. "Gender and the Timing of Marriage: Rural-Urban Differences in Java." *Journal of Marriage and the Family* 59, no. 2: 434–50.

Malkki, Liisa. 1992. "National Geographic: The Rooting of Peoples and the Territorialization of National Identity Among Scholars and Refugees." *Cultural Anthropology* 7, no. 1: 24–44.

Mam, Somaly. 2014. "Erwiana Sulistyaningsih." *Time 100 Most Influential People.* Accessed July 1, 2014. http://www.time.com/70820.

Manalasan, Martin. 2003. *Global Divas: Filipino Gay Men in the Diaspora.* Durham, NC: Duke University Press.

———. 2012. "Wayward Erotics: Mediating Queer Diasporic Return." In *Media, Erotics and Transnational Asia*, edited by Purnima Mankekar and Louisa Schein, 33–52. Durham, NC: Duke University Press.

Margold, Jane. 1995. "Narratives of Masculinity and Transnational Migration: Filipino Workers in the Middle East." In *Bewitching Women, Pious Men: Gender and Body Politics in Southeast Asia*, edited by Aihwa Ong and Michael Peletz, 274–98. Berkeley, CA: University of California Press.

Marsland, Rebecca, and Ruth Prince. 2012. "What is Life Worth? Exploring Biomedical Interventions, Survival, and the Politics of Life." *Medical Anthropology Quarterly* 26, no. 4: 453–69.

Martyn, Elizabeth. 2005. *The Women's Movement in Post-Colonial Indonesia: Gender and Nation in a New Democracy.* London and New York: Routledge Curzon.

Massey, Douglas, and Edward Taylor, eds. 2004. *International Migration: Prospects and Policies in a Global Market.* Oxford: Oxford University Press.

Massey, Douglas S., Joaquin Arango, Graeme Hugo, Ali Kouaouci, and Adela Pellegrino, eds. 2005. *Worlds in Motion: Understanding International Migration at the End of the Millennium.* Oxford: Clarendon. (Orig. pub. 1997.)

Mattingly, Cheryl. 2014. *Moral Laboratories: Family Peril and the Struggle for a Good Life.* Berkeley: University of California Press.

May, John. 2012. "GEP Indonesia: Angel Resource Institute Visits Indonesia." Global Entrepreneurship Program Newsletter. Issue 5, April. Accessed March 8, 2015. http://www.state.gov/documents/organization/182664.pdf.

McKay, Deidre. 2003. "Cultivating New Local Futures: Remittance Economies and Land-Use Patterns in Ifugao, Philippines." *Journal of Southeast Asian Studies* 34: 285–306.

———. 2005. "Migration and the Sensuous Geographies of Re-emplacement in the Philippines." *Journal of Intercultural Studies* 26: 75–91.

———. 2007. "Sending Dollars Shows Feeling: Emotions and Economies in Filipino Migration." *Mobilities* 2, no. 2: 175–94.

———. 2012. *Global Filipinos: Migrants' Lives in the Virtual Village.* Bloomsbury: Indiana University Press.

McKenzie, Sean, and Cecilia Menjívar. 2011. "The Meanings of Migration, Remittances and Gifts: Views of Honduran Women Who Stay." *Global Networks* 11, no. 1: 63–81.

McKinnon, Susan. 2001. *Relative Values: Reconfiguring Kinship Studies.* Durham, NC: Duke University Press.

McMahon, Paula. 2015. "Cruise Ship Worker Gets More Than 30 Years for Devastating Attack on Passenger." *Sun Sentinel*, January 7. Accessed March 9, 2016. http://www.sun-sentinel.com/news/crime/fl-cruise-ship-attack-sentenced-20150107-story.html.

McNevin, Anne, Antje Missbach, and Deddy Mulyana. 2016. "The Rationalities of Migration Management: Control and Subversion in an Indonesia-Based Counter-Smuggling Campaign." *International Political Sociology* 10, no. 3: 223–40.

Mills, Mary Beth. 1999. *Thai Women in the Global Labor Force: Consuming Desires, Contested Selves*. New Jersey: Rutgers University Press.

Miyazaki, Hirokazu. 2000. "Faith and its Fulfillment: Agency, Exchange, and the Fijian Aesthetics of Completion." *American Ethnologist* 27, no. 1: 31–51.

———. 2004. *The Method of Hope: Anthropology, Philosophy, and Fijian Knowledge*. Stanford: Stanford University Press.

Mukti, Hafizd. 2015. "17 WNI Telantar di Trinidad dan Tobago Usai Kapal Terbakar." *CNN Indonesia*. May 26. Accessed March 8, 2016. http://www.cnnindonesia.com/nasional /20150525220622-20-55623/17-wni-telantar-di-trinidad-dan-tobago-usai-kapal -terbakar.

Munjid, Achmad. 2012. "Is Indonesian Islam Tolerant?" *Jakarta Post*, September 14. Accessed March 9, 2016. http://www.thejakartapost.com/news/2012/09/14/is-indonesian-islam -tolerant.html.

Munro, Jenny. 2015. "'Now We Know Shame': Malu and Stigma among Highlanders in the Papuan Diaspora." In *From 'Stone-Age' to 'Real-Time': Exploring Papuan Temporalities, Mobilities and Religiosities*, edited by Martin Slama and Jenny Munro, 169–94. Canberra: Australian National University Press.

Nail, Thomas. 2016. *Theory of the Border*. Oxford: Oxford University Press.

Narotzky, Susana, and Nilo Besnier. 2014. "Crisis, Value, and Hope: Rethinking the Economy: an Introduction to Supplement 9." *Current Anthropology* 55, Supplement 9: S4-S16.

Nas, Peter. 2003. *The Indonesian Town Revisited*. Singapore and Germany: Institute of Southeast Asian Studies, LIT.

Nilan, Pam, Argyo Demartoto, and Alex Broom. 2013. "Masculinity, Violence, and Socioeconomic Status in Indonesia." *Culture, Society, and Masculinities* 5, no. 1: 3–20.

Nitibaskara, Ronny. 1993. "Observations on the Practice of Sorcery in Java." In *Understanding Witchcraft and Sorcery in Southeast Asia*, edited by C. W. Watson and R. F. Ellen, 123–34. Honolulu: University of Hawai'i Press.

Nugroho, Wahyu. 2015. "BNP2TKI Edukasi Mantan TKI Dengan Wirausaha." *Harnas*, April 9. Accessed August 3, 2015. http://www.harnas.co/2015/04/09/-bnp2tki-edukasi -mantan-tki-dengan-wirausaha.

Nur'aini, Desyinta. 2015. "210 Ribu ABK Indonesia Terjebak Praktik Illegal Fishing." *Jawa Pos*, June 16. Accessed March 8, 2016. http://www2.jawapos.com/baca/artikel /18978/210-Ribu-ABK-Indonesia-Terjebak-Praktik-Illegal-Fishing.

Oishi, Nana. 2005. *Women in Motion: Globalization, State Policies, and Labor Migration in Asia*. Stanford: Stanford University Press.

Ong, Aihwa. 2010. *Spirits of Resistance and Capitalist Discipline: Factory Women in Malaysia*. Albany: State University of New York Press. (Orig. pub. 1987.)

Özden, Çağlar, and Maurice Schiff. 2007. *International Migration, Economic Development and Policy*. Washington, DC: World Bank.

Palmer, Wayne. 2010. "Costly Inducements." *Inside Indonesia*, 100, April-June. Accessed March 10, 2016: http://www.insideindonesia.org/costly-inducements.

———. 2012. "Discretion in the Trafficking-Like Practices of the Indonesian State." In
    Labour Migration and Human Trafficking in Southeast Asia: Critical Perspectives,
    edited by Michelle Ford, Lenore Lyons, and Willem van Schendel, 149–66. London:
    Routledge.

———. 2016. *Indonesia's Overseas Labour Migration Programme, 1969–2010*. Leiden: Brill.

———. 2017. "Back Pay for Trafficked Migrant Workers: An Indonesian Case Study."
    International Migration. doi:10.1111/imig.12376.

Palomera, Jaime, and Theodora Vetta. 2016. "Moral Economy: Rethinking a Radical
    Concept." *Anthropological Theory* 16, no. 4: 413–32.

Paraskevopoulou, Anna. 2011. "Undocumented Worker Transitions: Family Migration."
    International Journal of Sociology and Social Policy 31: 110–22.

Parker, Lyn. 2008. "Theorising Adolescent Sexualities in Indonesia—Where 'Something
    Different Happens'." *Intersections: Gender and Sexuality in Asia and the Pacific* 18
    (October). Accessed September 9, 2017. http://intersections.anu.edu.au/issue
    18/parker.htm.

———. 2015. "The Theory and Context of the Stigmatisation of Widows and Divorcees
    (Janda) in Indonesia." *Indonesia and the Malay World* 44, no. 128: 1–20.

Parreñas, Rhacel. 2001. *Servants of Globalization: Women, Migration and Domestic Work*
    Stanford: Stanford University Press.

———. 2005. *Children of Migration: Transnational Families and Gendered Woes*. Stanford:
    Stanford University Press.

———. 2011. *Illicit Flirtations: Labor, Migration, and Sex Trafficking in Tokyo*. Stanford:
    Stanford University Press.

Patnistik, Egidius. 2014. "Pulang ke Indonesia, TKI tinggalkan Bayinya di Rumah Sakit di
    Saudi." *Kompas*, September 9. Accessed September 8, 2017. http://internasional
    .kompas.com/read/2014/09/25/09211061/Pulang.ke.Indonesia.TKI.Tinggalkan.Bayinya
    .di.Rumah.Sakit.di.Saudi.

Patunru, Arianto, and Rofi Uddarojat. 2015. *Reducing the Financial Burden of Indonesian
    Migrant Workers*. Center for Indonesian Policy Studies, CIPS Policy Recommendations
    1 (June 2015). Accessed August 3, 2015. https://cips-indonesia.org/en/publications
    /reducing-the-financial-burden-of-indonesian-migrant-workers-proposals-for
    -inclusive-growth-and-village-prosperity/.

Paul, Anju Mary. 2011. "Stepwise International Migration: A Multistage Migration Pattern
    for the Aspiring Migrant." *American Journal of Sociology* 116, no. 6: 1842–86.

———. 2015. "Negotiating Migration, Performing Gender." *Social Forces* 94, no. 1: 271–93.

Peletz, Michael. 1996. *Reason and Passion: Representations of Gender in a Malay Society*.
    Berkeley: University of California Press.

Pemerintah Kabupaten Cilacap. 2011. "Setengah Triliyun Remitance TKI Cilacap."
    Pemerintah Kabupaten Cilicap. Accessed July 1, 2014. http://cilacapkab.go.id/v2/?pilih
    =news&mod=yes&aksi=lihat&id=2371.

Pingol, Alicia. 2010. "Filipino Women Workers in Saudi: Making Offerings for the Here and
    Now and Hereafter." *The Asia Pacific Journal of Anthropology* 11, no. 3–4: 394–409.

Piper, Nicola. 2006. "Gendering the Politics of Migration." *International Migration Review*
    40, no. 1: 133–64.

Piper, Nicola, and Mina Roces. 2003. *Wife or Worker?: Asian Women and Migration*.
    Washington, DC: Rowman & Littlefield.

Platt, Maria. 2012. "Married Men Behaving Badly: Islam, Gender and Extramarital Relationships in Eastern Indonesia." *Intersections: Gender and Sexuality in Asia and the Pacific* 28 (March). Accessed September 9, 2017. http://intersections.anu.edu.au /issue28/platt.htm.

———. 2017. "Divorce and its Discontents." In *Indonesian Women Negotiating Unofficial Marriage, Divorce and Desire*. Abingdon: Routledge.

Platt, Maria, B. S. A. Yeoh, G. Baey, C. Y. Khoo, T. Lam, D. Das, and M. Ee. 2013. "Financing Migration, Generating Remittances and the Building of Livelihood Strategies: A Case Study of Indonesian Migrant Women as Domestic Workers in Singapore." Working Paper 10 (November). Asia Research Institute, National University of Singapore.

Potter, Lesley. 2009. "Oil Palm and Resistance in West Kalimantan, Indonesia." In *Agrarian Angst and Rural Resistance in Contemporary Southeast Asia*, edited by Dominique Caouette and Sarah Turner, 105–34. London and New York: Routledge.

Pratt, Geraldine. 2012. *Families Apart: Migrant Mothers and the Conflicts of Labor and Love*. Minneapolis, MN: University of Minnesota Press.

Prawiranata, Iwan. 2013. *Sustainable Microfinance in Indonesia: a Sociocultural Approach*. PhD diss., Victoria University.

Probo, Bayu. 2014. "Hasil Autopsi TKW Medan: Tulang Rusuk Patah." *Satu Harapan*, December 8. Accessed March 9, 2016. http://www.satuharapan.com/read-detail/read /hasil-autopsi-tkw-medan-tulang-rusuk-patah.

Prusinski, Ellen. 2016a. "'Because it is Our Fate': Migration Narratives and Coping Strategies among Indonesian Migrant Women Workers." *Asian Journal of Social Science* 44, no. 4–5: 485–515.

———. 2016b. "Becoming Siap Mental: Education for Transnational Labour Migration." *Ethnography and Education* 12, no. 3: 1–18.

Purbaya, Angling Adhitya. 2013. "Jumhur Ingatkan TKI Menabung dan Waspadai Majikan Genit." *Detik News*, July 21. Accessed September 9, 2014. http://news.detik.com/read /2013/07/21/074926/2309098/10/2/jumhur-ingatkan-tki-menabung-dan-waspadai -majikan-genit.

Puspito, Kusuma. 2014. *Bunuh diri Petani Di Kabupaten Gunungkidul* (2010–2014). Master's thesis, University Gadjah Mada, Yogyakarta.

Quiano, Kathy. 2011. "After Beheading, Indonesia Stops Sending Workers to Saudi Arabia." *CNN*, June 27. Accessed July 1, 2014. http://edition.cnn.com/2011/WORLD /asiapcf/06/22/indonesia.migrant.workers/index.html.

Rafael, Vicente. 1997. "'Your Grief Is Our Gossip': Overseas Filipinos and Other Spectral Presences." *Public Culture* 9: 267–91.

Ramadhani, Nurul Fitri. 2017a. "Polygamy Not Part of Islamic Teachings: Muslim Cleric." *Jakarta Post*, April 27. Accessed June 13, 2017. http://www.thejakartapost.com /news/2017/04/27/polygamy-not-part-of-islamic-teachings-muslim-clerics.html.

———. 2017b. "Female Ulema Issues Fatwa Obliging Muslims to Fight Early Marriage." *Jakarta Post*, April 27. Accessed June 13, 2017. http://www.thejakartapost.com/ news/2017/04/27/female-ulema-issues-fatwa-obliging-muslims-to-fight-early-marriage .html.

Rao, Nitya. 2014. "Migration, Mobility and Changing Power Relations: Aspirations and Praxis of Bangladeshi Migrants." *Gender, Place & Culture: A Journal of Feminist Geography* 21, no. 7: 872–87.

Reeves, Madeleine. 2011. "Staying Put? Towards a Relational Politics of Mobility at a Time of Migration." *Central Asian Survey* 30, no. 3–4: 555–76.

Republika. 2011. "RSUD Gunung Kidul Ajak WHO Tanggulangi Bunuh Diri." December 26. Accessed March 9, 2016. http://www.republika.co.id/berita/regional/ nusantara/11/12/26/lwtki2-rsud-gunung-kidul-ajak-who-tanggulangi-bunuh-diri.

———. 2012. "BNP2TKI Remikan Kampung TKI di Wonosobo." November 30. Accessed March 9, 2016. http://www.republika.co.id/berita/nasional/daerah/12/11/30/meahia -bnp2tki-resmikan-kampung-tki-di-wonosobo.

———. 2014. "Polisi Gali Informasi TKW Median Ditanam di Rumah." September 17. Accessed March 9, 2016. http://nasional.republika.co.id/berita/nasional/ hukum/14/12/17/ngozuf-polisi-gali-informasi-tkw-medan-ditanam-di-rumah.

———. 2015. "Femonema Lesbi Kian Marak di Kalangan TKW Hong Kong." July 20. Accessed March 9, 2016. http://www.republika.co.id/berita/nasional/umum/15/07/20 /nrseii-fenomena-lesbi-kian-marak-di-kalangan-tkw-hongkong.

Retsikas, Kostas. 2014. *Becoming—An Anthropological Approach to Understandings of the Person in Java.* London and New York: Anthem.

———. 2016. "The Other Side of the Gift: Soliciting in Java." *Heidelberg Ethnology: Occasional Paper* 4.

Rinaldo, Rachel. 2008. "Muslim Women, Middle Class Habitus and Modernity in Indonesia." *Contemporary Islam* 2: 23–39.

Rintel, Sean. 2013. "Crisis Memes: the Importance of Templatability to Internet Culture and Freedom of Expression." *Australasian Journal of Popular Culture* 2, no. 2: 253–71.

Robinson, Kathyrn. 2000. "Gender, Islam and Nationality: Indonesian Domestic Servants in the Middle East." In *Home and Hegemony: Domestic Service and Identity Politics in South and Southeast Asia,* edited by Kathleen M. Adams and Sara Dickey, 249–82. Ann Arbor: University of Michigan Press.

Rodriguez, Robyn. 2010. *Migrants for Export: How the Philippine State Brokers Labor to the World.* Minnesota: University of Minnesota Press.

Rodriguez, Robyn M., and Helen Schwenken. 2013. "Becoming a Migrant at Home: Subjectivation Processes in Migrant-Sending Countries Prior to Departure." *Population, Space and Place* 19, no. 4: 375–88.

Romero, Mary. 2002. *Maid in the U.S.A.* New York: Psychology Press.

Rosaldo, Michelle Z. 1980. *Knowledge and Passion: Ilongot Notions of Self and Social Life.* Cambridge: Cambridge University Press.

Rudnyckyj, Darmir. 2004. "Technologies of Servitude: Governmentality and Indonesian Transnational Labor Migration Assimilation." *Anthropological Quarterly* 77: 407–34.

———. 2010. *Spiritual Economies: Islam, Globalization and the Afterlife of Development.* Ithaca and London: Cornell University Press.

Salim, Delmus Puneri. 2015. *The Transnational and the Local in the Politics of Islam: The Case of West Sumatra, Indonesia.* Cham, Heidelberg, New York, Dordrecht, and London: Springer.

Salter, Mark. 2013. "To Make Move and Let Stop: Mobility and the Assemblage of Circulation." *Mobilities* 8, no. 1: 7–19.

Saraswati, Ayu. 2012. "'Malu': Coloring Shame and Shaming the Color of Beauty in Transnational Indonesia." *Feminist Studies* 38, no. 1: 113–40.

Sarigih, Bagus. 2014. "Adultery, Witchcraft, Land Workers on Death Row." *Jakarta Post*, January 25. Accessed July 1, 2014. http://www.thejakartapost.com/news/2014/01/25 /adultery-witchcraft-land-workers-death-row.html.

Schuster, Caroline. 2015. "Your Family and Friends are Collateral: Microfinance and the Social." Fieldsights—Theorizing the Contemporary, *Cultural Anthropology Online*. March 30, 2015. Accessed March 9, 2016. http://www.culanth.org/fieldsights/660-your -family-and-friends-are-collateral-microfinance-and-the-social.

Seekins, Donald. 1993. "Historical Setting." In *Indonesia: a Country Study*, edited by William Frederick and Robert Worden, 1–68. Washington, DC: Federal Research Division, Library of Congress.

Sen, Krishna. 1998. "Indonesian Women at Work: Reframing the Subject." In *Gender and Power in Affluent Asia*, edited by Krishna Sen and Maila Stivens, 35–62. London: Routledge.

Seruni. 2014. "Fenomena TKI Kabur Dari Majikan." Accessed February 2, 2014. http://www .seruni.or.id/2014/09/fenomena-tki-kabur-dari-majikan. (Link no longer active, but archived by the author and available on request).

Schiller, Nina Glick. 2012. "Unravelling the Migration and Development Web: Research and Policy Implications." *International Migration* 50: 92–97.

Schiller, Nina Glick, Linda Basch, and Cristina Szanton Blanc. 1995. "From Immigrant to Transmigrant: Theorizing Transnational Migration." *Anthropological Quarterly* 68, no. 1: 48–63.

Scott, James. 1976. *The Moral Economy of the Peasant: Rebellion and Subsistence in Southeast Asia*. New Haven: Yale University Press.

Scott, Karen. 2012. *Measuring Well-Being: Towards Sustainability?* New York, NY: Routledge.

Sijabat, Ridwan Max. 2013. "Jumhur Calls Report on Migrant Workers Misleading, Exaggeration." *Jakarta Post*, May 6. Accessed September 11, 2014. http://www .thejakartapost.com/news/2013/05/06/jumhur-calls-report-migrant-workers -misleading-exaggeration.html.

Silvey, Rachel. 2003a. "Spaces of Protest: Gendered Migration, Social Networks and Labor Activism in West Java, Indonesia." *Political Geography* 22: 129–55.

———. 2003b. "Gender, Socio-Spatial Networks, and Rural Non-Farm Work among Migrants in West Java." In *The Indonesian Rural Economy: Mobility, Work and Enterprise*, edited by Thomas R. Leinbach, 134–51. Singapore: ISEAS-Institute of South East Asian Studies.

———. 2004. "Transnational Domestication: State Power and Indonesian Migrant Women in Saudi Arabia." *Political Geography* 23: 245–64.

———. 2006. "Consuming the Transnational Family: Indonesian Migrant Domestic Workers to Saudi Arabia." *Global Networks* 6: 23–40.

———. 2007a. "Unequal Borders: Indonesian Transnational Migrants at Immigration Control." *Geopolitics* 12: 265–79.

———. 2007b. "Mobilizing Piety: Gendered Morality and Indonesian-Saudi Transnational Migration." *Mobilities* 2: 219–29.

Simoni, Valerio. 2016. "Economization, Moralization, and the Changing Moral Economies of 'Capitalism' and 'Communism' among Cuban Migrants in Spain." *Anthropological Theory* 16, no. 4: 454–75.

Singh, Khushwant. 2012. "Maid Killed Herself after Failing English Language Test." *The Straits Times*, February 9.

Siu, Beatrice. 2014. "Complexion 'Hid' Injuries of Erwiana." *The Standard* (Hong Kong), January 28. Accessed July 1, 2014. http://www.thestandard.com.hk/news_detail .asp?we_cat=4&art_id=141988&sid=41422485&con_type=1&d_str=20140128&fc=1.

Smith-Hefner, Nancy. 2007. "Javanese Women and the Veil in Post-Soeharto Indonesia." *The Journal of Asian Studies* 66, no. 2: 389–420.

Soeprobo, T.B.H, and Nur Hadi Wiyono. 2004. "Labour Migration from Indonesia." In *Empowerment of Indonesian Women: Family, Reproductive Health, Employment and Migration*, edited by Sri Harijati Hatmadji and Iwu Dwisetyani Utomo, 118–50. Depok, Indonesia: Demographic Institute, Faculty of Economics, University of Indonesia.

Solopos. 2012. "TKI Tewas Meninggal 9 Bulan Lalu Jenazah TKI Dede Akhirnya Dimakamkan." April 3. Accessed March 9, 2015. http://www.solopos.com/2012/04 /03/tki-tewas-meninggal-9-bulan-lalu-jenazah-tki-dede-akhirnya-dimakamkan -175599.

———. 2015. "Buku Ini Ulas 99 Cara Jadi TKI Sukses." March 18. Accessed March 7, 2016. http://www.solopos.com/2015/03/18/info-buku-buku-ini-ulas-99-cara-jadi-tki -sukses-585905.

Spaan, Ernst. 1994. "Taikongs and Calos: the Role of Middlemen and Brokers in Javanese International Migration." *International Migration Review* 28, no. 1: 93–113.

Steinwand, Dirk. 2013. "The Indonesian People's Credit Banks BPR." In *Southeast Asia's Credit Revolution: From Moneylenders to Microfinance*, edited by Aditya Goenka and David Henley, 95–112. London and New York: Routledge.

Stevanovic, Natacha. 2012. *Remittances and Moral Economies of Bangladeshi New York Immigrants in Light of the Economic Crisis*. PhD diss., Colombia University.

Stoll, David. 2013. *El Norte or Bust!: How Migration Fever and Microcredit Produced a Financial Crash in a Latin American Town*. Lanham, Boulder, New York, Toronto, and Plymouth, UK: Rowman & Littlefield.

Strathern, Marilyn. 1988. *The Gender of the Gift: Problems with Women and Problems with Society in Melanesia*. Berkeley: University of California Press.

Sudibyo, Triono Wahyu. 2015. "Pembunuh TKW Sri Hartati Ternyata Suami Sendiri Motifnya Tersinggung Diomeli." *Detik News*, May 25. Accessed March 9, 2015. http://news.detik.com/read/2015/05/25/163227/2924398/1536/pembunuh-tkw-sri-hartati -ternyata-suami-sendiri-motifnya-tersinggung-diomeli.

Sukamdi, Elan S., and Haris Abdul. 2004. "Impact of Remittances on the Indonesian Economy." In *International Migration in Southeast Asia*, edited by Aris Ananta and Evi Nurvidya Arifin, 137–65. Singapore: Institute of Southeast Asian Studies.

Susilo, Wahyu. 2007. "Maids Face Death Penalty." *Inside Indonesia*, July 26. Accessed March 9, 2016. http://www.insideindonesia.org/maids-face-death-penalty.

———. 2017. "Why the Ban on Sending Migrant Workers to the Middle East Isn't Working." *Indonesia at Melbourne*, February 7. Accessed September 10. http:// indonesiaatmelbourne.unimelb.edu.au/why-the-ban-on-sending-migrant-workers-to -the-middle-east-isnt-working/.

Suzuki, Nobue. 2003. "Transgressing 'Victims' Reading Narratives of 'Filipina Brides' in Japan." *Critical Asian Studies* 35: 399–420.

Tadiar, Neferti. 2004. *Fantasy Production: Sexual Economies and Other Philippine Consequences for the New World Order*. Hong Kong: Hong Kong University Press.

Tempo. 2014. "Menteri Hanif: Penampungan Calon TKI Mirip Tahanan." November 8. Accessed March 8, 2014. http://www.tempo.co/read/news/2014/11/08/173620556 /Menteri-Hanif-Penampungan-Calon-TKI-Mirip-Tahanan.

Thai, Hung Cam. 2014. *Insufficient Funds: The Culture of Money in Low-Wage Transnational Families*. Stanford: Stanford University Press.

Thieme, Susan, and Anita Ghimire. 2014. "Making Migrants Visible in Post-MDG Debates." *Sustainability* 6: 399–415.

Thompson, Edward P. 1971. "The Moral Economy of the English Crowd in the Eighteenth Century." *Past & Present* 50: 76–136.

Tjandraningsih, Indrasari. 2000. "Gendered Work and Labour Control: Women Factory Workers in Indonesia." *Asian Studies Review* 24, no. 2: 257–68.

———. 2013. "State Sponsored Precarious Work in Indonesia." *American Behavioural Scientist* 57: 403–19.

Tirtosurdarmo, Riwanto. 2003. "Population Mobility and Social Conflict: the Aftermath of the Economic Crisis in Indonesia." In *The Indonesian Crisis: a Human Development Perspective*, edited by Ananta Aris, 213–44. Singapore: Institute of Southeast Asian Studies.

Toyota, Mika, Brenda S. A. Yeoh, and Liem Nguyen. 2007. "Bringing the 'Left Behind' Back into View in Asia: a Framework for Understanding the 'Migration-Left Behind Nexus'." *Population, Space and Place* 13, no. 3: 157–61.

Tribunnews. 2011. "Warga Gunung Kidul Hobi Bunuh Diri?" January 16. Accessed March 9, 2016. http://www.tribunnews.com/regional/2011/01/16/warga-gunung-kidul-hobi -bunh-diri.

Tsay, Ching-lung. 2004. "Marriage Migration of Women from China and Southeast Asia to Taiwan." In *(Un)tying the Knot: Ideal and Reality in Asian Marriage*, edited by Gavin Jones and Kamalini Ramdas, 173–91. Singapore: Asian Research Institute, National University of Singapore.

Tufuor, Theresa, Anke Niehof, Chizu Sato, and Hilje van der Horst. 2015. "Extending the Moral Economy beyond Households: Gendered Livelihood Strategies of Single Migrant Women in Accra, Ghana." *Women's Studies International Forum* 50: 20–29.

United Nations Population Fund. 2013. "International Migration and Development: Contributions and Recommendations of the International System." Accessed September 4, 2016. http://www.unfpa.org/publications/international-migration-and -development.

University of Sydney Business School. 2015. *Entrepreneurship and Innovation Program: 2015 Annual Report*. Accessed September 6, 2017. http://sydney.edu.au/business/__data /assets/pdf_file/0011/268940/E_And_I_Annual_Report_2015.pdf.

Van Dijk, Rijk. 2010. "Social Catapulting and the Spirit of Entrepreneurialism: Migrants, Private Initiative, and the Pentecostal Ethic in Botswana." In *Traveling Spirits: Migrants, Markets and Mobilities*, edited by Gertrud Huwelmeier and Kristine Krause, 101–17. New York: Routledge.

Varisco, Daniel Martin. 2005. *Islam Obscured: The Rhetoric of Anthropological Representation*. New York: Palgrave Macmillan.

Velayutham, Selvaraj, and Amanda Wise. 2005. "Moral Economies of a Translocal Village: Obligation and Shame among South Indian Transnational Migrants." *Global Networks* 5, no. 1: 27–47.

Wang, Hong-zen. 2007. "Hidden Spaces of Resistance of the Subordinated: Case Studies from Vietnamese Female Migrant Partners in Taiwan." *International Migration Review* 41, no. 3: 706–27.

Warta Kota. 2015. "Sakit Hati, Jokowi Hentikan Pengiriman PRT ke Luar Negiri." February 14. Accessed March 7, 2016. http://wartakota.tribunnews.com/2015/02/14/sakit-hati-jokowi-hentikan-pengiriman-prt-ke-luar-negeri.

Waspada. 2013. "Tki Suka Dugem." 2013. Accessed July 1, 2014. http://waspada.co.id/index.php?option=com_content&view=article&id=295398:tki-suka-dugem&catid=77:fokur edaksi&Itemid=131.

Wee, Vivienne, and Amy Sim. 2004. "Transnational Labour Networks in Female Labour Migration: Mediating between Southeast Asian Women Workers and International Labour Markets." In *International Migration in Southeast Asia,* edited by Aris Ananta and Evi Nurvidya Arifin, 166–98. Singapore: Institute of Southeast Asian Studies.

Weiner, Annette. 1992. *Inalienable Possessions: The Paradox of Keeping While Giving.* Berkeley: University of California Press.

Weintraub, Andrew. 2008. "'Dance Drills, Faith Spills': Islam, Body Politics, and Popular Music in Post-Suharto Indonesia." *Popular Music* 27, no. 3: 367–92.

White, Douglas, and Thomas Schweizer. 1998. "Kinship, Property Transmission, and Stratification in Rural Java." In *Kinship, Networks and Exchange,* edited by Douglas White and Thomas Schweizer, 36–58. Cambridge: Cambridge University Press.

Wichelen, Sonja van. 2010. *Religion, Politics and Gender in Indonesia: Disputing the Muslim Body.* London and New York: Routledge.

Wieringa, Saskia. 2003. "The Birth of the New Order State: Sexual Politics and Nationalism." *Journal of Women's History* 15, no. 1: 70–93.

———. 2006. "Islamization in Indonesia: Women Activists' Discourses." *Signs* 32, no. 1: 1–8.

———. 2012. "Passionate Aesthetics and Symbolic Subversion: Heteronormativity in India and Indonesia." *Asian Studies Review* 26: 515–30.

———. 2015. "Gender Harmony and the Happy Family: Islam, Gender and Sexuality in Post-Reformasi Indonesia." *South East Asia Research* 23, no. 1: 27–44.

Wilson, Ian. 2012. "The Biggest Cock: Territoriality, Invulnerability and Honour Amongst Jakarta's Gangsters." In *Men and Masculinities in Southeast Asia,* edited by Michele Ford and Lenore Lyons, 121–38. London and New York: Routledge.

Winarnita, Monika. 2016. *Dancing the Feminine: Gender & Identity Performances by Indonesian Migrant Women.* Sussex: Sussex Academic Press.

Wise, Amanda. 2013. "Pyramid Subcontracting and Moral Detachment: Down-Sourcing Risk and Responsibility in the Management of Transnational Labour in Asia." *The Economic and Labour Relations Review* 24, no. 3: 433–55.

Wise, Raúl Delgado, and Humberto Márquez Covarrubias. 2009. "Understanding the Relationship between Migration and Development: Toward a New Theoretical Approach." *Social Analysis* 53: 85–105.

Wolf, Diane. 1988. "Female Autonomy, the Family, and Industrialization in Java." *Journal of Family Issues* 9, no. 1: 85–107.

———. 1992. *Factory Daughters: Gender, Household Dynamics, and Rural Industrialization in Java.* Berkeley: University of California Press.

Woodward, Mark. 1989. *Islam in Java: Normative Piety and Mysticism in the Sultanate of Yogyakarta.* Tucson: The University of Arizona Press.

——, ed. 1996. *Towards a New Paradigm: Recent Developments in Indonesian-Islamic Thought*. Tempe: Arizona State University Program for Southeast Asian Studies.

Wright, Kate. 2016. "Moral Economies: Interrogating the Interactions of NGOs, Journalists and Freelancers." *International Journal of Communication* 10: 1510–29.

Xiang, Biao. 2007. "How Far are the Left-Behind Left Behind? A Preliminary Study in Rural China." *Population, Space and Place* 13, no. 3: 179–91.

——. 2013. "Return and the Reordering of Transnational Mobility in Asia." In *Return: Nationalizing Transnational Mobility in Asia*, edited by Biao Xiang, Brenda S. A. Yeoh, and Mika Toyota, 10–29. Durham, NC: Duke University Press.

Xiang, Biao, Brenda S.A. Yeoh, and Mika Toyota, eds. 2013. *Return: Nationalizing Transnational Mobility in Asia*. Durham, NC: Duke University Press.

Xiang, Biao, and Johan Lindquist. 2014. "Migration Infrastructure." *International Migration Review* 48, Supplement 1: S122–48.

Yang, Kuo-Shu, and David Y. F. Ho. 1988. "The Role of Yuan in Chinese Social Life: A Conceptual and Empirical Analysis." In *Asian Contributions to Psychology*, edited by Anand C. Paranjpe, David Y. F. Ho, and Robert W. Rieber, 263–81. New York: Praeger Publishers.

Yeoh, Brenda S. A., and Shirlena Huang. 2000. "'Home' and 'Away': Foreign Domestic Workers and Negotiations of Diasporic Identity in Singapore." *Women's Studies International Forum* 23, no. 4: 413–29.

——. 2010. "Sexualised Politics of Proximities among Female Transnational Migrants in Singapore." *Population, Space and Place* 16, no. 1: 37–49.

Yeoh, Brenda S. A., and Theodore Lam. 2013. "Transnational Migration in Southeast Asia and the Gender Roles of Left-Behind Fathers." *ARROW for Change* 19, no. 1: 8–9.

Yeoh, Brenda S. A., Maria Platt, Choon Yen Khoo, Theodora Lam and Grace Baey. 2017. "Indonesian Domestic Workers and the (Un)Making of Transnational Livelihoods and Provisional Futures." *Social & Cultural Geography* 18, no. 3: 415–34.

Yosephine, Liza. 2016. "Indonesian Psychiatrists Label LGBT Mental Disorders." *Jakarta Post*, February 24. Accessed March 9, 2016. http://www.thejakartapost.com/news/2016/02/24/indonesian-psychiatrists-label-lgbt-mental-disorders.html.

Zelizer, Viviana. 2000. "The Purchase of Intimacy." *Law & Social Inquiry* 25, no. 3: 817–48.

Zigon, Jarrett. 2008. *Morality: an Anthropological Perspective*. Oxford: Berg Publishers.

——. 2010. "Moral and Ethical Assemblages: A Response to Fassin and Stoczkowski." *Anthropological Theory* 10, no. 1–2: 3–15.

——. 2014. "An Ethics of Dwelling and a Politics of World-Building: a Critical Response to Ordinary Ethics." *Journal of the Royal Anthropological Institute* 20, no, 4: 746–64.

Zubaidah, Neneng. 2015. "Indonesia Stop Kirim PLRT ke Timteng." *Sindonews*, May 5. Accessed March 7, 2016. http://nasional.sindonews.com/read/997318/149/indonesia-stop-kirim-plrt-ke-timteng-1430790652.

Index

CAROL CHAN is a postdoctoral fellow with the Interdisciplinary Program for Migration Studies (PRIEM) at Universidad Alberto Hurtado, Chile.

www.ingramcontent.com/pod-product-compliance
Lightning Source LLC
Chambersburg PA
CBHW070241290326
41929CB00046B/2271